"Incredible . . . Have you ever read a [...] hug the author?"

"This unrestrained memoir is a transporting experience and one of the most startlingly hopeful books I have ever read."
—**LISA TADDEO,** author of *Three Women*

"A story that . . . goes straight to the messy center of what it means to interrogate our own limitations and deepest desires, wherever that journey may take us." —**DANI SHAPIRO,** *New York Times*

"Christie Tate takes readers on a journey through her life-changing road to recovery and in turn finds hope, human connection, and a new take on life." —**CNN**

"Tate's candid path to healing is often hilarious and ultimately very touching." —*PEOPLE*

"*Group* sucked me in and never let go." —**SARAH HEPOLA,** author of *Blackout: Remembering the Things I Drank to Forget*

"Fearless candor and vulnerability." —*TIME*

"*Group* is an honest, addictive memoir about a woman's experience in group therapy. She held nothing back with them, and she holds nothing back with us." —*HELLOGIGGLES*

"This book will remind you how to come back to yourself even when you want to give up, will make you laugh, make you cry, help you breathe. This book will save lives."
—**LIDIA YUKNAVITCH,** author of *Verge*

"[A] dazzling debut memoir." —*PUBLISHERS WEEKLY* (starred review)

"A moving, raw account of healing, and one you'll definitely want to talk about in the group chat."
—*THE SKIMM*

NEW YORK TIMES BESTSELLER

AVID

READER

PRESS

GROUP

How One Therapist and a Circle of Strangers Saved My Life

Christie Tate

AVID READER PRESS

New York   London   Toronto   Sydney   New Delhi

AVID READER PRESS
An Imprint of Simon & Schuster, Inc.
1230 Avenue of the Americas
New York, NY 10020

This Avid Reader Press trade paperback edition June 2021

AVID READER PRESS and colophon are
trademarks of Simon & Schuster, Inc.

For information about special discounts for bulk
purchases, please contact Simon & Schuster Special Sales
at 1-866-506-1949 or business@simonandschuster.com.

The Simon & Schuster Speakers Bureau can bring authors to
your live event. For more information or to book an event, contact
the Simon & Schuster Speakers Bureau at 1-866-248-3049
or visit our website at www.simonspeakers.com.

Interior design by Lewelin Polanco

Manufactured in the United States of America

5   7   9   10   8   6   4

Library of Congress Cataloging-in-Publication
Data has been applied for.

ISBN 978-1-9821-5461-5
ISBN: 978-1-9821-5462-2 (pbk)
ISBN 978-1-9821-5463-9 (ebook)

*For my therapist and the
group members with whom I've
been privileged to share the circle*

Part 1

1

The first time I wished for death—like, really wished its bony hand would tap me on the shoulder and say "this way"—two bags from Stanley's Fruit and Vegetables sat shotgun in my car. Cabbage, carrots, a few plums, bell peppers, onions, and two dozen red apples. It had been three days since my visit to the bursar's office, where the law school registrar handed me a notecard with my class rank, a number that had begun to haunt me. I turned the key in the ignition and waited for the engine to turn over in the ninety-degree heat. I pulled a plum out of the bag, tested it for firmness, and took a bite. The skin was thick but the flesh beneath was tender. I let the juice dribble down my chin.

It was eight thirty. Saturday morning. I had nowhere to be, nothing to do. No one was expecting to see me until Monday morning, when I'd report for duty at Laird, Griffin & Griffin, the labor law firm where I was a summer intern. At LG&G only the receptionist and the partner who hired me knew I existed. The Fourth of July was Wednesday, which meant I'd face yet another stifling, empty day in the middle of the week. I'd find a 12-step meeting and hope that people would want to go for coffee afterward. Maybe another lonely soul would want to catch a movie or grab a salad. The engine hummed to life, and I gunned the car out of the parking lot.

I wish someone would shoot me in the head.

A soothing thought with a cool obsidian surface. If I died, I wouldn't have to fill the remaining forty-eight hours of this weekend or Wednesday's holiday or the weekend after that. I wouldn't have to endure the hours of hot, heavy loneliness that stretched before me—hours that would turn into days, months, years. A lifetime of nothing but me, a bag of apples, and the flimsy hope that stragglers after a recovery meeting might want some company.

A recent news story about a fatal shooting in Cabrini Green, Chicago's infamous housing project, flashed in my mind. I steered my car south on Clybourn and turned left on Division. Maybe one of those stray bullets would hit me.

Please, someone shoot me.

I repeated it like a mantra, an incantation, a prayer that would likely go unanswered because I was a twenty-six-year-old white woman in a ten-year-old white Honda Accord on a bright summer morning. Who would shoot me? I had no enemies; I hardly existed. Anyway, that fantasy relied too heavily on luck—bad or good, depending on how you looked at it—but other fantasies came unbidden. Jumping from a high window. Throwing myself on the El tracks. As I came to a stop at Division and Larrabee, I considered more exotic ways to expire, like masturbating while I hung myself, but who was I kidding? I was too repressed for that scenario.

I fished the pit out of the plum and popped the rest in my mouth. Did I really want to die? Where were these thoughts going to lead me? Was this suicidal ideation? Depression? Was I going to act on these thoughts? Should I? I rolled down the window and threw the pit as far as I could.

In my law school application, I described my dream of advocating for women with non-normative (fat) bodies—but that was only partly true. My interest in feminist advocacy was genuine, but it wasn't the major motivator. I wasn't after the inflated paychecks or the power suits either. No, I went to law school because lawyers work sixty- and seventy-hour weeks. Lawyers schedule conference calls during Christmas break and are summoned to boardrooms on Labor Day. Lawyers eat dinner at their desks surrounded by colleagues with rolled-up sleeves and pit stains. Lawyers can be married to their work—work that is so vital that they don't mind, or notice, if their personal lives are empty as a parking lot at midnight. Legal work could be a culturally approved-of beard for my dismal personal life.

I took my first practice law school admissions test (LSAT) from the desk where I worked at a dead-end secretarial job. I had a master's degree I wasn't using and a boyfriend I wasn't fucking. Years later, I'd refer to Peter as a workaholic-alcoholic, but at the time I called him the love of my life. I would dial his office at nine thirty at night when I was ready to go to sleep and accuse him of never having time for me. "I *have* to work," he'd say, and then hang up. When I'd call back, he wouldn't answer. On the weekends, we'd walk to dive bars in Wicker Park so he could drink domestic beers and debate the merits of early R.E.M. albums, while I prayed he'd stay sober enough to have sex. He rarely did. Eventually I decided I needed something all-consuming to absorb the energy I was pouring into my miserable relationship. The woman who worked down the hall from me was headed to law school in the fall. "Can I borrow one of your test books?" I asked. I read the first problem:

A professor must schedule seven students during a day in seven different consecutive time periods numbered one through seven.

What followed were a series of statements like: *Mary and Oliver must occupy consecutive periods* and *Sheldon must be scheduled after Uriah.* The test directions allotted thirty-five minutes to answer six multiple choice questions about this professor and her scheduling conundrum. It took me almost an hour. I got half of them wrong.

And yet. Slogging through LSAT prep and then law school seemed easier than fixing whatever made me fall in love with Peter and whatever it was that made me stay for the same fight night after night.

Law school could fill all my yearnings to belong to other people, to match my longings with theirs.

At my all-girls high school in Texas, I took a pottery elective freshman year. We started with pinch pots and worked our way up to the pottery wheel. Once we molded our vessels, the teacher taught us how to add handles. If you wanted to attach two pieces of clay—say, the cup and the handle—you had to score the surface of both. Scoring—making horizontal and vertical gouges in the clay—helped the pieces meld together when fired in the kiln. I sat on my stool holding one of my crudely sculpted "cups" and a C-shaped handle as the teacher demonstrated the scoring process. I hadn't wanted to ruin the smooth surface of the "cup" I'd lovingly pinched, so I smushed the handle on it without scoring its surface. A few days later, our shiny, fired pieces were displayed on a rack in the back of the studio. My cup had survived, but the handle lay in brittle pieces beside it. "Faulty score," the teacher said when she saw my face fall.

That was how I'd always imagined the surface of my heart—smooth, slick, unattached. Nothing to grab on to. Unscored. No one could attach to me once the inevitable heat of life bore down. I suspected the metaphor went deeper still—that I was afraid of marring my heart with the scoring that arose naturally between people, the inevitable bumping against other people's desires, demands, pettiness, preferences, and all the quotidian negotiations that made up a relationship. Scoring was required for attachment, and my heart lacked the grooves.

⁓

I wasn't an orphan either, though the first part of this reads like I was. My parents, still happily married, lived in Texas in the same redbrick ranch house I grew up in. If you drove by 6644 Thackeray Avenue, you would see a weathered basketball hoop and a porch festooned with three flags: Old Glory, the Texas state flag, and a maroon flag with the Texas A&M logo on it. Texas A&M was my dad's alma mater. Mine too.

My parents called a couple times a month to check on me, usually after mass on Sundays. I always went home for Christmas. They bought me a giant green Eddie Bauer coat when I moved to Chicago. My mom sent me fifty-dollar checks so I'd have spending money; my dad diagnosed problems with my Honda's brakes over the phone. My younger sister was finishing graduate school and about to become engaged to her longtime boyfriend; my brother and his wife, college sweethearts, lived in Atlanta near dozens of their college friends. None of them knew about my unscored heart. To them, I was their oddball daughter and sister who voted Democratic, liked poetry, and settled north of the Mason-Dixon Line. They loved me, but I didn't really fit with them or Texas. When I was a kid, my mom would play the Aggie fight song on the piano and my dad would sing along at the top of his lungs. *Hullaballo-canek-canek, Hullaballoo-canek-canek.* He took me on my college tour of Texas A&M, and when I picked it—primarily because we could afford it—he was genuinely thrilled to have another Aggie in the family. He never said so, but surely he was disappointed to learn that I spent home football games in the library highlighting passages in *Walden* while twenty thousand fans sang, stomped, and cheered loud enough that when the Aggies, scored the library walls vibrated. Everyone in my family and all of Texas, it seemed, loved football.

I was a misfit. The deep secret I carried was that I didn't belong. Anywhere. I spent half my days obsessing about food and my body and the weird shit I did to control both, and the other half trying to outrun my loneliness with academic achievement. I went from the honor roll in high school to the dean's list in college for earning a 4.0 for most of my semesters there to cramming legal theories into my brain seven days a week. I dreamed of one day showing up at 6644 Thackeray Avenue at my goal weight, arm in arm with a healthy functioning man, and my spine shooting straight to the sky.

I didn't think of disclosing to my family when my troubling wishes about death cropped up. We could talk about the weather, the Honda, and the Aggies. None of my secret fears and fantasies fit into any of those categories.

I wished passively for death, but I didn't stockpile pills or join the Hemlock Society's mailing list. I didn't research how to get a gun or fashion a noose out of my belts. I didn't have a plan, a method, or a date. But I felt an unease, constant as a toothache. It didn't feel normal, passively wishing that death would snatch me up. Something about the way I was living made me want to stop living.

I don't remember what words I used when I thought about my malaise. I know I felt a longing I couldn't articulate and didn't know how to satisfy. Sometimes I told myself I just wanted a boyfriend or that I was scared I would die alone. Those statements were true. They nicked the bone of the longing, but they didn't reach the marrow of my despair.

In my journal, I used vague words of discomfort and distress: *I feel afraid and anxious about myself. I feel afraid that I'm not OK, will never be OK & I'm doomed. It's very uncomfortable to me. What's wrong with me?* I didn't know then that a word existed to perfectly define my malady: lonely.

That card from the bursar with my class rank on it, by the way, said number one. Uno. First. *Primero. Zuerst.* The one hundred seventy other students in my class had a GPA lower than mine. I'd exceeded my goal of landing in the top half of the class, which, after my less-than-mediocre score on the LSAT—I never could figure out when Uriah should have his conference—seemed like a stretch goal. I should have been thrilled. I should have been opening zero-balance credit cards. Shopping for Louboutin heels. Signing the lease on a new apartment on the Gold Coast. Instead, I was first in my class and jealous of the lead singer of INXS who died of autoerotic asphyxiation.

What the hell was wrong with me? I wore size-six pants, had D-cup breasts, and pulled in enough student loan money to cover a studio apartment in an up-and-coming neighborhood on the north side of Chicago. For eight years, I'd been a member of a 12-step program that taught me how to eat without sticking my finger down my throat thirty minutes later. My future gleamed before me like Grandma's polished silver. I had every reason to be optimistic. But self-disgust about my stuckness—I was far away from other people, aeons away from a romantic relationship—lodged in every cell of my body. There was some reason that I felt so apart and alone, a reason why my heart was so slick. I didn't know what it was, but I felt it pulsing as I fell asleep and wished to not wake up.

I was already in a 12-step program. I'd done a fourth-step inventory with my sponsor who lived in Texas and made amends to the people I'd harmed. I'd returned to Ursuline Academy, my all-girl high school, with a one-hundred-dollar check as restitution for money I stole while managing parking-lot fees junior year. Twelve-step recovery had arrested the worst of my disordered eating, and I credited it with saving my life. Why was I now wishing that life away? I confessed to my sponsor who lived in Texas that I'd been having dark thoughts.

"I wish for death every day." She told me to double up on my meetings.

I tripled them, and felt more alone than ever.

2

A few days after I learned my class rank, a woman named Marnie invited me to dinner following a 12-step meeting. Like me, she was a recovering bulimic. Unlike me, she had a super-together life: She was only a few years older, but she worked at a lab focused on cutting-edge experiments for breast cancer treatments; she and her husband had recently painted the entryway of her colonial Sherwin-Williams's Osage Orange; she was tracking her ovulation. Her life wasn't perfect—her marriage was often stormy—but she chased what she wanted. My instinct was to say no to her dinner offer so I could go home, take off my bra, and eat my four ounces of ground turkey and roasted carrots alone in front of *Scrubs*. That's what I usually did—beg off—when people after meetings invited me to join them for coffee or dinner. "Fellow-ship," as they called it. But before I could decline, Marnie touched my elbow. "Just come. Pat's out of town, and I don't want to eat alone."

We sat across from each other at the type of "healthy" diner that serves sprouted bread and sweet potato fries. Marnie seemed extra buoyant. Was she wearing lip gloss?

"You seem happy," I said.

"It's my new therapist." I chased a spinach leaf around my plate with my fork. Could a therapist help me? I let the hope flicker. The summer before law school, I availed myself of eight free sessions with a social worker, courtesy of an Employee Assistance Program. I'd been assigned a meek woman named June who wore prairie skirts without irony. I didn't tell her any of my secrets because I was afraid of upsetting her. Therapy, like being truly close to people, seemed like an experience I had to stand on the outside of, my face pressed to the window.

"I'm doing an all-women's group."

"Group?" My neck tensed immediately. I had a deep mistrust of groups after a bad experience in fifth grade when my parents transferred me to a local public school from my small Catholic school where class size was dwindling. At the new school, I fell in with the popular girls, led by Bianca, who gave out Jolly Ranchers every lunch period and had solid gold orbs on her add-a-bead necklace. I once spent the night at Bianca's house, and her mom took us in her silver Mercedes to see *Footloose*. But Bianca turned on me midyear. She thought her boyfriend liked me because we sat near each other in history. One day at lunch, she offered everyone at the table a Jolly Rancher except me. She slipped a note under my lunch bag: *We don't want you at our table.* All the girls had signed it. By then, I knew something was off in the connection between me and other people. I sensed in my gut that I didn't know how to stay connected, how not to be cast aside. I could tolerate 12-step groups because the membership at every meeting shifted. You could come and go as you pleased, and no one knew your last name. There was no one in charge at a 12-step meeting—no Queen Bee Bianca who could oust other members. A set of spiritual principles held a 12-step group together: anonymity, humility, integrity, unity, service. Without those, I never would have stayed. Plus, the cost of a meeting was basically free, though they suggested a two-dollar donation. For the cost of a Diet Coke I could spend sixty minutes acknowledging my eating disorder and listening to other people's pain and triumphs around food.

I speared a chunk of tomato and considered interesting topics I could raise with Marnie—the execution of Oklahoma City bomber Timothy McVeigh or whatever Colin Powell was up to. I felt the urge to impress her with my knowledge of current events and display some togetherness of my own. But I was curious about her therapy group. I feigned nonchalance as I asked what it was like.

"It's all women. Mary's going deaf, and Zenia's about to lose her medical license because of alleged Medicare fraud. Emily's father is a drug addict—he harasses her with hate mail from his one-bedroom apartment in Wichita." Marnie lifted her arm and pointed at the soft, fleshy underside of her forearm. "Our new girl is a cutter. Always wears long sleeves. We don't know her story yet, but for sure, it's dark as hell."

"Sounds intense." Not what I'd pictured. "Are you allowed to tell me all this?"

She nodded. "The therapist's theory is that keeping secrets is a toxic process, so we—the group members—can talk about whatever we want, wherever we want. The therapist is bound by doctor-patient confidentiality, but we're not."

No confidentiality? I sat back and shook my head. I twisted the napkin around my wrist under the table. No way could I do that. I once hinted to my high school social justice teacher Ms. Gray that my eating was screwed up. When Ms. Gray called my parents to suggest counseling, my mom was furious. I was polishing off a plate of biscuits and watching Oprah interview Will Smith when my mom stormed into the living room, madder than a one-winged hornet. "Why would you tell people your business? You *must* protect yourself!" My mom is a proper Southern woman raised in Baton Rouge during the 1950s. Telling other people your business was tacky and could have adverse social consequences. She was convinced I'd be ostracized if other people knew I had mental problems, and she wanted to protect me. When I started going to 12-step meetings in college, it took all the courage I had to trust that the other people would take the anonymity part of the program as seriously as I did.

"How does anyone get better?" Marnie was clearly doing better than I was. If we were a tampon commercial, I'd be the one scowling about odors and leakage; she'd be doing a jeté in white jeans on her heavy flow day.

She shrugged. "You could check it out."

I'd had other therapy. In high school, there was a short stint with a woman who looked like Paula Dean and wore pastel pantsuits. My parents sent me to Paula D. after Ms. Gray called about my eating, but I was so busy obeying the command to protect myself that I never said anything about how I felt. Instead, we chitchatted about whether I should get a mall job over the summer. Express or Gap? Once, she sent me home with a five-hundred-question psychological test. Hope coursed through my fingers as I filled in each answer bubble; these questions would finally reveal why I couldn't stop eating, why I felt like a misfit everywhere I went, and why none of the boys were interested in me when all the other girls were French-kissing and getting felt up.

Paula D. read the results in her perfectly modulated therapist voice: "'Christie is perfectionistic and afraid of snakes. An ideal occupation for Christie would be watch repairperson or surgeon.'" She smiled and cocked her head. "Snakes are pretty scary, huh?"

It never occurred to me to show her my tears and panic. To open up, I needed a therapist who could hear the echoes of pain in my silences and see the shirttail of truth under my denials. Paula D. didn't. After that session, I sat my parents down and told them that I'd graduated from therapy. All better now. My parents beamed with pride, and my mom shared her life philosophy: "You just make up your mind to be happy. Focus on the positive; don't put any energy into negative thoughts." I nodded. Great idea. On the way down the hall to my bedroom, I stopped in the bathroom and threw up my dinner, a habit I developed after reading a book about a gymnast who threw up her food. I loved the feeling of emptying myself of food and the rush of adrenaline from having a secret. At age sixteen, I thought bulimia was a genius way to control my ruthless appetite, which led me to binge on crackers, bread, and pasta. Not until I got into recovery did I understand that my bulimia was a way to control the unending swells of anxiety, loneliness, anger, and grief that I had no idea how to release.

Marnie dragged another fry through the smear of ketchup. "Dr. Rosen would see you—"

"Rosen? Jonathan Rosen?"

I *definitely* couldn't call Dr. Rosen. Blake saw Dr. Rosen. Blake was a guy I'd met at a party the summer before law school. He took a seat next to me and said, "What kind of eating disorder do you have?" He pointed at the carrot sticks on my plate and said, "Don't look at me like that. I've dated an anorexic and two bulimics who wished they were anorexic. I know your type." He was in AA, between jobs, and offered to take me sailing. We rode bikes to the lakefront to watch Fourth of July fireworks. We lay on the deck of his boat, shoulder to shoulder, staring at the Chicago skyline and talking about recovery. We sampled the vegan food at Chicago Diner and went to the movies on Saturday afternoons before his AA meeting. When I asked if he was my boyfriend, he didn't answer. Sometimes, he'd disappear for a few days to listen to Johnny Cash albums in his darkened apartment. Even if I could see the same therapist as Marnie, I could *not* see the same therapist as my ex-whatever-Blake-was. What, was I going to call up this Dr. Rosen and say, "Remember the girl who had anal sex last fall with Blake to cure his depression? Well, that was me! Do you take BlueCross-BlueShield?"

"How much does this therapy cost?" Couldn't hurt to ask, though I had no conscious intention of joining a therapy group.

"Super cheap—only seventy bucks a week."

I blew a hot breath out of my cheeks. Seventy bucks was chump change to Marnie, who ran a lab at Northwestern University and whose husband was the heir to a small family fortune. If I skimped on groceries and took the bus instead of driving, I *might* have an extra seventy bucks by the end of the month. But each week? I made fifteen dollars an hour at my summer internship, and my parents were Just Be Happy people, so I couldn't ask them. In two years, I'd have a job locked down, but on my student budget, where would the money come from?

Marnie said Dr. Rosen's phone number out loud, but I didn't write it down.

But then she said one more thing.

"He just got remarried—he smiles all the time."

Instantly, I pictured Dr. Rosen's heart: a red grammar school cutout for Valentine's Day with hash marks etched across the surface like bare tree branches in winter. I projected onto Dr. Rosen, a man I had never met, a gut-wrenching divorce, lonely nights in a sublet efficiency with freezer-burned microwaved dinners, but then a twist: a second chance at love with a new wife. In the chest of a smiling therapist beat a scored heart. My chest filled with curiosity and a slim, quivering hope that he could help me.

As I lay in bed that night, I thought about the women in Marnie's group: the presumed cutter, the felon, the daughter of the drug addict. I thought about Blake, who had formed tight bonds with the men in his group. After his sessions, he would come home brimming with stories about Ezra, who had a blow-up doll for a girlfriend, and Todd, whose wife dumped all of his possessions out on the sidewalk when she wanted a divorce. Was I really worse off than these folks? Was my malady, whatever it was, so impossible to cure? I'd never given bona fide psychiatry a chance. Psychiatrists have medical degrees—maybe whatever was wrong with me required the skills of someone who'd dissected a human heart during his training. Maybe Dr. Rosen would have some advice for me—something he could impart in a single session or two. Maybe there was a pill he could prescribe to take the edge off my despair and score my heart.

3

I found Dr. Rosen's number in the phone book and left a message on his machine two hours after my dinner with Marnie. He called me back the next day. Our conversation lasted less than three minutes. I asked for an appointment, he offered me a time, and I took it. When I hung up, I stood up in my office, my whole body shaking. Twice I sat down to resume my legal research, and both times I popped out of my seat thirty seconds later to pace. My mind insisted that making a doctor's appointment was no big deal, but the adrenaline coursing through me hinted otherwise. That night I wrote, *I got off the phone & burst into tears. I felt like I said the wrong stuff & he doesn't like me & I felt exposed and vulnerable.* I didn't care if he could help me; I cared about whether or not he liked me.

The waiting room consisted of bland doctor's office fare: an Easter lily, a gray-scale photograph of a man stretching his arms outward and turning his face toward the sun. The bookshelf held titles like *Codependent No More* and *Vandalized Love Maps* and dozens of AA newsletters. Next to the inner door, there were two buttons: one labeled "group" and one labeled "Dr. Rosen." I pressed the Dr. Rosen button to announce myself and then settled in a chair along the wall facing the door. To calm my nerves, I grabbed a *National Geographic* and flipped through pictures of the majestic Arctic sea wolf galloping across a treeless plain. On the phone Dr. Rosen had sounded serious. I heard East Coast vowels. I heard an unsmiling gravitas. I heard a stern, humorless priest. Part of me had hoped he'd be too booked to see me for a few weeks or months, but he offered an appointment forty-eight hours later.

The waiting room door swung open at exactly one thirty. A slight middle-aged man in a red Tommy Hilfiger golf shirt, khaki pants, and black leather loafers opened the door. His face wore a slight smile— friendly but professional—and what was left of his wiry grayish hair stuck up all over his head, slightly reminiscent of Einstein. If I passed him on the street, I would never look twice. From a quick glance, I could tell he was too young to be my dad and too old to want to fuck, which seemed ideal. I followed him down a hall to an office where northern windows looked out over the multistory Marshall Field's building. There were several patient seating options: a scratchy-looking upholstered couch, an upright office chair, or a black oversize armchair next to a desk. I chose the black armchair. A slew of framed Harvard diplomas drew my eye. I respected the Harvard thing. I'd had Ivy League dreams but state school finances and test scores. To me, those Ivy League certificates signified that this guy was top tier. Elite. Crème de la crème. But it also meant that if he couldn't help me, then I was truly and deeply fucked.

Once I settled in the chair, I took a good look at his face. My heartbeat accelerated as I took in his nose, eyes, and the straight line of his lips. I put them altogether and realized: I knew him. I pressed my lips together as the knowledge sunk in. I totally knew this guy.

This Dr. Rosen was the same Jonathan R. I'd met in a recovery meeting for people with eating disorders three years earlier. In 12-step meetings, people go only by their first name and last initials to preserve their anonymity. Twelve-step meetings for people with eating disorders are like AA meetings—members gather in church basements where they share stories about how food is ruining their lives. Like our more famous AA brethren whose meetings have been depicted in Meg Ryan movies and referenced in TV shows from *The West Wing* to *NYPD Blue*, food addicts collect serenity coins and get sponsors to learn how to live without bingeing, purging, starving, and maiming their flesh. Unlike AA, most of the 12-step meetings I'd attended were filled with women. In ten years, I'd seen only a handful of men in my meetings. One of them was the Harvard-educated psychiatrist sitting two feet away from me, waiting for me to open my mouth.

I knew things about Jonathan R. as a person. A man. A man with an eating disorder. I remembered things he'd shared about his mother, his chronically ill child, his feelings about his body.

A therapist is supposed to be a blank slate. There were smudges all over Dr. Rosen.

I swiveled my body so he could see me head-on. Once he recognized me, would he kick me out right away? His expression remained open, curious. Five seconds passed. He didn't seem to recognize me and was waiting for me to speak. Now the Harvard thing intimidated me. How could I come across as both witty and tortured, like Dorothy Parker or David Letterman? I wanted this Dr. Rosen to take seriously my newly developed fantasies about dying, yet still find me irrepressibly charming and maybe also a little bit fuckable. I figured he'd be more willing to help me if he found me attractive.

"I suck at relationships and am afraid I'll die alone."

"What does that mean?"

"I can't get close to people. Something stops me, like an invisible fence. I can feel myself holding back, always holding back. With guys, I always fall for the ones who drink until they puke or pass out—"

"Alcoholics." Not a question but a statement.

"Yes. My first love in high school smoked pot every day and cheated on me. In college, I fell for a beautiful Colombian fraternity boy who was alcoholic and had a girlfriend, and then I dated a pot addict. There was a nice guy after him, but I dumped him—"

"Because?"

"He walked me to class, bought me copies of his favorite books, and asked permission to kiss me. He made my skin crawl."

Dr. Rosen smiled. "You're afraid of emotionally available men. I suspect women too." More statements.

"Stable guys who express interest in me make me want to vomit. I guess that's true about women too." My mind flashed to a scene from the previous Christmas when I was in Texas visiting my family, and I'd run into a high school friend at Banana Republic. When Lia called out my name, I stood next to the blazers and oxford shirts, frozen, as she hugged me warmly. When she pulled away, a stricken look passed across her face—like *I thought we were friends*—and then she asked me about Chicago and law school. As we chitchatted among the shoppers looking for after-Christmas bargains, my mind insisted that she didn't want to be talking to me because she was now a successful physical therapist without an eating disorder or a weird affliction that made her clam up when someone from her past offered her a hug. Lia and I had been close in high school, but I pulled away senior year when my eating disorder revved up and I became consumed with getting my first boyfriend to stop cheating on me.

"Are you bulimic?"

"I'm in recovery—twelve-step," I said quickly, hoping not to trigger his memory of hearing me introduce myself as *Christie, recovering bulimic.* "The steps helped me with the bulimia, but I can't fix this relationship thing—"

"Not by yourself. Who's in your support system?"

I mentioned my sponsor Cady, a stay-at-home mom of grown kids who lived in the rural Texas town where I went to college. I was closer to her than anyone—I called her every three days but hadn't laid eyes on her in five years. There was my random assortment of women like Marnie with whom I connected during and sometimes after recovery meetings. Law school friends who didn't know I was in recovery. Friends from high school and college in Texas who tried to keep in touch with me, but I rarely returned their phone calls and never accepted their invitations to visit.

"I'm starting to have fantasies about dying." I pressed my lips together. "Ever since I found out I'm first in my class at law school—"

"Mazel tov." His smile was so genuine that I had to turn my head to his diplomas to keep from bursting into tears.

"It's not Harvard or anything." He raised his eyebrows. "And anyway, so I'll have a great career, so what? There won't be anything else—"

"That's why you picked law." His confident diagnoses were both disarming and comforting. He was no Paula D. with her questions about snakes.

"What's the story in your head about how you became you?" Dr. Rosen asked.

"Every family has a fuckup." I don't know why I said that.

"Valedictorian of your law school class, and you're a fuckup?"

"Being valedictorian doesn't mean shit if I'm going to die alone and unattached."

"What do you want?" he asked.

The word *want* echoed in my head. *Want, want, want.* I groped for a way to speak my longing in the affirmative, not just blurt out how I didn't want to die alone.

"I want—" I stalled.

"I would like—" More stopping.

"I want to be real. With other people. I want to be a real person."

He stared at me like *what else?* Other strands of desire floated through my mind: I wanted a boyfriend who smelled like clean cotton and went to work every day. I wanted to spend less than 50 percent of my waking hours thinking about the size of my body. I wanted to eat all of my meals with other people. I wanted to enjoy and seek out sex as much as the women on *Sex and the City.* I wanted to return to ballet class, a passion I dumped when I grew breasts and fleshy thighs. I wanted to have friends to travel the world with after I took the bar exam in two years. I wanted to reconnect with my college roommate who lived in Houston. I wanted to hug high school friends when I ran into them at the mall. But I didn't say any of that because it seemed too specific. Corny. I didn't yet know that therapy, like writing, relied on detail and specificity.

He said he'd put me in a group. I shouldn't have been surprised, but the word *group* landed like a punch between my ribs. A group would be filled with people, people who might not like me, who would pry into my business and violate my mother's edict not to expose my mental anguish to other people's scrutiny.

"I can't do a group."

"Why not?"

"My mother would flip. All those people knowing my business—"

"So don't tell her."

"Why can't I do individual sessions?"

"Group's the only way I know how to get you where you want to go."

"I'll give you five years."

"Five years?"

"Five years to change my life, and if it doesn't work, then I'm out of here. Maybe I'll kill myself." I wanted to wipe that smirk off his face, and I wanted him to know I wasn't going to stick around indefinitely, schlepping downtown to talk about my feelings with other broken people, if there weren't material changes in my life. In five years I'd be thirty-two. If I still had a slick, unattached heart at thirty-two, I would off myself.

He leaned forward. "You want intimate relationships in your life within five years?" I nodded, willing to bear the discomfort of eye contact. "We can do that."

I was scared of Dr. Rosen, but was I going to second-guess the Harvard-educated psychiatrist? His intensity scared me—that laughter, those statements—but it also intrigued me. Such confidence! *We can do that.*

As soon as I agreed to group, I became convinced that something catastrophic would happen to Dr. Rosen. I pictured the number twelve bus mowing him down in front of Starbucks. I pictured his lungs riddled with malignant tumors, his body succumbing to ALS.

"If you meet the Buddha on the road, kill him," Dr. Rosen said in our second session when I told him my fears.

"Aren't you Jewish?" There was the Jewish surname, the mazel tov, the needlepoint with Hebrew letters hanging across from the diplomas.

"The expression means you should pray that I die."

"Why would I do that?"

"If I die"—he clasped his hands together and smiled like a manic elf—"someone better will come along." His face burst with joy, as if he believed that anything—anything at all—could happen, and it would be glorious and better than what came before it.

"I was once in an accident on a beach in Hawaii. Someone I was with drowned." I felt a rise in my chest as I watched his eyes expand before my detonated bomb.

"Jesus. How old were you?"

"Three weeks shy of fourteen." My body buzzed with anxiety as it always did when Hawaii came up. That summer, the sweet spot between eighth grade and starting a new, all-girls Catholic high school, my friend Jenni invited me to join her family for a vacation in Hawaii. We spent three days exploring the main island—black sand beaches, waterfalls, a luau. On the fourth day, we went to a secluded beach at the edge of the island, and Jenni's father drowned in the surf. I never knew how to talk about the experience. My mom called it "the accident," other people called it "the drowning." The night it happened, Jenni's mom called family members back in Dallas, sobbing into the phone: "David's been killed." I didn't have the words for what happened or how it felt to carry the memory of dragging his limp body out of the ocean, so I didn't talk about it.

"Do you want to say more?"

"I'm not praying that you die."

⁓

If you Google "see Buddha kill," you'll find a link to a book titled *If You Meet the Buddha on the Road, Kill Him! The Pilgrimage of Psychotherapy Patients.* Apparently, psychotherapy patients, who were now my people, must learn that therapists are nothing more than struggling human beings like their patients. It was an early signal that Dr. Rosen was not going to give me answers, that he might not have them to give. I added to my fantasy reel of Dr. Rosen's grisly demise an image of me driving a wooden stake into Dr. Rosen's heart, which was unsettling, and not just because I'd confused Buddha with Dracula.

Freshman year of college, some lively, popular girls from Austin invited me to road-trip to New Orleans with them. The plan was to stay at one of the girls' cousin's place and party in the French Quarter until it was time to drive back to campus. I told them I needed to think about it, even though I knew my answer. I cited homework as an excuse, even though it was the second week of school, and my only assignment was to read the first half of *Beowulf*, which I'd read in high school.

Groups intimidated me, even all those years after Bianca and her Jolly Ranchers. Where would I sleep in New Orleans? What if I didn't understand their jokes? What if we ran out of things to say? What if they figured out I wasn't as rich or cool or happy as they were? What if they found out I wasn't a virgin? What if they knew I'd slept with only one guy? What if they learned my secrets around food?

How could I possibly do a group with the same people every week?

"I know you. From meetings." I blurted it out in the middle of my second session. I was afraid that he would one day remember me and then have to kick me out of his practice because we'd sat in meetings together. "From years ago when I lived in Hyde Park."

He cocked his head to the side and narrowed his eyes. "Ah, right. I thought you looked familiar."

"Does this mean you can't treat me?"

His shoulders shook as he burst into elfin laughter. "I hear the wish."

"What?" I stared at his jolly face.

"If you're thinking about committing to treatment with me, you're going to start coming up with excuses about why it won't work."

"It was a legitimate fear."

More laughter.

"What?"

"If you join one of my groups, I want you to tell the group every single thing you remember me sharing during meetings."

"But your anonymity—"

"I don't need you to protect me. That's not your job. Your job is to tell."

My journal entry after the second session was strangely prescient: *I feel nervous about being exposed in therapy about the way I eat . . . I've got a lot of emotion about Dr. Rosen & his role in my life. Fear about my secrets coming out. Fear is so huge.*

Dr. Rosen spoke in koans.

"The starving person isn't hungry until she takes her first bite," he said.

"I'm not anorexic." Oh, sure, I'd wished for an attack of anorexia all through high school when I couldn't stop bingeing on Pringles and Chips Ahoy, but that was never my deal.

"It's a metaphor. When you let the group in—take that first bite—only then will you feel how alone you've been."

"How do I 'let the group in'?"

"You share with them every aspect of your life that deals with relationships—friendship, family, sex, dating, romance. All of it."

"Why?"

"That's how you let them in."

⌁

Before starting group, you got three individual sessions. In my last one, my shoulders relaxed as I curled into Dr. Rosen's black leather armchair. I twirled my bracelet with my index finger and slipped my foot in and out of my shoe. I was used to Dr. Rosen; he was my strange old pal. Nothing to fear here. I'd told him that I knew him from meetings, and he said it wasn't a deal breaker. The only thing left was to hammer out the particulars, like which group would he put me in? He offered a Tuesday morning coed group full of doctors and lawyers that met from seven thirty to nine. A "professionals" group. I hadn't been picturing men in my group. Or doctors. Or lawyers.

"Wait, what's going to happen to me when I start group?"

"You're going to feel lonelier than you ever have in your life."

"Hold the phone, Harvard." I bolted straight up in my chair. "I'm going to feel *worse*?" I'd just met with the dean of students at law school to take out a private health-care loan at 10 percent interest to pay for my new therapy. Now he was telling me that group would make me feel worse than the morning I drove around dribbling plum juice and praying for a bullet to my brain?

"Absolutely." He nodded like he was trying to knock something off the top of his head. "If you're serious about getting into intimate relationships—becoming a real person, as you said—you need to feel every feeling you've been stifling since you were a kid. The loneliness, the anxiety, the anger, the terror." Could I go through this? Did I want to? Curiosity about this man, his groups, and how they might score my heart inched out my resistance, but just barely.

"Can I call you to let you know?"

He shook his head. "I need your commitment today."

I gulped, stared at the door, and considered my options. The commitment scared me, but I was more afraid of walking out of his office empty-handed: no group, no other options, no hope.

"Fine. I commit." I grabbed my purse so I could slink back to work and fret over what I'd just committed to. "One last question. What's going to happen to me when I start group?"

"All of your secrets are going to come out."

4

"*Top or bottom?*" *A portly, balding guy with giant green eyes* and wire-rimmed glasses lobbed this opening salvo at me during my first group session. Later, I learned that the guy who started my hazing was Carlos, a sharp-tongued gay doctor in his late thirties who'd been seeing Dr. Rosen for a few years.

"In sex. Top or bottom?" he said.

Out of the corner of my eye, I saw Dr. Rosen shifting his gaze from one member to another, like a sprinkler on a timer. I smoothed the front of my skirt. If they wanted bawdy, sex-positive Christie, I'd serve her up.

"Definitely top."

Of course, this Christie was a fabricated version of me who welcomed intrusive questions from strangers with a smile. Underneath my skittering nerves and accelerated pulse, I felt like crying because the authentic answer to the question was that I had no idea how I liked to have sex. I didn't date guys capable of consistent sex, thanks to their depression and addiction. I said top because I had a foggy memory of pleasure with my high school boyfriend, the basketball star slash pothead who boned me regularly in the front seat of my dad's Chevy.

Dr. Rosen did a theatrical throat clear.

"What?" It was the first time I looked straight at Dr. Rosen since

group started. He'd opened the waiting room door and led me, Carlos, and two other people to a corner office on the opposite end of
the hallway from the room where'd I'd had my individual sessions. In
the fourteen-by-fourteen group room, there were seven swivel chairs
arranged in a circle. Sunlight striped the room from the slats in the
mini blinds. In one corner there was a bookshelf, lined with titles on
addiction, codependency, alcoholism, and group therapy. On the bottom
shelf, a motley assortment of stuffed animals and a nun with boxing
gloves spilled over the edge. I'd selected a chair facing the door, which
was nine o'clock to Dr. Rosen's high noon position. The chair was hard
on my ass and squeaked faintly when I swiveled left and right. Honestly,
I'd expected spiffier accommodations from a Harvard alum.

"How about an honest answer?" Dr. Rosen said. His grin broadcast
a challenge, like he knew without a doubt I'd begun my group career
masquerading as a sexually healthy woman.

"Such as?"

"That you don't like having sex at all." My face flushed. That was
not how I would have described myself.

"That's not true. I love having sex, I just can't find anyone to have sex
with." I'd had orgasms and toe-curling sex before—in college there was
that Colombian alcoholic who touched my face as he kissed me, lighting
me up like a supernova. And I genuinely liked being on top those few
times with my high school boyfriend, tilting my pelvis just so, charging
forward into my sexuality as only a drunk-on-Zima seventeen-year-old
could. I didn't know where those buried parts of me went or why I
couldn't hold on to them.

A grandpa-aged guy with a military buzz cut and a Colonel Sanders
goatee—a retired proctologist—piped in. "A pretty girl like you? That
can't be true." Was he leering at me?

"Guys don't . . . respond to me." Tears threatened. Two minutes into
the session, and I was cracking. I remembered when my all-girls Catholic high school sent us on a spiritual retreat sophomore year, and my retreat leader opened with a story about her bulimic past. I responded by
bursting into tears and confessing my bulimia to a roomful of fourteen-
year-olds, whom I then swore to secrecy. It was the first time I'd told

anyone about my purging. Sitting across from Colonel Sanders, I felt the confusion from the retreat sidle up next to me, hovering: Would opening my mouth to spill the truth to strangers salvage my life or would it destroy me as my mother predicted?

"What do you mean, 'respond'?" Colonel Sanders was definitely leering.

"Guys *always* approach my friends, but never me. It's been like that since high school." In co-ed groups at bars or parties, I would stand slightly off to the side, never sure what to do with my hands, finding it impossible to laugh in my normal pitch or join the conversation because I was trying to imagine how to get the guys to like me. It wasn't just American guys. My college roommate Kat and I traveled all over Europe after college, and not one single guy hit on me. Not even in Italy. Meanwhile, guys from Munich, Nice, Lucerne, and Bruges fell all over Kat and ignored me.

A buzzer rang, and Dr. Rosen pressed a button on the wall behind him.

Three seconds later, a smiling woman in her late forties with chipped turquoise nail polish, overprocessed orange hair, and a raspy smoker's voice walked in. Her fringy rayon shirt was more Woodstock than downtown Chicago. I'd seen her a few times in 12-step meetings. "I'm Rory," she said to me and another older guy sitting across from me, who was apparently new to the group as well. Like a den mother, she pointed everyone out and told us their names and occupations. Colonel Sanders's given name was Ed. Carlos, a dermatologist. Patrice, a partner in an obstetrics practice. Rory was a civil rights attorney. The new guy, Marty, had Groucho Marx eyebrows and a habit of sniffing every ten seconds. He introduced himself as a psychiatrist who worked with Southeast Asian refugees.

"So you're here to have more sex?" Colonel Sanders said.

I shrugged. Literally, moments before I admitted as much, but now I was backing away because of messages embedded in my marrow: Nice girls don't want *it*. Feminists don't need *it*. Good girls don't talk about *it* at all, especially in mixed company. My mother would die if she knew I was talking about *it* with these strangers.

From there, the conversation ping-ponged to Rory, who mentioned she'd asked her father for money to pay her bills. Dr. Rosen steered Rory to her father's Holocaust survival story, which involved hiding in a trunk in Poland for several years. Abruptly, the conversation pivoted to Carlos's patient who refused to pay his bill.

As the group zigzagged from issue to issue, I shifted from butt cheek to butt cheek on that hard-ass chair. I sighed and cleared my throat in frustration. Nothing was resolved. Didn't anyone want any answers? Resolutions? Worse, as the newcomer, I had no context for any of the stories. Why did Carlos's assistant quit? Why did Rory seem so anti-Semitic when her dad survived the Holocaust in a footlocker? What was the deal with her overdue Visa bill?

At some point in the session I fingered the beads of my pearl bracelet like a rosary strand to soothe myself. Dr. Rosen watched me, his newest lab rat. Would he later write a note for my file? *CT manipulates jewelry with her digits during group discussion. CT demonstrates all the classic signs of someone with major intimacy issues, severe repression. Tough case.*

I'd left my three individual sessions feeling that, despite his cockiness and strange sense of humor, Dr. Rosen and I had a bond. I believed he understood me, but now it felt like we were total strangers. I called him an asshole in my head.

There were unwritten group rules.

"You crossed your legs," Colonel Sanders said. I stared down at my right thigh crossed over my left. Everyone turned toward me.

"So what?" I asked, defensive.

"We don't do that here." Colonel Sanders eyed my legs. I uncrossed them quickly.

"Why not?" If making me feel stupid was a way to get better, I'd be cured by Christmas.

"It means you're not open." That was Carlos.

"It means you're ashamed." That was Rory.

"You're shutting down emotionally." That was Patrice.

The group room was a fishbowl. There was nowhere to hide from the six pairs of eyes around the circle. They could read my body. Make assessments. Draw conclusions. They could *see* me. The exposure made me want to cross my legs until the end of the session. Until the end of time.

Dr. Rosen came to life and spoke. "What are you feeling?"

Instead of blurting out a bullshit answer that I thought would win me points—*I feel empowered by the group dynamics*—I took a breath and searched for the truth. I'd lost my bearings, but decided that the truth could function like a home base. It had worked in 12-step meetings—I was alive because I'd told the truth about my bulimia over and over in meetings. Nothing in my life had empowered me—not good grades, not a thin body, not dry-humping a beautiful Latin fraternity boy—like speaking the raw truth about vomiting up my meals. The first true, full-bodied sensation of power I ever felt was after my first 12-step meeting when I sat on a bench with a woman from the meeting and told her that I'd been bingeing and purging food I'd stolen all over campus. I felt the power of turning my back on my mother's proscription about telling other people my business. I released a secret, not caring who in my family might abandon me, because I finally understood that keeping the secret was an act of abandoning myself. If there was a way to health in group therapy—and I wasn't sure there was—the foundation had to be built on truth. There was no other way. And none of these people knew my mother or any of her friends. So no more fronting.

"Defensive." How was I supposed to know that *we* don't cross our legs?

Dr. Rosen shook his head. "That's not a feeling."

"But that's exactly . . ." Now I was pissed, and I was *positive* that was a feeling.

Another rule: "Feelings have two syllables or less: ashamed, angry, lonely, hurt, sad, afraid—" Dr. Rosen explained feelings like Fred Rogers talking to a preschooler. Apparently, once you veer beyond two syllables, you are intellectualizing, effectively darting away from the simple truth of your feelings.

"And happy," Rory said.

"But you won't feel that in here," Carlos said. Everyone laughed. The corners of my mouth rose in a smile.

Dr. Rosen nodded in my direction. "So what's 'defensive'?"

My first pop quiz. I wanted to give the right answer. It felt as hard as figuring out Sheldon's conference on the LSAT practice test. I ran through the roster of feelings. *Frustrated* came to mind, but that was three syllables. *Furious?* Nope, three syllables. Three blind mice. Three times the cock crowed. Three times Jesus fell. Three was holy. Three was biblical. Why couldn't I use a three-syllable word? My top choice: *adios*.

"Angry?" I said.

"I heard something else. How about shame?"

I said it aloud: "Ashamed?"

I thought of shame as something survivors of incest or ritual abuse had to work through. Shame belonged to people who had committed grave sexual sins or who did embarrassing things in public while naked. Did it belong to me? I always wore my clothes, even to bed—I often wore a bra during sex. Was *shame* the word for the feeling that everything about me was wrong and had to be buried under perfect test scores? Is shame what I felt as a little girl in ballet class when I pined for a petite body like the Jennifers and Melissas? Was that the name of the body disgust I felt in my gut growing up when I sat next to my friends and my younger sister, and compared the vast expanse of my thighs with their delicate, birdlike bones?

I wanted to be valedictorian in therapy like I was in law school. The problem with being number one, of course, was that it didn't cure my loneliness or bring me one inch closer to other people. Then there was the fact that I hadn't a clue how to be "good" at group therapy.

The cardinal rule in Rosen-land, of course, was no secret keeping among group members, which came up when Carlos discussed a woman named Lynne who was in another Rosen group. According to Carlos, Lynne planned to leave her husband because, in part, of his erectile dysfunction. I scrunched up my nose and shot a look at Dr. Rosen. How could he allow us to talk about some innocent man's broken penis? What if I knew him? When Marnie mentioned the no-secrets business, I didn't realize Dr. Rosen would actually condone gossip about other patients *in the middle of a session*.

"What about confidentiality?" I said.

"We don't do that here," Rory said. Patrice and Carlos confirmed with vigorous nodding. The memory of my mother scolding me in high school flashed in my mind. I'd bent the vow to let 12-step people in, but they were bound by the spiritual principle of anonymity, which was right there in the name of the program. What were these jokers bound by?

"How are we supposed to feel safe?"

"What makes you think confidentiality makes you safe?" Dr. Rosen looked energized, ready to school me.

"Group therapy's always confidential." My authority on group therapy was one friend from graduate school who had to sign a confidentiality agreement when she joined a group. "Maybe I don't want my secrets all over your group grapevine."

"Why not?"

"You don't get why I want privacy?" There were zero expressions of outrage on the faces staring back at me.

"You might want to look at why you're so invested in privacy."

"Isn't it standard practice?"

"It might be, but keeping secrets for other people is more toxic than other people knowing your business. Holding on to secrets is a way to hold shame that doesn't belong to you."

On one level I understood what he was saying. Food addicts in recovery meetings got well when they told their stories. But at the beginning of every 12-step meeting, there is a reminder: *What you hear here, when you leave here, stays here.* When that line is read, people in the meeting respond: *here, here!* Dr. Rosen was ethically bound to keep my secrets as my psychiatrist, but there were five other people who would hear every word I said. The walls of the group room were not a barrier to the information flowing out. What if I one day embezzled money from my future law firm? What if I developed irritable bowel syndrome and shit my pants on Michigan Avenue? What if I slept with someone who couldn't use punctuation properly? How was I going to feel knowing that some Joe Schmo in the Wednesday men's group might know details about the acrobatic sex I one day hoped to have?

"What am I going to get out of this?" I didn't know then that this question would come out of my mouth so many times that it would become part mantra, part catchphrase.

"A place to come where everything is speakable, and you are not asked to hold any secrets for anyone. Ever."

At the end of the session, Dr. Rosen pressed his palms together. "We'll stop there for today." Everyone stood up. To me, Dr. Rosen said, "We close the same way they close twelve-step meetings, holding hands in a circle saying the Serenity Prayer. If you are not comfortable with that, you don't have to participate."

I flashed him my "this ain't my first rodeo" smile. I'd just sat through ninety minutes of group therapy; if anyone needed the Serenity Prayer, it was me. The familiar prayer was meant to help addicts get in touch with a power greater than themselves without invoking any particular religious tradition: *God, grant me the serenity to accept the things I cannot change, courage to change the things I can, and the wisdom to know the difference.*

After we recited the prayer, everyone turned to the person next to them and embraced. Rory and Patrice. Marty and Ed. Carlos and Dr. Rosen. I watched them, unprepared to step forward and press my body to theirs, but when Patrice opened her arms to me, I stepped forward and let her hug me. My arms hung at my sides like empty sleeves. Dr. Rosen stood in front of his chair, and my group members stepped over to hug him, one by one.

I stepped forward and wrapped my arms around Dr. Rosen's shoulders and gave a quick squeeze—too quick to smell him or to retain memory of his arms around my body or mine around his. So quick it felt like it didn't happen. There was no imprint on my body. I hugged him because I wanted to fit in, do what everyone else was doing, and not draw any attention to myself. Years later, I'd watch new patients come in and refuse to hug anyone, especially Dr. Rosen, and my jaw would drop open, realizing it never once occurred to me *not* to hug him. I didn't have that kind of *no* anywhere in my body.

After group, I rode the Red Line train north to school, my head buzzing with the new faces, the new feelings vocabulary, the new world I'd just joined. Dr. Rosen acted like he knew all about me. His definitive statement—*you don't like having sex at all*—stung. So cocky! Just because he was a fancy psychiatrist didn't mean he knew everything. I'd once been open to pleasure, and if he ever bothered to ask me about it, I would look him and each of the group members in the eye with my legs uncrossed and tell them all about it.

and

The night of my first big O the spring weather in Texas was pleasant enough that I had my bedroom window open at 6644 Thackeray Avenue.

I couldn't sleep, so I flipped on the radio and heard, "*Sexually Speaking*, you're on the air." *Ooooh*. This radio program was *not* for kids. I burrowed deeper under the covers. Sister Mary Margaret told us that sex was only for married couples trying to make a baby—having sex under any other circumstances would lead to hell, far away from God, our parents, and our pets. My mom affirmed that Catholic truth over dinner one night when she explained that there were two sins that would get you a one-way ticket to eternal damnation: "Murder and premarital sex."

It was not hard to imagine myself slipping from God's favor as I scooched up the volume on the radio.

A caller confessed that she was unable to reach orgasms with her partner. What followed were Dr. Ruth Westheimer's instructions on how to get to know your body through masturbation. Helpfully, Dr. Ruth explained where the clitoris was and what it did. It was almost like she knew she was talking to a fourth grader.

I couldn't let all that sage advice go to waste. I slid my hand between my legs and touched the delicate pearl that sometimes hurt when I rode my bike for too long. Slowly, I circled it with my finger until I felt something happening—a warm wave building, making my legs go stiff. My fantasy reel: Tad Martin from *All My Children* kissed my face and told me he loved me more than all the women in Pine Valley. I rubbed myself harder. The extra pressure didn't hurt. My body climbed toward its first glorious sexual release. Then my whole body shuddered with pleasure just as Dr. Ruth promised. For the first time in my life, I thought: My body is exquisite and powerful.

There in the balmy, darkened privacy of my childhood bedroom, I tripped into my sexuality under the gentle tutelage of Dr. Ruth. I felt grown-up to have discovered the sexual secrets of adulthood. This touching myself and the warm wave of intense body pleasure must have been naughty because nobody ever talked about doing it. Masturbation was the grossest-sounding word I could imagine, and I'd never ever say it.

By fourth grade, I'd been marinating in body hatred for a few years. My stomach was too big—that was the message I received starting at age four from my beloved ballet teacher. "Christie," she'd say. "Stomach." A reminder to suck it in, make it disappear. She favored the girls whose leotards didn't bulge and whose upper thighs didn't quite touch. I wanted more than anything to be a ballerina and to be adored by my teacher, and the one thing holding me back on both fronts was the size of my body. I also suspected that my mother's sighs when I modeled new clothes in the Joske's and Dillard's dressing rooms were proof that she wished I was thin-boned. I know I did. I believed that slim, lithe girls like my sister and the Jennifers and Melissas in ballet class were happier because of their smaller bodies. They were certainly better loved. In attempts to become one of those small-bodied girls, I engaged in minor skirmishes with my appetite—trying to eat half a sandwich at lunch or skipping dessert—but my appetite always won. Every day, I'd enter the kitchen with the intention of getting a glass of water and three Club crackers, yet ended up consuming a fistful of Chips Ahoy and knocking back half a pitcher of grape Kool-Aid. Why couldn't I control my appetite? Why was my body keeping me from being who I was supposed to be?

I was a sensitive kid already gearing up for a years-long war with my body through bulimia, but in my dark room with my hand between my legs, I experienced unalloyed body pleasure. For those few minutes, I could make peace with my flesh and drift off to sleep.

Dr. Rosen didn't know about little Christie's forays into self-pleasure. That little girl had the guts to turn up the radio and explore.

5

"*Christie, why don't you tell the group what you ate yesterday,*" Dr. Rosen said.

"No!" My voice ricocheted off the walls. I jumped out of my chair and hopped around in the middle of the circle like I was trying to put out a fire. "No, no, no! Please, Dr. Rosen. Don't make me!" I begged like a child. *Not this; please not this.* I'd never acted like this before. But no one had ever asked me point-blank about my food.

"Jesus, woman. If you're going to act like that, then you have to tell us," Carlos said.

We hadn't even been talking about food. We'd been talking about the medical bills for Rory's ferret.

I was one month into treatment. In four Tuesday sessions, the group and I had gone through all the getting-to-know-you rituals. They knew I came to group because I struggled with relationships. They knew about the bulimia, and they knew about me and Dr. Ruth. But this? Telling the seven people in front of me what I'd eaten the day before? Impossible.

My eating disorder was no longer the stuff of a *Lifetime* movie—I didn't go from drive-through to drive-through eating and puking, but I ate like a weirdo. Exhibit A: Every single morning I ate a slice of mozzarella cheese rolled up in a cabbage leaf, along with a bowl of microwaved apple pieces that I poured skim milk over and ate with a spoon. "Apple Jacks," I called them. This had been my breakfast for almost three years straight. Never a Sausage McMuffin, chocolate croissant, or granola bar. If I couldn't have my secret special breakfast, alone in the privacy of my kitchen, then I skipped breakfast. This breakfast was safe. It never, ever beckoned me toward a binge.

My law school friends saw my odd lunch every day because I couldn't hide it: a can of tuna in springwater over a bed of green cabbage doused with French's Classic Yellow Mustard. They justifiably made fun of me for how disgusting and unimaginative it was. A normal person would never eat this lunch more than once; I ate it every single day. At lunchtime, the other students would saunter across campus for subs loaded with pink-and-white meats and cheeses, dripping with chunky jardinière sauce, while I sat back in the student lounge eating like a rabbit at a ballpark, prepping for the next class. They didn't know that before I got into recovery, my relationship with food led me to crouch, face-to-toilet, after most meals. The body memory of losing control of my appetite and ending up literally in the toilet haunted me. I almost met my ignominious death in college. You could say a lot about my lunch—it was flavorless, deprivational, and guaranteed to induce heartburn—but it kept me from losing control. Could those fancy subs do that?

For dinner, I ate sautéed ground turkey mixed with broccoli, carrots, or cauliflower and a tablespoon of Parmesan cheese. Every now and then I'd mix it up and use ground chicken instead of turkey. Once I tried ground lamb, but it was greasy and made my apartment smell gamy. When I got into recovery for bulimia, I picked a handful of foods that seemed "safe" because I'd never binged on them. I didn't have the courage to veer from my safe foods.

The bingeing popped up elsewhere, though. That was the secret rotting inside me. Every night, for "dessert," I'd have three or four red apples—often more. Sometimes as many as eight. When I hinted at my apple consumption to my sponsor Cady back in Texas, she assured me that as long as I didn't eat white sugar, it didn't matter if I ate a bushel of apples three times a day. White sugar was the devil's poison to many people in recovery—it would lead you to a death by doughnuts. Cady gave me permission to keep apples on the "safe food" list no matter how many bushels I went through per week.

I spent more on apples than I spent on cable, gas, and transportation combined. Apples were the reason I didn't have a roommate—I was terrified of being found out, but I also couldn't imagine eating only a single apple every night.

"Tell us," Rory said, her voice soft and gentle.

I squeezed my eyes shut and spoke fast, like an auctioneer at a cattle sale. "Cheese, cabbage, apple, milk, cabbage, tuna, mustard, an orange, chicken, carrots, and spinach." I paused, scared to go on. I couldn't imagine telling them about the apples, but keeping the secret suddenly felt unbearable. They would say I had had no recovery, that I hadn't properly worked the steps, and that I was a failure. Inwardly, I screamed hysterically. But somehow, I blurted out: "Then I ate six more apples."

Hard to say which shame burned hotter: eating half a dozen apples after dinner or that the villain of my food diary was the innocuous darling of the produce section. I'd sat in hundreds of 12-step meetings listening to people report bizarre and appalling things they did with cherry cheesecake, black licorice, scalloped potatoes. And there was me with a bag of apples on my lap.

The previous night's binge had been routine. I ate one apple right after dinner and swore I was done eating for the day. But there was a stirring in my belly: Was I still hungry? Was it a somatic signal that I needed more calories? I had no idea. A woman I knew from recovery always said that if you craved food after dinner, you should sit on your bed until it passed. I tried it—sitting cross-legged atop my comforter listening to sounds on the street below—but the craving for apples drew me off the bed and into the kitchen, where I grabbed another one from the fridge drawer. I ate another apple, fast, like maybe it wouldn't count if I ate it in under sixty seconds. Then the shame—the buzzword I'd learned in group—of speed-eating an apple alone in my apartment crested, so I ate two more. My belly was tender to the touch. What the fuck was I doing? I didn't know, but I ate two more Red Delicious. When I finally crawled under the covers to sleep, the sharp edges of the apple bits I'd failed to chew properly poked the edges of my stomach. Acid burned my throat.

How in the world could I call myself "in recovery" around food when I did this to myself every night? How would anyone love someone who ate like me? I'd been doing this for years. How would it ever stop?

Dr. Rosen asked if I wanted help. I nodded slowly, terrified he would suggest I eat bison burgers and artichoke pizza or a pint of Ben & Jerry's every night like a normal lonely person. Or worse, that I stopped eating apples.

"Call Rory every night and tell her what you ate."

Rory met my eyes with a smile so kind I had to look away or I would cry—like Dr. Rosen's mazel tov for my class rank. Head-on kindness warmed my solar plexus like a heat lamp and made me tear up.

Having my ritual revealed at last, in detail, was like having a layer of skin removed. The defining feature of my eating was secrecy. In kindergarten, I snuck cookies from the snack bin. Thanksgiving weekend of junior year in high school, I snuck-ate the top layer off a pecan pie. I stole food from every roommate I'd ever had. Even in recovery, I let go of the vomiting, but I kept the secrecy. And some version of the bingeing.

"I'm not trying to keep you from eating apples," Dr. Rosen said. "Eat as many as you want. The apples aren't killing you; the secrecy is. And the point is"—he leaned close and lowered his voice—"if you can let this group into your relationship with food, you will be closer to intimate relationships. You'll start with Rory."

I looked at Rory and imagined telling her about every morsel I put in my mouth. My whole body clenched, mostly with fear, but there was also hope. Here was a chance to be known inside the messiness of my eating, something I'd never truly let myself have before.

It wasn't a total surprise that my food stuff and relationship stuff sprouted from the same broken parts of me. What surprised me was that Dr. Rosen understood that. Paula D. hadn't seen it, and I was actively vomiting back then.

"Will calling Rory cure my apple binges?"

"You don't need a cure. You need a witness."

I wanted a cure. Apples were expensive.

⁓

Sophomore year in college I fell for the soulful Colombian with dimples deep as watering holes. He would drunk-dial me after the bars closed, and we would make out behind the Kappa Kappa Gamma house. He was the guy who taught me everything a kiss could be. Before him, I couldn't grasp the big deal about touching my lips to someone else's, but when his soft tongue met mine, I understood in an instant. A good kiss can reach every organ, every cell. It can steal your breath and make a cathedral of your mouth. Those kisses woke me up.

And then they fucked me up. The Colombian was a double whammy—an alcoholic with a serious girlfriend. The one time I slept over at his apartment, he was so drunk that he pissed in his closet because he thought it was the bathroom. Where was I when he relieved himself four feet from the bed at two A.M.? In his kitchen, shoving left-over birthday cake into my mouth. When I headed out for my walk of shame a few hours later, I ignored the amphitheater of black cake crumbs and the smear of frosting on the linoleum floor.

I was his secret side dish when his real girlfriend, the willowy Chi Omega with the straight blond hair, visited her parents in San Antonio.

The weekend of the Colombian's fraternity spring formal in Galveston, Texas, I ran by his apartment. Like a creepy stalker I watched him and the Chi Omega load up his Ford Bronco with cases of Shiner Bock. He patted her ass; she threw back her hair.

Devastated, I ran back to my dorm and consumed every calorie in our tiny cinder-block room: Teddy Grahams, pretzels, popcorn, Pop-Tarts, and leftover Halloween candy my roommate kept in her closet. Then I walked the halls, scavenging food from the common trash bins. I pulled some other kid's discarded pepperoni pizza out of the trash and popped it into the microwave for thirty seconds. While I waited for the cheese to melt, I devoured a batch of stale oatmeal raisin cookies that were still in a FedEx box from someone's mom in Beaumont.

I'd been bingeing and purging since seventh grade; I didn't need to use my finger. All I had to do was bend over the toilet. When I was done purging, I ran the shower to clean myself up before my roommate returned from a study group. My stomach felt like it would split open lengthwise. Steam billowed in the tiny bathroom, and I hugged the wall, waiting to see if more vomit was coming. Black dots swirled in my vision. I sank into the floor, half in the shower and half out. Before everything went black, I thought: This is it; this is how I die, bingeing myself into oblivion and moping over a boy.

I dialed Rory's number. Mercifully, her recorded voice greeted me, and then the beep. My turn. In a voice barely above a whisper, I recounted all the cabbage and the five postdinner apples. After I hung up, I threw my phone across the bedroom. It clattered across the hardwood floors. "Goddammit!" I yelled into my apartment, as I punched my pillows. In one moment, I thought: Why am I doing this? It hurts too much. Then: Why didn't I get to Dr. Rosen sooner?

I called Rory again the next night, and it wasn't one bit easier. My hands still shook and I threw my phone across the room when I was done telling her voice mail what I'd eaten. My arms ached with phantom pain as if I'd literally wrestled to keep hold of my precious secret. By the third night, when the voice mail beeped, I almost said "ditto from yesterday," I forced myself to enumerate each apple and cabbage leaf.

The fourth night was the worst. Seven apples. Enough for a prize-winning pie at the state fair. I wanted to hide the reality of those seven apples, but I was midway on a tightrope. If I told her, could I scurry, quick like, to the platform ahead? Either way, I wanted off the tightrope.

It's not going to work if you don't do the hard thing, I told myself. Deep breath. "Seven fucking apples."

6

Dr. Rosen was a snake charmer. He could ask a pointed question and secrets from our past would slither out. He'd coax Rory into recounting details of her father's harrowing escape from Poland, urging her to speak in her father's Old World accent. At Dr. Rosen's urging, Colonel Sanders described the dubious therapy he had with an unlicensed doctor who treated him for PTSD after his service in Vietnam. Dr. Rosen could get Carlos talking about the stepbrother who abused him after Sunday school, and Patrice misting up over her brother who hanged himself in the family orchard. Dr. Rosen sensed where our shame and grief was hidden and knew how to extract it. He prodded me to talk about Hawaii and bulimia almost every session.

Every Tuesday morning, I rode the train eleven stops from my apartment to the Washington stop on the Red Line, where I would climb to the street level around seven ten. Twenty minutes early. The day I'd committed to joining a group, I stopped sleeping through the night. I could fall asleep around ten, but then I'd bolt awake at two or three, and never get back to sleep, so it was easy to get downtown early. But I didn't want to drag my anxious, furiously beating heart to the waiting room to sit there among addiction books waiting for the door to swing open. I'd walk around the block—past Old Navy, down to Carson Pirie Scott, and then east toward the El tracks on Wabash. Sometimes I made two loops, assuring myself: *You're just a woman going to therapy; you're going to sit in a circle and talk for ninety minutes. Easy peasy.*

Sometimes sessions were as emotionally charged as a juicer demonstration at Sam's Club. One week we spent an *entire* session discussing the insurance forms that Carlos wanted Dr. Rosen to sign. Another time, when Patrice showed up with two different colored knee-high stockings (one midnight indigo, the other ebony), we debated for fifteen minutes whether it was progress for fastidious Patrice to mess up her hosiery or whether she was backsliding into self-neglect. There was no tidy conclusion, no resolution.

There were disclosures. There was feedback. There was looking, seeing, and being seen. There were no answers.

I wanted answers.

Pivots happened without warning. One second, quiet Marty, the guy who started the same day I did, would be crying as he described his disturbing cache of death mementos—namely, the cyanide tablets he kept in his bedside table in case he ever wanted to end it all—and then suddenly the group conversation pinged to the time I had pinworm in kindergarten. Pinworm, a common childhood parasite, produces agonizing nighttime anal itching. I told the group how, at five years old, alone in my room at 6644 Thackeray Avenue, I scratched my ass like a feral dog for hours into the night, long after my parents flipped off *The Tonight Show* and went to sleep.

"Did your parents know you had it?" Rory asked.

"Wait," I said, holding up my hands. "We were talking about Marty's cyanide." How had the group landed on my five-year-old butt?

"The group has a way of uncovering things you might need to let go of," Dr. Rosen said.

Dr. Rosen loved detail, so I took a deep breath and described how my parents gave me a tube of Desitin for pinworm, but it didn't relieve the itching. By morning, the stinky white paste was ground under my fingernails and smeared all over my sheets, my nightgown, my butt, and my vagina, which was not where the pinworms were, but everything got confused during the long night of scratching. My mauled vagina, the cream that smelled like fertilizer, and my itchy ass were excruciating. But worse than the physical discomfort was the horrific knowledge that there were live worms in my butt.

"Desitin is a topical solution for diaper rash, and pinworm is a parasite. You would have needed mebendazole," Dr. Rosen said, sounding super doctor-y and looking very Harvard, with his furrowed brow. I longed to dart to someone else's issues, but the group snared me with its questions. Like why I didn't tell my parents Desitin didn't work.

"I thought it was my fault the medicine wasn't working." I wasn't supposed to scratch—they told me not to, but I did. All night long. Plus, who wants to talk about butt worms? Shame, a word I didn't know at five, had clamped my mouth shut.

"You were already committed to doing things alone by age five," Dr. Rosen said like it was a big revelation, but it didn't feel like one. When I had pinworm, I was embarrassed—in Rosen-speak *ashamed*—about being a dirty girl with worms in my butt, worms that weren't crawling through my brother's or my sister's asses. Worms were proof that my body was defective and disgusting. Dr. Rosen pressed me to describe how it felt to be a little girl alone in a fight with an anal parasite.

I shuddered and squeezed my eyes shut. From a distance of two decades, I could smell the Desitin and feel the infernal itching between my legs. I'd never discussed pinworm with anyone, much less a rapt audience of six.

Without opening my eyes, I told them, unprompted, "I felt shame."

"Shame's a cover. What's underneath?" Dr. Rosen said.

I put my head in my hands and scanned my body for an answer. I lifted the corners of shame to see what lurked beneath. I saw my five-year-old face twisted in horror in my childhood bedroom as I scratched past midnight. Horror that I didn't know how to ask for help. That eventually I had to visit the pediatrician, a tall, middle-aged man with fat thumbs and a deep voice, and tell him all about my butt. That during reading circle at school I had to wedge the heel of my tennis shoe into my butt crack to ease the itching without anyone noticing. That I was dirty and lived in a body filled with food I couldn't stop eating and worms that made my butt itch. Most of all, horror that my body was a filthy problem, a problem that no one else had.

"Horror," I answered.

Dr. Rosen nodded his head in approval. "You're getting closer."

"To what?"

"Yourself and your feelings." He swept his arms around the room. "And of course us."

"How will this trip down memory lane help me?"

"Look at Patrice and ask her if she can identify." Patrice looked startled and shook her head like *don't look at me*. After a beat, she launched into a story about a medically administered enema that went wrong. Then Rory mentioned her distaste for anal sex, and Marty contributed a story about the intractable constipation he'd suffered as a kid. By the end of group, everyone had shared a butt story.

A few days after this session, I called my parents. My dad and I discussed my car's sticky brakes, the Aggies' prospects for the Cotton Bowl, and the unseasonably cool weather in Chicago. Then I pulled a Rosen: out of the blue, I asked him about my pinworm history. What did he remember? (not much) How many times did I get them? (several) Did my siblings ever have them? (no) In the background, I heard my mother's voice: "Why is Christie asking about pinworm?" I gripped the phone harder. The confession that I'd joined a therapy group gathered in my mouth, but dissolved when I imagined *her* horror upon realizing that I'd discussed my butt worm history with a group of people. Plus, if I told her about Dr. Rosen and group, I'd have to admit that I'd failed at both willing myself to be happy *and* not telling other people my business.

"Why are you asking?" my dad said.

"Just curious."

One Tuesday morning, no one said a word during the entire ninety-minute session. All of us literally sat in silence, listening to the El train lumber below, car brakes screeching, and someone shutting a door down the hall. We didn't catch each other's eyes or giggle. During the first half, I plucked lint off my sweater, jangled my leg, and picked my cuticles. I looked at the clock every thirty seconds. The silence made me feel exposed, antsy, and unproductive. *I could be reading my Constitutional Law assignment.* Gradually, I stilled and watched Lake Michigan out the window. The quiet space we were holding felt as vast as the ocean or outer space. The light streaming in the room seemed holy; the intimacy among us sacred. At nine, Dr. Rosen folded his hands and said his usual "We'll stop there for today."

As I walked down the hall with my group members, I carried the quiet calm in my body, though once we reached the street, I shook Carlos's arm: "What the fuck just happened in there?"

Whatever it was, through the rest of the day, I carried a quiet calm and sense of awe that I could sit with six other people in total silence for ninety minutes.

Dr. Rosen gave a lot of prescriptions, though rarely for drugs. He wasn't a pill guy. Carlos got a prescription to bring his guitar to group and play a song for us to help allay his fears about expanding his practice. Patrice got a prescription to rub strawberries on her husband's stomach, lick them off, and then report the results to group. And because Dr. Rosen thought that the prescription Rory's internist gave her for anxiety was suppressing her sexual feelings, he gave her his own: "Put one pill between each of your toes while your husband goes down on you."

I'd been following my prescription to call Rory every night to tell her my food for a few weeks. I no longer cried after I hung up the phone, and my apple consumption was down to a modest five per night. It was time for another prescription.

"Can I have something for my insomnia. I can't think straight." My second year of law school was under way, and when I wasn't sitting in group, I was interviewing with Chicago's biggest law firms for a summer internship, which I hoped would lead to an offer for full-time employment. Not sleeping well for weeks meant that fatigue pressed against my skull, making it hard to stay awake for classes and interviews. At Winston & Strawn, I'd pinched the inside of my arm to stay awake while a white-haired managing partner described the time he argued before the Supreme Court.

I'd already confessed that my eating was a hot steamy mess; now I admitted I couldn't sleep. I was a newborn baby stuck in a twenty-seven-year-old's body.

Dr. Rosen sat up and rubbed his hands together like a mad scientist. "Call Marty tonight before you go to sleep and ask for an affirmation."

"Before or after I call Rory to tell her what I ate?"

"Doesn't matter."

"I'm going to the opera tonight, so call me before seven," Marty said.

At six fifty that night, I stood on the train platform at Belmont, exhausted from the long day of classes and a five-hour interview at Jones, Day, where again I'd pinched in the inside of my arm to stay awake while talking to senior partners. I dialed Marty's number as wind slapped my hair into my face.

"I'm calling for my affirmation," I said into the phone as the lights of an incoming northbound train rose toward the platform.

"You have great legs, toots." Marty wasn't skeevy, like Colonel Sanders. He wept every time he opened his mouth in group and seemed genuinely astonished when we asked to know more about what made him so sad. He always said, "I just can't believe anyone is listening to me."

I laughed into the roar of the oncoming train and prayed his words would work like an extra-strength Ambien.

The next morning I hesitated before opening my eyes, afraid to see that it was only two A.M. I heard morning sounds. My neighbor's door slamming. Birdsong. A car starting. I opened my left eye and saw the clock—five fifteen. I'd gotten an unprecedented seven hours of sleep. I pumped my fist like a champion.

Maybe Dr. Rosen was brilliant.

7

As winter descended on Chicago, I practiced bringing mundane issues to group. A prickle of shame skidded down my spine when I asked my group to weigh in on matters I should know how to handle as a reasonably intelligent twenty-seven-year-old, like whether I should use some of my financial aid money to go on a ski trip organized by my college roommate Kat. The group unanimously voted yes to the trip. Dr. Rosen pressed me for a good reason *not* to go.

"It's all couples. I'll be the eleventh wheel."

"Be open," Dr. Rosen said.

I can't believe it! You never come to anything! Kat wrote when I accepted her invitation.

On the Tuesday morning between Christmas and New Year's, I dialed Rory's cell from a cabin in Crested Butte. It was my first time missing a session.

"Hi, sweetie, let me put you on speaker." I heard a rustling and then Rory's voice, slightly muffled: "Everyone say hi to Christie." A chorus of hellos in the background.

"What're y'all doing?" I asked, picturing each of them in their regular spots, the gray Chicago sky out the window.

"It's boring without you," Carlos said.

"Y'all miss me?" Weren't they grateful to have a break from me and my pitiful stories of too many apples, too many worms?

"Everyone's nodding," Rory said. "Even Dr. Rosen."

My heart soared up over the Rocky Mountains and zoomed across the plains to the fourteen-by-fourteen room where they sat, where there was an empty chair my body usually fit, where they held me in their minds.

As a kid, my siblings and I would take turns visiting our paternal grandmother, who lived in a big yellow farmhouse in Forreston, Texas. I loved those weeks—I could roam around her property, looking for treasures by the creek and picking through bones at the cow graveyard. Once, I called home halfway through my visit. I can't remember why. I think I was testing my ability to make a long-distance call. The phone at 6644 Thackeray Avenue rang and rang. *Maybe they're at the neighborhood pool or in the backyard.* I tried again that night. No answer. Where could they be?

When my dad called that weekend to arrange a time to pick me up, I grabbed the phone from my grandma. "Where were y'all? I tried to call two nights ago."

"We went to Oklahoma for a few days."

They took a vacation without me? My vision blurred as tears gathered. I'd never been to Oklahoma, and suddenly I was desperate to go—to see whatever they'd seen. Cool stuff like authentic tepees tended by women in long black braids and working oil rigs dotting a straight dusty highway. How could they travel—cross the state line!—without me? This clearly meant I wasn't an integral part of my family, and the realization made me want to curl up and bawl.

On the other end of the phone my dad explained that they'd gone to pick up an antique armoire from a family friend in Ponca City. "The Howard Johnson's a/c was broken, and your mother is still mad at me for making her eat at a Kentucky Fried Chicken, where we watched a dog eat a rat in the parking lot." He spoke as if the trip was a disaster, but all I could hear was that magical, wondrous things happened in this land called *Oklahoma*. And I heard this: *You don't matter. We vacation without you, because you don't matter.*

For years, my mother would shudder whenever the trip to Oklahoma came up. There was not a single picture, and no member of my family harbored a happy memory from their weekend jaunt to Oklahoma. And yet I too would shudder at the mention of the state due north of Texas because it was proof that I could be left behind.

⌒

Winter also brought my first date since joining group. Carlos set me up with his friend Sam, an attorney who was fresh out of a relationship. In our first phone conversation, Sam and I established an easy rapport. He admitted that he'd never seen an episode of *Survivor*, and I confessed I abandoned *Harry Potter* after the first chapter. When I got off the phone because my book club meeting was about to start, he sounded impressed that a busy law student would also take the time to read for pleasure.

I had every reason to believe that Sam and I would hit it off. We both adored Carlos and had mixed feelings about the legal profession. I watched out the window as he parked his car in front of my apartment at eight o'clock sharp. My belly stirred with excitement. In the bathroom, I applied one more coat of the lipstick Carlos picked out for me at Barneys.

When I opened the door, I thought we'd hug, but he stuck out his hand and smiled in a clinical way that didn't reach his eyes. He then turned quickly to head down the stairs, like a man who had double parked in front of a hydrant. I didn't despair, though. The whole night stretched before us full of possibility and, perhaps later, physical contact.

Sam hadn't made a reservation and offered no suggestions about where to go. An awkward silence hung between us until I suggested a Cuban place on Irving Park near my apartment. As we drove, the only sound in the car was my voice giving him directions. Had I made up the chemistry I felt on the phone?

At Café 28, Sam left his wool Burberry scarf wrapped around his neck and was curt with the waitstaff. By the time our food came, it was clear this was going nowhere. The disappointment made me want to smash my fist into the stupid potatoes and hurl my salmon across the room. I'd bought lipstick and a sweater for this. I'd been going to group, calling Rory, calling Marty, and "letting the group in" as Dr. Rosen suggested. Where were the results? Why was Sam so remote and uninterested?

We rode home in silence so complete it was nuclear. Sam did not walk me to the door; he did not cut the engine. Maybe he stuck his hand out for a closing handshake, but I'd turned my back on him after thanking him for dinner. When I walked into my apartment, the clock read eight fifty.

My date hadn't even lasted an hour.

I dialed Dr. Rosen's number; his was number one, the valedictorian of my speed dial. To his voice mail, I announced my conclusion. "Therapy isn't working. Please call me tomorrow. I'm sinking." I paced in circles around my apartment, wondering why Sam hadn't given me a chance. I shared the humiliation with Rory when I called with my food report, and Marty when I called for my affirmation.

"It's not your fault the date sucked," they promised. "Some dates just suck."

The next day I did something I'd never done in my entire educational career: Skipped class to huddle under the covers and stare into the void. I didn't watch TV, read a book, or review any notes for class. Around noon, my closest friend from law school, Clare, left a voice mail. "Hey, no one can remember the last time you didn't show up for class. Call me."

The familiar stuckness I'd felt most of my life shut out every other thought, every other sensation. It felt like it would always be there, obstructing my breath, my blood, my desire. Stuck, stuck, stuck. Therapy was supposed to change things, open me up. A cry was forming somewhere in my chest, like a hurricane gathering force way off the coast of Florida. The stuckness felt like my fault. How would this ever change? I sank into self-hate as I counted ridges on my popcorn ceiling. What was the point of those Tuesday sessions if I was going to remain this stuck?

At three fifteen, Dr. Rosen's number glowed on my phone's screen.

"Can you help me?" I said instead of hello.

"I hope so."

"Why was my date such a disaster?"

"Who says it was a disaster?"

"It was fifty minutes long. I didn't even go to school today—I'm in bed."

"Congratulations."

"For what?"

"When was the last time you made this much space for your feelings?"

"Um." He knew the answer was never.

"You deserve space to feel."

"But what should I *do*?"

"What were you doing before I called?"

"Staring at the ceiling."

"Do that. And come to group tomorrow."

"That's it?"

He laughed. "*Mamaleh*, that's plenty."

It didn't feel like enough. But my body unclenched when I got off the phone. Rational thoughts filled my head: Sam was one of thousands of men in Chicago. There was nothing wrong with me. It was one lame date. Big deal. It wasn't a reason to slip into catatonia.

In group, Dr. Rosen affirmed that all I had to do was keep coming to sessions. To him, the ninety minutes I sat in the circle with him and my group mates were the be-all and end-all of emotional transformation. To him, they were potent enough to score my still-smooth heart. To him, it was enough.

Not to me. I wanted a new prescription. Something bold and hard. Something that would require all my courage. Dr. Rosen wasn't taking my distress seriously. He didn't understand how it felt in my body. I was a window painted shut, a jar lid that wouldn't budge no matter how much you banged it on the counter.

I had to show him.

Andrew Barlee called me out of the blue. I remembered him from a holiday party as a quiet guy with lapis-blue eyes who laughed at my jokes.

I agreed to meet him for brunch. Over eggs and potatoes, I studied his rough hands and his haircut that was almost a mullet. Did I like him? The gut answer was no. We had nothing in common, there was zero chemistry, and I couldn't stop wondering about his unironic eighties haircut. But I pushed that no down below my ribs with a list of his positive traits: He was kind, solvent, sober, and interested in me. So what if he didn't like to read? So what if he didn't seem interested in current events that didn't involve the Bears' prospects for the Super Bowl? So what if my body convulsed with resistance when he grabbed my hand on the way to his car?

Andrew offered to make dinner for me at his place for our second date. On the drive to his new condo in Rogers Park, the Friday-afternoon traffic crawled down Western. Frustrated after sitting through two green lights without moving forward an inch, I pounded on the steering wheel and screamed at the top of my lungs. I screamed so long and so loudly that my voice sounded hoarse for the next two days. I didn't want to go to Andrew's house, but I'd made myself say yes, because saying no meant I subconsciously wanted to be alone. *Andrew was a nice guy!* I screamed at myself. *Give him a chance!* How could I claim to be desperately lonely and then decline a date with a nice, sober man?

After a tour of his bright, tasteful one-bedroom apartment, Andrew grilled two chicken breasts and emptied a bag of lettuce into a ceramic bowl after dousing it with Hidden Valley Ranch. I smiled at his earnest efforts, even though my stomach was churning with that no that longed to rise up and fly out of my mouth.

We sat on his couch, balancing our plates on our knees and making polite small talk about his work and my family in Texas. When I looked at him head-on, I couldn't tell he had a mullet, but making conversation felt like bone grinding on bone—our words didn't flow naturally. Neither of us was witty or charming. This wasn't what I wanted: Dry-ass chicken breasts with a nice-enough guy whom I could barely talk to.

When we were done eating, I panicked. There was no more small talk inside me, so I scooted toward him and put my lips on his, hoping that kissing might spark something—something that might make me want to be there with him.

Andrew's eyes widened in surprise and then excitement. He kissed me back. I turned into a mechanical doll with no heat, no heart. I wanted to go home and hated myself for it. I also hated myself for rejecting Andrew for dumb reasons like his haircut. No wonder I was alone; I was a bitch. The no pulsed in my gut, but I pushed it down. Here was a nice guy sitting right in front of me, and if I didn't like him or wasn't into him, that was my own fault.

"Do you have a condom?" I said. Maybe I could fuck my way out of this stuckness. Maybe sex would make me feel an attraction to him.

I still had on my sweater, bra, underwear, jeans, socks, and boots. Andrew's red flannel shirt was tucked tightly into his belted jeans. His shoes were still tied. Moving from a chaste ninety-second make-out session to intercourse made as much sense as robbing the 7-Eleven on the corner. But between us, we lacked the skills or desire to slow down and figure out what the hell was actually happening.

There was no music. No mood lighting. Zero ambience, unless you counted the occasional wafts of charred chicken. Andrew pulled down his pants and slipped the condom on. I shimmied my jeans over my hips.

He moved on top of me. I bit my lower lip and stared at his ceiling. Poisonous thoughts ran through my head: *This is all you get. You will never feel anything. You are broken. Faulty score.* When I blinked, tears spilled out of both eyes. I held the sob back and composed the story I would tell in group: *Look what I did. Do you get it now? This is serious.*

Andrew struggled to get inside me. More stuckness. I tilted my hips to give him a better angle and speed things up. In three or four thrusts it was over. I felt nothing outside the thrum of self-hate. My breath never changed rhythm.

His phone rang as he was finishing up. Emergency at work. Andrew yanked his pants up. "Sorry, but I have to go." I didn't even know what his job was.

Back in my car, I dialed Dr. Rosen's number. I told his answering machine about the chicken breasts, the no in my gut, the sex that I instigated. "I tried to tell you. Please hear me."

Four days later in group: My eyes locked with Dr. Rosen's. My fists were tight with rage. How many more guys did I have to fuck for him to take me seriously? What would it take to wipe that smirk off his face?

"You think I can't see you." Dr. Rosen said.

"Do you get that I'm in a lot of pain?"

"Christie, I get that you are in a lot of pain."

"Can you help me?"

"Yes."

"What do I need to do?"

"You're doing it."

"It's not enough."

"Yes, it is."

"It hurts!" I banged my fists on the arms of the chair. "I hurt."

"I know."

"I never want to fuck like that again."

"You never have to fuck like that again."

"This isn't enough."

"Christie, it is enough."

How could it possibly be enough? The night with Andrew was a disaster on every level, and it was my fault. Yet I was the one who had a high-powered therapist and five supportive group members supposedly steering my life in a better direction.

"What's the point in all of this? The brass ring is just more shitty sex and disconnection."

"You're not at the brass ring yet," Dr. Rosen said. "But you're on your way."

I swept my arm around the room. "How come they're all ready and I'm not?" Every other person in group had a significant other next to whom they fell asleep every night. "How long is this going to take?" I imagined myself growing old and feeble as I waited for the miracle of group therapy to transform my life.

"I don't know how long it's going to take. Can you celebrate the steps you've taken so far?"

No, I couldn't. I didn't want to celebrate until I knew how much was left to do. The realization that there was no shortcut to the mental health I was working toward crushed my spirit. I'd ceded to the group my isolation and my secret eating rituals. Those were my long-cherished coping mechanisms. Now, for every interaction, including every single date, I had to show up without my primary defenses, which sounded healthy in theory, but what it felt like that morning in group was a stunning, irrevocable defeat. There would be no more solace in apple binges, no retreats to my hermetically sealed life. There would be the bright light of Dr. Rosen's and my group mates' gaze illuminating all my deficits, but no secret cave to stash my feelings. So I had them right there in my chair: I wept for how lonely I felt and how deeply afraid I was that my life would never truly change or, worse, that true change would ask more of me than I could give. And had the session not ended at nine, I'm certain I could have cried my way to the lunch hour.

8

"You should tell the group about the Smoker," Carlos said.

On the elevator ride up to group, I'd told Carlos about the Smoker—so named because he loved his cigarettes and because he was smoking hot—my newest crush at law school. He had a girlfriend, but she was never around. Her name was Winter, and she was a waitress. I'd hoped that she was ugly or dirty or mean, but when I finally saw her serving pitchers at John Barleycorn, I couldn't deny that she was a willowy, fresh-faced beauty who offered a genuine smile to all of her customers.

The Smoker and I had struck up a friendship because we both spent hours in the computer lab, typing up our notes between classes. In our first encounter, he asked me to watch his books while he stepped out to smoke. Of course I said yes. I loved his five o'clock shadow, his smoky-smelling sweater, the shy way he looked away when he laughed.

"The Smoker?" Dr. Rosen cocked his head.

"This guy at school. Has a girlfriend. Smokes like a chimney. Drinks heavily. I'm falling in love with him."

"He's unavailable," Patrice said.

Dr. Rosen paused, covered his mouth with his hand, shifted his position, and then put his hands on the arms of his chair. Finally he said, "Next time you're with him, tell him the truth."

"Which is?"

"That you're a cocktease."

I looked at Carlos. Was Dr. Rosen for real? Everyone in the circle shook their heads, like *No, Dr. Rosen, she can't say that.* Rory blushed from behind her hands.

"You want me to tell the guy I have the hots for that I'm a 'cocktease'? Then what?" Wasn't the Smoker the tease? He was the one flirting with me despite his apple-cheeked girlfriend. If you would have asked me before this session if Dr. Rosen, my middle-aged psychiatrist with the rubber-soled brown shoes who knew nothing of pop culture ("Who's Bono?" he once asked), knew the term *cocktease*, I would have sworn he didn't. Now, as part of my therapeutic treatment, he was telling me to drop it into conversation with the guy I wanted to bed.

"We'll find out."

Two nights later, I sat in a speeding yellow taxi going west on Lake Street with the Smoker and his affable sidekick, Bart, a jokey kid from our law school class. The air was sticky but the sky was clear. A sliver of moon smirked at me. We rolled the windows down to cut the stench of the tree-shaped potpourri dangling from the rearview mirror. I leaned out the window and turned my face to the inky sky and its cheerful moon. A laugh caught in my throat—I held it for a few seconds and then let it out. Over the pulsing music, I sat upright, squared my shoulders, and turned toward the Smoker, who was sitting between me and Bart.

"I'm a total cocktease." The "total" I added as a personal flourish to prove I wasn't a mindless Rosen automaton.

The Smoker stopped chewing his postcigarette gum and froze. Then a smile spread across the horizon of his beautiful face. He kept his eyes fixed straight ahead. My skin tingled as I watched him take in my words. I wanted to wrap my legs around him and rock myself against him and his perfectly frayed Levi's.

Bart craned his head around the Smoker's chest and peered over at me.

"Say what?"

"You heard me," I said, turning my head toward the window.

"No, I didn't," Bart said.

"Then why are you so determined to get me to say it again—"

"Because—"

"Because you heard me the first time."

"Damn. You crazy, girl." Bart's cackle was picked up by the wind, and it dissolved into the night, right along with my pride.

The Smoker kept smiling and drumming his fingers on his long, ropy thighs. Mortification slowly set in as I realized the Smoker wasn't going to make a move on me. He would hang out with me and Bart for another hour and then go home and slip between the covers to wait for Winter's shift to end so they could fuck until dawn. I focused on the buildings we whizzed by along Milwaukee Avenue. Furniture stores, taco joints, Myopic Books. People waiting in line to hear a band at Subterranean. None of them knew what I'd said. Below the humiliation I felt the bud of something else: pride that I'd done what Dr. Rosen said. Saying those words had been a high-dive plunge, requiring all the courage I could summon. Now that a few minutes had passed, I realized that saying those words stitched me closer to Dr. Rosen and my group. And in four days I would sit in the circle and recount this night during which I had triumphed over my nerves—and better judgment—to follow Dr. Rosen's advice.

When we got to the Bucktown bar, we found that there was no room on its outdoor patio, so the Smoker lit up a cigarette on the sidewalk. Bougainvillea spilled over the fence and smelled faintly sweet.

"Want one?" he asked, holding out his pack of Marlboros.

Oh, how I wanted to say yes so we could have a perfect moment together sucking in and puffing out like beautiful people in the movies, people with no mental health issues, no sexual hang-ups, no eating disorders, no worms. If I said yes, he would lean in close and light my cigarette. His smell—the smoke, the gum, the day's residue—would become part of my memory.

But I couldn't make myself take one. Dr. Rosen had recently explained to Rory, when she mentioned how much she missed cigarettes, that when you smoke you are inhaling toxic self-hatred.

"No thanks," I said.

The following Tuesday, I rode the Red Line train downtown before group as the sun inched over the tree line. I'd been up since four—despite calling Marty for an affirmation the night before—and decided to head downtown to sit in a coffee shop.

I nursed a cup of tea and stared out the window on Madison Street. A bright yellow backpack—like one you'd expect Curious George's handler to wear—caught my eye. The man wearing it walked a half beat slower than everyone else, as if he were touring an English garden. He looked shorter than average—barely my height—and his lips were moving slightly like he was having a conversation with himself. I took him for a tourist and fished the tea bag out of my cup. Not until he was almost out of view did it hit me: Dr. Rosen.

It definitely was him—that untamed hair, those slightly hunched shoulders. How was he so puny? In group, he seemed so huge—larger than life—as I begged him for prescriptions, solutions, and answers.

I watched until he disappeared down Madison, taking his sweet time, mumbling to himself.

Why did he walk so slowly? He was headed to work—to *my* group session—not on a pilgrimage to Medjugorje. Why the mumbling? Where'd he get that god-awful backpack?

By the time I'd finished my tea and headed to group, I faced the harder question: Was my therapist a complete freak? Why did I take his advice on what to say to the Smoker? Why did I give that strange little man so much power?

As I walked toward group, I prayed, "Please kill the Buddha."

9

Everyone else in group got a special sex assignment. Colonel Sanders got a prescription to rub his wife's back without pressuring her for sex. Patrice got a prescription involving sex toys. Carlos had been advised to get naked and hold his fiancé, Bruce, for ten minutes every night. Marty was supposed to invite his live-in lady friend, Janeen, to take a shower with him. Dr. Rosen renewed Rory's prescription to have her husband go down on her while she put her Adderall between her toes.

I listened and burned with envy. "I want a sex assignment but I don't have a partner."

Dr. Rosen rubbed his hands together as if he'd been waiting weeks for me to ask. "I suggest you bookend your masturbation with Patrice."

I rubbed my temples and squeezed my eyes shut. "Do what?"

"Call up Patrice." Dr. Rosen pretended to dial a phone and then held his hand like a receiver. "Say, 'Hi, Patrice. I'm going to masturbate now. I'm calling because I want your support with my sexuality. It's worked really well with my food and now I'd like to work on my sexuality.' Then, when you're done, call her back and say, 'Thank you for your support.'"

"No." I stood up. "Absolutely not."

Intellectually, I understood there was nothing wrong with masturbation—Dr. Ruth taught me that. Pleasure was nothing to be ashamed of. In theory. But in practice, I could manage pleasure only in secret, hidden under the covers in the dark of night. I had never—and could never—talk about self-pleasure. The ghosts of all the nuns who told me that sex was only for procreation with my Catholic husband haunted me. In sixth-grade health class Sister Callahan spent several awkward minutes explaining that masturbation was a "grave sin because each wasted sperm could have been a new life." Sister Callahan didn't mention the possibility that girls might engage in such behavior, which seemed like proof that girls didn't—and shouldn't—ever masturbate. It was unspeakable.

The technical term for my condition was *sexual anorexia*. The anorexia most people are familiar with is someone who severely restricts her food. A sexual anorexic like me starved herself of sex by chasing unavailable alcoholics, who usually had girlfriends, who did not or could not be intimate, or by forcing herself to have sex without any attraction to her partner. The label intrigued me—as a chubby kid, I'd longed for a sleek label like "anorexic." Now I wasn't sure I loved the label, but it made me feel less alone. If there was a name for me and my condition, that meant I wasn't the only one.

There was no way I could "bookend my masturbation." I stared at Dr. Rosen and shook my head.

"But you call me about your apples," Rory said.

"This is different."

"How so?" Dr. Rosen said.

"You can't see the difference between apples and masturbation?" My neck contracted into my clavicle at the thought of calling Patrice. Calling Patrice about *that* was lighting up a flare: *Guess what, world! I'm wacking off!* It violated the Catholic Church's anti-onanism rules and my mother's don't-tell-people-your-business rule. The prescription was outrageous, perverted, impossible.

"Do you want my take?" Dr. Rosen said. "Eating ten apples after dinner—"

"I'm down to four—"

"Okay, four, but eating those apples wasn't pleasurable. You wanted it to stop. Stopping a negative behavior is radically different than getting support for starting a pleasurable one. You are more resistant to pleasure. That's why I'm giving you this prescription—"

"Which I cannot do." I should quit group.

"You have other choices," Dr. Rosen said.

Rory tapped my foot with the tip of her boot and suggested I ask for something gentler. I took a deep breath. Was I going to drown in despair or was I willing to ask for what I needed?

"Can you dial it down?" I whispered.

Dr. Rosen smiled and paused. "How about this? You bookend taking a bath with Patrice."

"No requirement that I do or touch or rub anything while I'm in there?"

"Strictly utilitarian."

"Done." My whole body relaxed. I could take a goddamn bath. I was back in the game.

Dr. Rosen stared at me.

"What?" I asked.

"When was the last time you told someone that you weren't ready for what they were asking you to do?"

Senior year of high school, I dated Mike D., a basketball star who smoked pot daily. He was my first real boyfriend, and I wanted desperately to be a good girlfriend, whatever that meant. Before me, Mike dated a cheerleader who, apparently, gave amazing head. When he hinted he missed her deep throat, I felt summoned to suck his dick. But at seventeen, I'd only visited first base briefly, three years earlier. Blow jobs were third-base territory, and my ignorance about them made my throat constrict with panic. Where would my hands go? How long would I have his penis in my mouth? What would it taste like? When he pushed my head under the blankets, I shoved my fear down my throat and into my belly. When I tried to come up for air to ask for a performance review, Mike pushed my head back down. I've revisited my sweaty head under that blanket thousands of times, always wondering why I felt bereft of choices, words, and the right to lift the blanket and take a breath. Or to not suck his dick in the first place. I did it because I wanted to be a good girlfriend and good girlfriends say yes.

In college, my roommate Cherie graduated a semester ahead of me. Free-spirited Cherie's postcollege plans entailed couch surfing in Colorado until she started graduate school. When she asked me to drive her Jetta to Denver after graduation, I should have said no. I was supposed to be in Dallas visiting family and working a part-time mall job. Driving Cherie, her bike, and her duffel bag full of tie-dyed shirts to the Mile High City was inconvenient and expensive. But I said yes because the thought of saying no made my stomach clench. I wanted to be a good friend. Good friends say yes.

Before moving to Chicago for graduate school, I got a job at Express in my college town, selling skorts to sorority girls. I got promoted to assistant manager after a few months. My supervisor often showed up to work with long, bloody scratches on her forearms—either from a feral cat or a serious self-harm habit—and would ask me to cover for her several times a month. Saying yes meant I had to work ten hours without a break—assistant managers were not allowed to leave the store unattended, even to run over to Chick-Fil-A for a snack. My supervisor would be at home engaging in mysterious physical behavior, and I'd be asking a stock boy to cover the registers so I could pee. It never occurred to me to say no, though. I wanted to be a good employee, and good employees say yes.

Yes was who I thought I was supposed to be as a girlfriend, friend, employee. A girl, and then a woman, in the world. When someone asked me to jump I prepared to leap without thinking about whether I was hungry or knew the route to Denver or knew what the fuck to do with a penis in my mouth.

I told Dr. Rosen I wasn't in the habit of saying no. He asked if I knew what that cost me. I shook my head. Costs? People liked me because I was a Yes Girl. If I went around saying no, then what? They'd be mad at me. Disappointed. *Unhappy.* I couldn't tolerate that. That kind of audacity belonged to other people, like guys and hot women with no emotional baggage.

"If you can't say no in relationships, then you can't be intimate," Dr. Rosen said.

"Say that again." I held still so that each word would seep inside me, past my skin and muscle, and settle in my bones.

"If you can't say no, there can be no intimacy."

People said no to me all the time, and I still loved them. Is this what people were learning in high school when I was bingeing on Girl Scout Thin Mint cookies and making mixtapes with Lionel Richie and Whitney Houston songs?

ur

As my old claw-footed bathtub filled with sudsy, lavender-scented water, I left Patrice a voice mail completing part one of the "bookend." I'd purposely dialed her cell phone because she turned it off at night. I held my breath as I slid into the nearly scalding water. The bubbles made tiny rustling sounds. I leaned my head against the hard porcelain edge and exhaled. My breath hitched—a hint I might cry, but I squeezed my eyes shut and shook my head. I didn't want to blubber through this—I wanted to be a normal fucking woman taking a bath to relax. After two minutes, I wanted to get out. I'd filled the prescription, swallowed the medicine. Now I had things to do, like make three phone calls to three different group members.

But then I put my palms over my heart and took a deep breath. Tears welled in my eyes, and I let them come. What I felt was relief. Intense, cascading, pure relief. *No might belong to me too.*

Everybody else said no. My college roommate Kat was blunt, sassy, and secure. In college, she told a handsy Phi Delt to "fuck off" when he asked her for a blow job. There was no fist of anxiety in her stomach telling her she had to give him head. At age five, my headstrong brother had an hour-long stand-off with my parents when they insisted he eat a bite of tuna sandwich. He won the tuna showdown while I forced myself to eat every awful, mayonnaise-filled bite, crust and all. Carlos pushed back on Dr. Rosen insisting he was never going to bring in his guitar and sing for the group.

Meanwhile, I considered quitting group so I wouldn't have to look at Dr. Rosen and say, "Nope. I can't bookend my masturbation with Patrice."

I cupped water into my hands and let it drain through my fingers. I'd always hated baths. What's so relaxing about submerging in water when there's nothing to stare at except a tiled wall or parts of my body beneath the suds? I hated looking at my body. I always ended up picking it apart—unshaven legs, unpedicured toes, unperky breasts, untoned stomach, and unsmooth thighs. All that scrutiny and shame drowned whatever pleasure I was supposed to be deriving from taking a bath, the pastime that was supposedly beloved by all womankind.

I still saw those things—the chipped red polish, the hairy legs, the lumpy flesh. And I still felt the heat of shame prickling my skin. But alongside it, a spark of something lighter and cooler chased the tail of the shame, and I had the barest sliver of a notion that I could have a different relationship with and to my body and then maybe with other people.

My fingertips pruned as the water cooled to room temperature. A shiver ran down my neck as I sat up. I wrapped myself in a pink-and-white striped beach towel and sat on the edge of the bathtub.

I dialed Patrice's cell. "I did it. Good night."

I called Rory to report my food.

I called Marty to collect my affirmation. "You've got what it takes, kiddo," he said in Groucho Marx accent.

I laughed. My neck and shoulder muscles were warm and loose from the bath. I had a woozy, half-asleep feeling. "I love you," I said, cupping the phone with my still-pruned fingers. The words just slipped out.

"Of course you do, sweetie. I love you too. Isn't this fun?" I smiled. *Fun* was not quite the word I would have used for the warm expansive feeling spreading across my chest, but I couldn't think of better one.

In bed, I had a vision: My group members' hands tucked under me like in the childhood game Light as a Feather, Stiff as a Board. They worked together to invoke whatever spirits would help lift me up, up, up. I could feel Dr. Rosen's hands cradling my head, Carlos and the Colonel at my shoulders, Patrice and Rory on each hip, and Marty at my feet. I did love them. For their presence, their effort, and their strong hands on my body. They were etching themselves into my life.

It thrilled me, made me want to bawl, and it scared me to death.

10

Fat tears rolled down Marty's face one spring Tuesday. There was a silver tin in his lap, the size and shape of a small drum or a container of Williams-Sonoma Christmas cookies. He said he was sick of all the death. He didn't want it anymore.

This was good work for Marty. He appeared congenial and functional on the outside, but we all knew about his stash of cyanide. Dr. Rosen mentioned it almost every session and urged him to bring it to group.

"It looks like you're ready to let that go," Dr. Rosen said, gesturing at the tin.

"What's in there?" the Colonel asked.

Marty held the tin up to his heart. "The remains of a child."

I dug my heel into the carpet and scooted my chair back. Babies were supposed to be fat-cheeked and loud—cooing, squalling, crying. They weren't supposed to sealed up in a tin can.

Marty explained that the baby, who died when he was less than a month old, had been the son of one of his first patients in his psychiatry practice. The patient had asked Marty to keep the remains years ago while he worked through his grief, but then the patient died. Now Marty was asking Dr. Rosen what to do with this memento mori.

Dr. Rosen loved to stir up everyone's feelings around death. If you made a pie chart of group topics, the two biggest pieces were sex and death. And if there was a trauma connected to a death experience, then Dr. Rosen would nudge you about it on at least a bimonthly basis. Rory had to talk about the Holocaust every other time she told a story, even if the decimation of European Jews in the 1940s had seemingly nothing to do with the late fees on her Citibank card. When Patrice struggled with a complex issue at work, Dr. Rosen pivoted right to her brother's suicide. Naturally, he nudged me to discuss the accident in Hawaii regularly. Usually, I backed away and reminded him to focus on my sex life, not my great misfortune of witnessing a death on a trip to the beach when I was thirteen.

Marty handed the tin to Dr. Rosen, who inspected it and said something in Hebrew. Dr. Rosen told Marty that if he was ready to let go of his preoccupation with death, he'd be able to embrace his life more fully, and he'd grow closer to his longtime partner, Janeen.

A somber silence fell over the group. A wave of feeling swelled in my chest—memory flashes from Hawaii—but I pushed it down; I was convinced it was just sadness I was manufacturing to match the group mood.

Meanwhile, I had an urge to cross my legs in defiance. Where was Dr. Rosen's magic trick for me? What had I stashed in my closet that I could bring to group and voilà! I'd be ready for intimacy and closeness? Marty and I had started on the same day, and now he was lapping me. I'd come to Dr. Rosen wishing for death because I was chronically and fundamentally alone, but Marty had *cyanide pills* in his bedside table. And somehow he was leaping forward? I let the jealousy and anger rise, but said nothing.

With only fifteen minutes left in the session, Dr. Rosen turned his attention to Marty's tin. "Pick someone to hold that for you." I gazed at the splotchy carpet as Marty scanned the room. Surely he would pick Patrice, the Mama Bear of the group.

"Christie."

Holy flaming Freud balls. I narrowed my eyes at Marty, afraid and annoyed that he picked me to hold a baby who never got to grow up, whose flesh and bones were now sealed up in a silver tin. I scowled at Dr. Rosen for orchestrating this whole morbid affair. I wanted to stand up and beat my head with my fists and scream until my throat was shredded: "I'm not here for death and bones and ashes! I'm here for life! I WANT TO LIVE!"

How did it make sense that I, a random woman from Marty's therapy group, was suddenly the custodian of this tin? Didn't the baby deserve to be in the hands of someone who loved him or his parents dearly? The randomness was unbearable.

Dr. Rosen directed Marty to look at me and ask if I would take the tin. When Marty and I locked eyes, I saw his pain but couldn't bear it. I turned to Dr. Rosen.

"How about I take Marty's cyanide pills?"

"I don't think so," said Dr. Rosen. A pause. Then, "You don't have to do that, you know."

"What?"

"Make a joke when you're scared or upset or angry. Deflect."

"How's this? Fuck you, Dr. Rosen." Dr. Rosen rubbed his heart with his palm, a gesture I'd seen before. He once explained that when someone shared their anger with him directly, it was a sign of love that he folded into his heart as a blessing.

"Better."

"Okay," I whispered, chastened. I asked Marty what the baby's name was.

"Jeremiah."

I couldn't abandon Baby Jeremiah. Some part of that beloved child was still in that tin, and I wouldn't turn my back on him. I was selfish and self-absorbed, but I was not a total monster. My outstretched arms reached for the tin.

Dr. Rosen passed the tin to Patrice, who handed it to me. I took it into my hands and held it perfectly still. I did not want to *feel* the contents inside. As I lowered the tin into my lap, I imagined it filled with tiny seashells. I tried really hard not to think about bones. An image of me rocking and sobbing, while cradling the tin, flashed through my mind, but a plume of anger at Dr. Rosen snuffed out the tender grief.

"Question," I said to Dr. Rosen. "Marty gets closer to Janeen if he lets Jeremiah go, but what happens to me if I take him?"

After uttering a few *mmm*s and *umm*s at the ceiling, he said, "For you, these ashes represent your attachment to this group. You need the group's support to lean into death, to stop running from it." He leaned forward as if he was afraid I couldn't hear him. "You want to move forward? Start feeling."

"I don't know." My shaking hands gripped the tin.

"You don't know what?"

"How to do it. Or if I can."

"*Mamaleh,* it's already happening."

Two weeks later, Marty pulled out an envelope and presented it to Dr. Rosen.

"My pills," Marty said. He poured the yellow disks into his palm and offered them to Dr. Rosen, who stood up and said, "We're going to have a funeral." We followed Dr. Rosen to the small bathroom just outside the group room. Rory held Marty's hand until he was ready to let them go. Dr. Rosen announced that he would now recite the Mourner's Kaddish.

"What are we mourning?" I asked.

"The death of Marty's suicidality."

"*L'chaim,*" Carlos said.

"That means 'to life,'" the Colonel said to me, putting a gnarled hand on my shoulder.

"I've seen *Fiddler on the Roof,*" I said, moving his hand off me.

"*L'chaim* indeed," Dr. Rosen said, glowing at Marty, who dropped the pills into the toilet and watched them swirl until they disappeared.

After we flushed Marty's pills, we took our seats back in the group room. Dr. Rosen stared at me.

"You ready?" he said.

"For what?"

"You know what."

"I don't."

"I think you do."

Of course I did.

11

My luggage tag read "Christie Tate-Ramon." When Jenni's dad, David, handed it to me, he said, "I've always wanted two daughters." He hugged me, and then shooed me and Jenni into the taxi idling in the driveway. There were five of us: Jenni, her dad David, her mom Sandy, her brother Sebastian, and me. Freshman year of high school was six weeks away.

When we landed in Honolulu, everyone at the airport wore flowered shirts and greeted us with "Mahalo." On the drive to the hotel, we repeated it over and over like a blessing.

For three days, we explored the lush main island, stopping on the side of the road to marvel at waterfalls sprouting from the wall of a mountain, eating macadamia nuts, and snapping pictures of black sand beaches. The second night we attended an obligatory luau, where we all poked at the poi and wore fresh orchid leis.

On the fourth day, just after lunch, David loaded us kids into the rental sedan, along with towels and boogie boards. We were headed to a secluded black beach at the end of the highway, which we had seen during our first day of sightseeing. Sandy stayed at the condo to do laundry.

"Surf, surf, surf," David chanted as we drove along the curvy road that hugged the side of a mountain. Sebastian pushed a cassette into the tape deck and cranked the volume. The Cure sang moodily of beaches and guns. We rolled down the windows and sang at the top of our lungs, letting the breeze hit the back of our throats.

David parked the car and headed toward a shaded path where a "No Trespassing" sign hung on an iron fence, partially obscured by a flowering vine. I paused for a nanosecond, fear prickling my spine. We were breaking a rule. David continued to whistle. Above, the blue sky portended nothing but fresh air and a refreshing swim once we reached the beach. Bad things didn't happen in places with this many flowers.

We filed down in a straight line, me in the rear. My flip-flops strained to support me as I made my way down the steep mountain path.

When the trail leveled off and opened up to an expanse of wild grass, we could see the surf rolling to the shore. Black sand crystals glinted in the sunlight. David found a flat, dry spot for us to dump our stuff. There were no other people on the beach—no lifeguard chair, no laid-out beach towels, no signs of life. It felt like freedom to have this expanse of paradise all to ourselves. I peeled off my T-shirt and shorts. I adjusted the straps of my one-piece Ocean Pacific bathing suit, and Sebastian dove into the surf. Jenni and I trotted after him.

"I'll meet you down there." David hunched over his contact lens case with a travel-size bottle of saline solution.

The waves looked gentle, not unlike the swells at Padre Island on the Gulf Coast of Texas, where my family vacationed. The sky remained a harmless blue bowl. My biggest problem was that I wished my body was as lean as Jenni's.

Once I'd waded far enough that the water hit my midthighs, a wave knocked me over. My whole body sunk below the waterline, and the undertow dragged me downward. I struggled to get upright, but as soon as I cleared the surface of the water, another wave pushed me down again, and I somersaulted through the surf. Salt water stung my eyes and rushed up my nose. It felt like an invisible force below the sand was pulling me under, daring me to fight. Every time my head popped out of the water, I'd try to catch my breath, but would get knocked down before I could fill my lungs with air. Every effort to get myself upright failed.

I had to get out. Frantic, I flailed my arms and bicycled my legs, but the undertow continued to suck me back. When I finally landed in a spot where I could stand up, I gasped and coughed, almost doubled over with exhaustion. My head pounded from the effort of fighting the sea. I staggered out of the water.

Once I was onshore, my chest heaved with the effort of my escape. My arms ached from trying to claw my way through the water. Jenni emerged and walked toward me. We agreed that sunbathing would be more fun.

"Where's my dad?" she said, scanning the water.

I raised my hand to my forehead and surveyed the ocean—left, right, and left again. No sign of David. The fear prickled again, straight up my spine, nesting at the base of my neck.

"Oh my God!" Jenni pointed straight ahead and took off into the water. Ten yards in front of us, an orange object lolled in the water. David's board. Something large and white floated beside it.

David was facedown. A wave surged forward and delivered him to us in shin-deep water. We turned him over, and his eyes stared, unblinking, up at the sky. My breath came in shallow gasps. Water gushed from David's nose and mouth. So much water poured out of him. As if he contained half the ocean.

Jenni and I each grabbed an arm. We pulled him to the shore. Neither of us knew CPR, but we pumped his chest like we imagined we should. We screamed maniacally for Sebastian. With every thrust to David's chest, more water gushed out of his mouth and nose. His eyes stared unblinking at the sky, at nothing at all.

My teeth chattered uncontrollably, and my arms spasmed. I ran in place when I wasn't pumping David's chest because standing still meant that the truth of his open eyes and gushing mouth could find me and settle in. My mind spun out lies: *He'll be fine. People don't die on vacation. We'll laugh on the way home about that mean old Hawaiian surf.* I could still hear him whistling.

If we could just pump enough water out of him, he would sit up and cough.

"Oh my God!" Sebastian arrived, dripping wet and panting. He pressed on his dad's chest with his two open palms.

"I'll go get help," I said, and took off running, barefoot, still shaking—my legs desperate to be in motion. In stillness, the truth loomed, so I pumped my legs and hurled my body back up the mountain. The ghost of David whistling down the path just thirty minutes earlier haunted each step. Halfway up the trail, I tripped on a root and landed spread-eagle on the path. A long red gash opened on my knee. It looked like it should hurt, but I felt nothing. I was all heartbeat and panic. I'd flown out of my body and was already up the mountain begging someone to help us.

"No! No! Daddy, no!" Sebastian and Jenni's keening reached me from the beach. I scrambled to my feet. I had to keep running to drown out the unbearable sound of their mourning. Every time I stopped to catch my breath, I heard their cries. Picturing the two of them alone on the beach with their father's limp body drove me up the mountain.

When I made it to the top, I collapsed at the feet of four elderly golfers. I lay eye to eye with their white spiked shoes and the hems of their plaid pants. One of them bent over and stuck his face in mine. "You okay, little lady?"

"Someone's drowned—he's not dead," I insisted. To me, at that point, there was a difference between drowning and dying. "His kids are down there alone with him."

The four of them shuffled off, leaving me propped up against a boulder.

"He's not dead." A scream, a whisper, a dispatch straight from my trembling heart.

Stillness was terrifying. I scrambled to my feet and ran up the paved road for more help. Little pebbles gouged my feet but didn't pierce the skin. I ran faster. I found an abandoned cabin set back from the road. When no one answered my knocking, I burst through the unlocked door, screaming, "Phone! Phone!" In the darkened room, there was only a wooden table, a couple of chairs, and a stout bookshelf. No people, no light, no phone.

Back out on the road, I couldn't see the beach or hear Jenni and Sebastian. I stood in my bathing suit waiting for something to happen, shaking and twitching, with nowhere to run. A low guttural moan escaped from my throat, a nonsense word, mashing up "no, no, no" and "please, please, please." My hands held each side of my head as if it would split apart if I let go.

A family from Kansas—mom, dad, and teenage son—stopped at the lookout point. I waved my hands: "Help! Please!" Good news: the dad was a cardiologist. He and the son disappeared down the trail while the mother offered me a can of root beer and invited me to sit in her car. I sipped the sugary drink, still shaking, my body absorbing the awful truth.

A highway patrolman cruised by in a black truck, and the mother jumped out of the car to stop him. He stuck his head out of the window, and she whispered something to him. He peered at me and then promised to send help.

Thick gray clouds rolled in out of nowhere. Rain splattered the car. The rain turned to hail. I flinched as each ice pellet tapped the window. And still I shook. It felt like my molars would fall out from the chattering. I could still my body for a few seconds by holding my breath, but as soon as I gasped for air, the shaking started again.

Overhead, helicopter blades whirred in a staccato rhythm, a giant metal bird gliding toward the beach. The mother winced and grabbed my hand. She knew what it meant. The golfers appeared at the head of the footpath. I bolted from the car, hopeful still, about news from the beach, even though the two in front shook their heads. No, he didn't make it. No, he's dead. No, there is no more hope.

"The children are coming up behind us." Hope finally drained out of my body.

I could hear the hum of the blades even when there was nothing to see but the gray expanse of sky. The helicopter rose up over the mountain with a long rope hanging from its belly. At the end of the rope was a black body bag, swaying like a weighted tail. It sailed across the sky until it was only a tiny dot on the horizon.

12

After sharing all the awful details in one unbroken narrative, I felt lighter. I believed that taking up that space and letting my witnesses know what I experienced was all the healing I needed. Now my group knew about the Cure tape, David's contact lenses, the ravenous ocean, my bare feet on the trail, the root beer, the rain, the helicopter.

The next week, as I walked from the elevator to the group room, I imagined that Dr. Rosen would allude to the good work I'd done around Hawaii the week before. It was a wish: I wanted a gold star for finally letting the group witness the awful images I carried around from that traumatic summer. But as I reached the waiting room, I felt something else, something seemingly unrelated: anxiety about Dr. Rosen's upcoming vacation. He would be out for the next two weeks. Without these weekly sessions to anchor myself, I'd be pulled under by a wave of loneliness. Two weeks without group felt like two weeks without oxygen. Underneath the anxiety, I also felt angry. How could he abandon us for two whole weeks?

"Get on the floor and grab Carlos's leg," Dr. Rosen suggested fifteen minutes into the session when I shared how I felt about his upcoming absence. Grabbing Carlos's leg was supposed to soothe and ground me. It did neither.

The group energy had been frenetic and unfocused from the first moment. We zipped from Carlos's patient to Marty's wedding planning to Rory's sex life. Multiple side conversations broke out every time we switched topics, detracting from the main discussion. Dr. Rosen insisted it was our collective anxiety about not meeting for two weeks.

I wrapped my right arm around Carlos's shin and picked at the carpet with my left hand as Marty discussed life post–cyanide stash, when suddenly, the urge to scream at the top of my lungs came over me—it crept slowly upward from my stomach through my sternum and to the edge of my throat. It was too strong to hold down—like a sneeze or an orgasm. It flew out of me and stopped all movement in the room. *Aaaahhhhhhhhhhhh!* It was from my deep-down guts and it shook the walls.

"What the fuck?" Carlos said, peering down from his chair.

"I don't know what that was," I said, embarrassed by my primal wail that seemed to have no narrative, no trigger, and no explanation.

Unfazed, Dr. Rosen said, "Sure you do."

I heard the helicopter buzzing and felt my body constrict with panic. My mind zoomed to Hawaii, right above the waves and the black sand.

"Where do you think I'm going on vacation?"

"No idea."

"You have a picture in your head—"

"'Vacation' is a word, not a picture."

"Am I going skiing?"

"It's July."

"So where am I going?"

I blurted out, "Mexico. Fucking Playa del Carmen."

"What's in Mexico?"

"Pesos." Dr. Rosen didn't budge. The right answer blared in my head. "Beaches."

He slapped his hands together with an *ahhh*. "Do you have any feelings about me going to the beach?"

Pieces of the Hawaii story had trickled out during the first year of group, leading up to the gush of the previous session. Every time the subject arose, Dr. Rosen prodded me to express my feelings about it, and I resisted. I defended against the emotions by insisting it wasn't *that* big of a deal. *He wasn't my dad. It was so long ago.* It felt dramatic and somehow fake to wade into my feelings about Hawaii. I had so many excuses to scurry away from the subject. Plus, I didn't want to talk about being alone in my bathing suit, running uphill to get help, my bloody leg, David's vacant eyes, and the seawater pouring out of his face. None of the words I knew added up to the terror I felt, nor could they contain my grief.

And this: when we returned from Hawaii, Jenni and I started our freshman year at Ursuline Academy. Six weeks from that black sand beach where we watched David's limp body sway under the helicopter's belly, we put on our red-and-navy pleated uniform skirts and our penny loafers and shuffled from algebra and world history to PE and English. I sat in algebra watching Ms. Pawlowicz put complicated equations on the board and sat at lunch listening to other girls plan their outfits for the Michael Jackson concert. *Who cares? We're all going to die. None of this matters.* Those first few months, half of me was still in Hawaii, waiting for David to cough and wake up so I could resume a normal teenage life that revolved around my crush on Joe Monico or whether to get bangs. After school I slept for hours, and my parents grew concerned about my emotional state. I saw them staring at me during dinner, when I rested my heavy head on my open palm, and in the afternoon when I couldn't get off the couch. But we never talked about "the accident" in Hawaii. One evening, my parents knocked on my door and found me lying on my bed listening to the radio. They attempted small talk with me about homework and an upcoming home football game. I could tell from the way my mom gripped the doorknob and my dad leaned in against my dresser that they were working up to something substantive.

"Can you please do us a favor?" My mom stood in my doorway, her eyes, brown like mine, pleading in a way that was startling in its novelty.

"I guess. What is it?"

"Can you try to act normal? Just try it. For us. Would you try to act normal? All this moping around, it's not good for you—"

"Okay." I knew what she meant. Since Hawaii, I'd been drained of energy. There was the extra sleeping and the disinterest in all the new opportunities arising with the start of high school. All of it was passing me by. To them, my listlessness looked like childish "moping" that I could—and should—snap out of before I lost a whole year of my life. My parents firmly believed that I could make up my mind to be happy. I understand now that they were offering me the tools they relied on: willpower, optimism, and self-reliance. But those tools kept slipping out of my grasp, so I reached for the more reliable bingeing and purging to tamp down the emotions trying to surface. My parents and I wanted the same thing: for me to be normal. I longed for a "normal me" more than they did, but none of us understood that I wasn't "moping" and that the attempts to stuff my feelings might come at a high cost. I also heard an implied request that I bury Hawaii and all its terrifying images. Beneath my parents' request thrummed a subtext: *Don't think about it, or you'll get upset. Don't get upset, or you'll fall behind on the important work of being a normal teenage girl. Don't talk about it, or you'll upset yourself. Don't talk about it, or you'll upset me.* I wanted to be a dutiful daughter, so I buried it the best I could.

cvr

"Not everyone gets to come home." My voice cracked. Dr. Rosen asked if I could scream some more. I didn't think I could, but then I bent over and rested my forehead on the stiff carpet and guttural moans from a previous decade rose up and spilled out of me in waves.

"What happened after the helicopter took David's body away?" Dr. Rosen asked. I'd never talked about what happened after we left the beach. In my mind, the story ended as soon as the helicopter disappeared over the mountain with David's body in the long black bag.

I started to shake as I had in the Kansas woman's car.

"Were you cold in the police station?"

"The floor was cold under my bare feet and I didn't have any of my clothes. One officer offered me a foamy yellow blanket, and a different officer led me to a private room so I could call my parents. They were at the movies with friends, so I told my brother what had happened."

"What did you do when you left the police station?" Rory asked.

"Sebastian drove us back to the condo. We were over an hour away. Then he missed a turn, and we drove miles out of our way—on and on we drove down this two-lane highway. No one said a word. I sat by my-self in the backseat and stared out the window at the stupid ocean and the brilliant Hawaiian sunset, all purples, pinks, and oranges. The Cure tape played over and over. When one side finished, there were several clicks, then the other side would start playing. It took several sides to get to the condo."

"The police let the three of you leave all alone?" Dr. Rosen asked.

"Sebastian was almost eighteen."

"His dad had just died," Rory said, her voice breaking. "You were children."

"The police should have taken care of you." Patrice reached out for my hand. I grabbed it and she squeezed it like she had that first morning during the closing prayer.

"And when you made it back to the condo?" Dr. Rosen asked.

"We had to tell Sandy. We knocked on the door because we'd lost the keys. When she looked through the peephole, she understood the terrible math. One of us was missing. She started screaming, 'No! No! No!'"

"Jesus, Christie," Carlos whispered.

I'd pushed past them in the doorway and hid in the bathtub—no water running—so I could get out of their way. Behind the shower cur-tain, I picked at the dried mud and blood caked on my legs, trying to bear their grief. They remained in the doorway, holding each other and sobbing, until the last beams of daylight faded to darkness.

"What did it sound like?" Dr. Rosen asked.

I opened my mouth to imitate their wailing. Nothing came out. When I tried again, the sound froze inside me, my aperture for grief sealed up inside my throat.

"You did it a minute ago. You can hear it in your head," Dr. Rosen said.

I could hear it, the three of them, huddled and wailing, but no sound would come out. That terror and grief were a part of me, an organ that covered everything, like skin or hair. Like a stain. I didn't know how to let it go. I managed a few guttural barks. I shook my head. "I can't."

I'd long ago accepted that I'd carry Hawaii—those screams and the terrified clenching of every muscle when I thought of the ocean—for the rest of my life. It was the price of having survived. What would it look like to heal? I couldn't conjure a version of me that wasn't haunted by the ocean gushing out of David.

Dr. Rosen suggested an experiment. "Repeat after me: 'I did not kill David.'"

I shook my head. "Jesus, Dr. Rosen, I don't think I killed him. This isn't an ABC after-school special."

"You feel responsible."

"That's ridiculous. I was thirteen—"

"The sign."

"You always mention it, hon," Rory said.

"Sign?" I said, my gaze darting around the room.

"The 'No Trespassing' sign," Rory said.

I slumped back in my chair as if I'd been hit. Did I really think it was my fault? "That's what I've been carrying all these years?"

"It's one of many stories that you carry."

We were never supposed to be on that beach. The whisper that had been echoing through me since 1987 roared in my ears: You could have stopped it. Should have. I might have been thirteen, but I could read. I understood we were breaking the law. I knew what "No Trespassing" meant.

"Ready to repeat after me?" Dr. Rosen said. I nodded. "Look at Rory and say: 'I did not kill David.'"

"I did not kill David."

"It's not my fault he died."

"It's not my fault he died."

"I don't have to blame myself."

"I don't have to blame myself."

"It's not my fault."

"It's not my fault."

"Now breathe," Dr. Rosen said. My lungs expanded underneath my ribs. When I exhaled, my breath came out jagged, its edges caught on the hooks of the resistance I'd built up over seventeen years.

"So this trauma has kept me alone all these years?"

"Your buried feelings about it has driven you away from people."

"Why?"

He leaned toward me and spoke slowly. "If you get into an intimate relationship, your intense feelings are going to come out just like they did this morning. You'll attach to someone." He pointed at himself. "He might go to the beach. He might not come back. Love will lead you to the beach a thousand times a day for the rest of your life."

"I'm never getting over this."

Dr. Rosen shook his head. "Christie, you will never get over this."

Dr. Rosen closed the session in the usual way, and Patrice and Rory both turned to me and wrapped me in their arms. Carlos stood just to the side, waiting for his turn. So did Marty and the Colonel. Each of them held me tight. Dr. Rosen also held me for a few seconds longer than usual. Just below the surface of my skin, I could still feel my body shaking with the memory of the waves hitting the black sand beach.

13

In August 2002, I celebrated my first anniversary in group by anxiously refreshing my e-mail with an index finger every three minutes in the student lounge where I was camped out with other law students. I'd finished a ten-week summer internship at Bell, Boyd & Lloyd, and the hiring coordinator said they'd e-mail us about permanent job offers by the end of the day. Over the summer, I'd written memos, researched principles of contract law, and stayed past nine several nights to prove my commitment. I also cheered at a Cubs game and sipped club soda at happy hours to prove that one future day I would be capable of socializing with blue-chip clients. But now I needed a job offer.

At four thirty, I gave the mouse one last press. My eyes seized on the e-mail from the firm: *The committee still hasn't voted.* Every other year in the firm's history, all of the interns were offered postgraduation jobs at a boozy party in the conference room overlooking downtown Chicago. This year, we'd primly sipped cranberry juice and nibbled roasted almonds as the managing partner talked about the economic downturn with a tight smile. Now this e-mail proved that the rumors that had spooked us all summer were true: they didn't have enough jobs for all of us.

My third year of law school had just started. Graduation loomed nine months ahead. The dot-com bubble had burst, and law firms typically did not hire third-year students—they hired the interns who worked for them over the summer. Some law firms were imploding; there one day and gone the next. My school, Loyola, was in the second tier, so I was competing with students who hailed from the University of Chicago and Northwestern, both of which were in the top ten. When I graduated, my debt was going to total over $120,000. If I didn't have a job, a good one, then how would I pay for rent, student loans, and therapy?

I race-walked to the career services center, where several other students were flipping through job listings in big white binders. A paltry list of firms scheduling interviews with third-year students was pinned to a bulletin board. Someone had scribbled *We're Fucked* at the bottom. Two organizations were interviewing third-year students: The Judge Advocate General (JAG) Corp. and Skadden, Arps, a top-ranked firm, famous for having the highest starting salaries in the country. The JAG Corp. was out because I didn't want to disclose my mental-health treatment or the three times I'd smoked pot to the federal government. As for Skadden, it was a powerhouse law firm stocked with thoroughbred attorneys from Ivy League schools who routinely worked sixty-hour weeks. Skadden was the Harvard of law firms. They would never hire me.

I fought the urge to vomit on the white binder.

My closest law school friend Clare pooh-poohed my fears. "You're first in our class! You have it made." Yes, as valedictorian, I would land a job, but if it only paid thirty grand, I would sink under the weight of my debt. I'd taken out a private loan, at 10 percent interest, to pay for treatment with Dr. Rosen. My law school debt was considerable. How would my life work if I had an extended job search? Would I have to move back to 6644 Thackeray?

In group, Dr. Rosen was insistent. "Interview at Skadden."

I balked. I saw myself as second tier, a middle-of-the-pack lawyer. My law school was second tier, as was Bell, Boyd & Lloyd. The Skadden partners argued before the Supreme Court and helmed complex commercial litigation covered in multipage *Wall Street Journal* articles. They wore custom-made suits with Italian leather shoes. I was a little girl with pinworms, a college student who almost died from self-induced vomiting, a young woman with an apple fetish barely in remission.

"Skadden's not for me, Dr. Harvard."

"Yes, it is."

What the hell did he know? He sat around with psychologically broken people all day. Skadden would expect me to perform at my highest level around other people who were doing the same and had been since they graduated summa cum laude from Princeton. I was a Loyola Rambler.

"You're brilliant. Skadden is going to want you."

Brilliant was a word to describe Madame Curie, Steve Jobs, or Dr. Shirley Ann Jackson, the female physicist who invented caller ID. It was not a word for me. Being first in my class made me a workhorse who desperately wanted achievements with which to wallpaper over the holes in her personal life, *not* brilliant. I had the LSAT score to prove it.

Patrice nudged me in the forearm and then exaggerated the motion of rubbing her chest like Dr. Rosen always did when someone gave him a compliment *or* an insult. I rubbed my chest halfheartedly. But some part of that *brilliant* penetrated just below my breastbone, a sliver of it nested in the soft part of me that was willing to receive it.

At home, I opened my closet door and stared at my navy Calvin Klein suit and Cole Haan flats. Of course I'd wear the lipstick Carlos picked out. At least I could get the costume right.

A week later, I sat across from a balding white guy in his sixties who stood in his stocking feet, leaning on oak bookshelves where his children smiled from chunky silver picture frames. Head of Skadden's litigation department. He winked and asked me where I saw myself in five years, chuckling as if the question was bullshit. I told him the truth: "I hope to be moving toward partnership." I didn't mean firm partnership necessarily, but he didn't know that.

The next partner who interviewed me had the most sumptuous charcoal-gray suit I'd ever seen. I studied it so I could describe it to Carlos later. During our thirty-minute conversation, he rolled up five separate pieces of Scotch Tape—sticky side up—and daubed at invisible dust specks on his desk. When he shook my hand at the end of the conversation, he said, "I promise we can give you exciting work."

The male associates had quirky artifacts in their offices: a framed vintage Cubs jersey, a Gorbachev bobblehead doll, a signed Bruce Springsteen album. None of them seemed psycho or incapable of talking about their lives outside of work. The only woman I met, Leslie, had an open smile and an easy laugh. I felt myself sink into the chair in a way I hadn't in the men's offices. When I asked her if it was possible for a woman to succeed at Skadden, she nodded her head slowly. "Yes, I think so."

For lunch, two junior associates, Jorge and Clark, hailed a cab that whisked us to Emilio's for tapas. Jorge had a regal bearing and wore a bow tie and cuff links. Clark was baby-faced, slightly disheveled, and recently married. Once we were seated, Jorge suggested we each order four plates to share. I'd never had tapas. I'd never eaten chorizo and Manchego cheese for lunch, or any other meal. I'd never shared twelve plates of food with two men while trying to land a job.

When the food arrived, I calmed my breath and took bites from each of the plates: grilled goat cheese on toast points, Spanish sausage, tricolored olives glistening with oil, sautéed escargots, and grilled potatoes. As the savory bites slid down my throat, my belly quivered with pleasure and shock. This was a long way from cabbage, tuna, and mustard. I worried the corner of a white linen napkin between dishes and thought about Rory's mind exploding when I reported my food later that night.

Even if I didn't get the job, the meal was a miracle.

They assured me they had lives outside of work: Jorge had a fiancée, Clark an abiding fondness for hours-long poker games. As I chewed my last bite, I felt desire stir in my chest. I wanted to work at Skadden too. I wanted to breathe the rarefied air of a fancy law firm just like Clark and Jorge were.

We parted ways outside Emilio's, and I walked down Ohio Street toward Michigan Avenue. My smart navy shoes clicked on the sidewalk as I turned down Michigan Avenue, past Tiffany, Cartier, and Neiman Marcus. My feet fell into a perfect staccato rhythm, and my spine was pillar straight. My stride was that of a woman who was first in her law school class. It might have been a second-tier school, but only one person had done it. The truth of that number—one—sizzled through my body, finally something more than abstraction or shame. It was energy, and it belonged to me.

By the time I slipped my key into my door, I believed I deserved an offer from Skadden—in part, because I was first in my class, but also because down the street was a wacky doctor with an impressive pedigree who told me I was brilliant. And even if I didn't believe I was brilliant, I did believe that he believed I was.

I ended up with two job offers: one from Bell, Boyd & Lloyd, where I'd done my internship, and one from Skadden. Clare said I should go back to the smaller firm because Skadden would work me to death. Hadn't the point of therapy been to keep me from taking a job that would suck the life out of me? I didn't want a life consumed by work. My favorite law school professor told me to go for Skadden because I was young and energetic and it was too good an opportunity to pass up.

With twenty-four hours left to make the decision, I took it to group. I'd left lunch with Jorge and Clark, high on serrano ham and convinced I could succeed at Skadden, but doubt crept in. Would Skadden suck me dry with billable hours? Skadden could be my nightmare come true if work left me no time to work on my relationships.

Dr. Rosen disagreed. "It will be easier to practice law around other brilliant people." There was that word again. "You could call now and accept the offer."

It was one thing to tell a hot guy from school that I was a cocktease, but it was quite another to turn a decision like this—the genesis of my legal career—over to Dr. Rosen. I told him I needed a few minutes to think about it. He did his "suit yourself" shrug and turned his attention to someone else.

With fifteen minutes to go in the session, that stirring of desire and ambition in my chest returned—quivering, translucent, fragile as a bubble. After my first year of law school, before my initial call to Dr. Rosen, I downloaded the application for Northwestern Law School. With my class rank, I could have transferred there and enrolled at the number eight law school in the country. I filled out the application and put the pages into a thick manila envelope. But at the mailbox in front of the law library, my fingers wouldn't grab the small metal handle on the door. My elbows wouldn't bend, my biceps wouldn't curl. The future that beckoned on the other side of that mail chute required more of me than my body could give. I didn't belong there. I was a second-tier person. I walked ten paces back toward the library and chucked the envelope in the trash.

Skadden was prestigious, and I didn't know if I belonged, but my fear of not measuring up was suddenly not as strong as the propulsive yes in my chest. It seemed absurd to let insecurity and fear hold me back from all Skadden was offering. Plus, they would pay me enough that I could afford rent, student loans, and therapy.

As the group session ticked down, I stared at the peak of the sooty Jewelers' Building a few blocks away. I held still to keep this brand-new vision from evaporating: My business card on heavy white card stock. My five-figure bonuses. My updated wardrobe. My Tumi briefcase. My cases and clients. Could I take all of this in? Could I try?

I wanted to try.

I held up my phone like a torch. "I want Skadden."

Dr. Rosen gestured with his hands, like *go right ahead.*

I flipped open my phone and dialed, but hesitated before pushing send. Patrice scooted her chair toward me and put out her hand. I placed mine into her open palm.

The recruiting partner's voice mail picked up. When it beeped, I looked to Dr. Rosen for a boost. He nodded.

I inhaled quickly. On the exhale, I stepped into my future.

"I hope you know what you're doing," I said, when I flipped the phone shut. "This is my life."

"Maybe you'll meet your husband there." Dr. Rosen smirked. I freed my hand from Patrice's and flipped him the bird. I wasn't taking a job to find a husband. He laughed and rubbed his chest with gusto.

I had a new job to go with my new home.

A few weeks earlier, Clare, my friend from law school, called and announced: "Tater, I need a new roommate." I thought she'd ask her boyfriend, our fellow classmate Steven, to move in, but she said they weren't ready for that step yet.

Clare's Gold Coast condo had a marbled lobby, a twenty-four-hour doorman, and a pool. It was walking distance to school and three El stops from Dr. Rosen. Deep purple curtains held by gold velvet sashes hung in her living room. I'd have access to the gym and a parking spot. My whole body trilled with pleasure at the invitation. She offered to charge me the same rent I paid for my efficiency with the clanking radiator, the water-stained ceiling, and the decades-old kitchen appliances. How could I say no? Ten minutes later, I flipped through the yellow pages and hired a moving company.

The night I committed to Skadden, I stretched out on my bed and took stock of my life. A new job. A new home. In the event of my death, Clare could alert the authorities. Or the doorman. I wouldn't die alone.

14

Carlos from group was my first male best friend. He would call me on the way to the gym, ranting that his fiancé, Jared, spent too much on Italian shoes or antique linens. He whisked me to restaurants in his tiny silver BMW and introduced me to foods I'd never had (pad thai, sturgeon) or heard of (cassoulet, shawarma). Without Carlos, I never would have tasted spanakopita or stepped foot in Barneys. As I headed into my second year of group, my relationship with Carlos was one of the brightest features of my steadily brightening life. When I bragged in group that Carlos and I had never had any conflict, Dr. Rosen piped up. "Pray for a fight."

"Why?"

"Because you want a truly intimate relationship."

"That means fighting?"

"If you aren't willing to fight, how can you can be intimate?"

Did wrestling with my brother at 6644 Thackeray over the remote control count? I searched my memory for a good old-fashioned throwdown—a slammed door, a fist curled, a throat raw from bellowing. I found nothing. In high school, my friend Denise snuck out of my house so she could have sex with her senior boyfriend at Caruth Park. I didn't get mad at her for potentially getting me in trouble by fleeing out my window. I swallowed my anger and let her back in when she tapped on the sill. Freshman year of college, my friend Anne invited the guy I was dating over to watch a movie with her while I was at the library. I never said a word. Instead, I moved out two months later. And when my friend Tyra confronted me for leaving her theater performance before her final curtain call, I felt hot plumes of anger shoot up from my stomach to my mouth. She ignored that I brought her flowers, stayed until she'd delivered all of her lines, and left because I had the stomach flu. Part of me wanted to get up in her wounded face and say, real vicious-like, "Could you think about someone else for one hot second?" Instead, I said, "I'm so sorry. I promise I'll be at the next one."

When it came to anger, I swallowed, pretended, ignored, withdrew. I knew nothing about fighting.

"I think you should join the Monday men's group," Dr. Rosen said to Carlos one Tuesday morning about thirteen months into my treatment. "It will help you prepare for your marriage."

I asked if I should join a second group too and Dr. Rosen shook his head and said I wasn't ready. Shame pinned me to my chair, and I remained silent for the rest of group. I didn't know whether I wanted to join a second group, but that wasn't the point. Dr. Rosen offered something to Carlos that he didn't offer me. For the rest of the session, noxious thoughts scrolled through my mind:

He likes Carlos more than me.

I'm not doing this right.

I suck at therapy.

I left group in a wordless, huffy silence. I avoided Carlos's calls—first, because I was jealous that he was the favored son, and then because I was ashamed of my petulance. We didn't speak until Sunday night, when I confessed my jealousy. "Don't be jealous of a second group, girl," he said. "It's just going to cost more money and create more hassle."

That night, I left Dr. Rosen a message asking him to call me before group so I could get his feedback on my intense reaction to Carlos's invitation to join a second group. Dr. Rosen often returned my calls between sessions. I assumed I'd hear from him.

All day Monday, I carried my phone turned up in my palm like a heart transplant patient waiting for news about a donor. By sundown, I lost hope. I called Marnie while browning a chicken breast on the fancy stove-top range in Clare's condo. She still saw Dr. Rosen, so I thought she'd understand how I was feeling

Before I could tell her anything, her other line beeped. "Hey, that's Dr. Rosen. Let me call you back."

Click. Marnie was gone.

I grabbed the skillet handle and the hot cast iron seared my fingers. "Dammit!" I cradled my burned fingers and hopped in pain, still cursing under my breath. I sat down in the middle of the kitchen and rocked back and forth. The chicken and oil hissed in the pan.

Five minutes later, Marnie called back. I took a deep breath. Maybe Dr. Rosen had called her back because she'd recently gotten pregnant after a miscarriage—maybe things weren't going well. Maybe she was cramping or had gotten bad news at the doctor.

"Everything okay?" I asked, genuinely concerned.

"It's our stupid contractor. He put in the wrong door—we ordered oak, not mahogany. Dr. Rosen coached me on how to talk to him tomorrow."

The air whooshed out of my lungs, and I doubled over. I pressed freezer-burned ice into my burned hand while glowing, newly pregnant Marnie discussed how to boss around laborers from a custom-upholstered settee in her four-story house.

Why would Dr. Rosen help her and not me?

As I dialed his number, my whole body shook. At the beep: "I can't believe you! You FUCKING ASSHOLE. You've been teaching me to ask for help. To reach out. To 'LET YOU AND THE GROUP IN.' But you don't reach back? Fuck you!" On and on, I yelled at Dr. Rosen's voice mail as my hand throbbed.

His voice mail beeped. I'd talked until the end of the message and then smashed the phone down on the floor. I wanted to smash everything: Clare's beautiful plum-colored Pottery Barn plates, the wine chiller in the corner, the vase of dried flowers, the framed Jazz Fest print above the table. Everything was throbbing: my head, my heart, my throat, my hand. I hated everything about Dr. Rosen: his smug face, his dumb elfin laughter, his arrogant prescriptions. Fuck him and that circle of chairs in that eighteenth-floor office.

ur

During the first few minutes of group, I avoided eye contact with everyone. I folded my hands in my lap, my gaze fixed on an oval-shaped stain on the carpet. Marty filled us in on his mother's hip operation, and Dr. Rosen did his routine of shifting his gaze from one person to the next.

"Did you leave me a message?" I looked up, and Dr. Rosen was staring at me. I nodded and felt light-headed.

"Do you want to tell the group about it?" He beamed at me like he did when Rory reported finishing a chapter of her dissertation. Around the room eager faces met my glance.

"I was upset and said some things that were not very nice—"

"Not very nice? Don't minimize! You were vicious!" Dr. Rosen gestured with his hands and bounced in his seat. He rubbed his heart and closed his eyes like he was savoring a great meal. "We should all go into my office and listen to it."

Everyone stood up. Field trip! It was my first time in his office since starting group and everything looked the same: the framed Harvard diplomas, the needlepoint, the uncluttered desk against the wall.

As Dr. Rosen held the receiver and punched in the passcode to his voice mail, Carlos whispered, "What the hell did you say?"

Dr. Rosen pressed the speaker button and there was my voice, shrill and clear. "You don't give two shits about me! Marnie has EVERYTHING! What about me?" My voice went on for three minutes. The group huddled around the phone.

When my voice finally shut up, he clicked the phone off. "Can you celebrate this?" He enunciated each word as if I was new to the English language.

Celebrate anger? That was rarer than fighting. I have no memory of yelling at my parents for any reason. Not even as a teenager. We weren't yellers. We were silent treatment people; we did huffy sighs and quiet seething. When my parents forbade me from attending Troy Tabucci's New Year's party sophomore year because they suspected there would be underaged drinking, I holed up in my room, making mixtapes of sad songs. When they told me that I had to go to college in Texas, I threw away the dog-eared Dartmouth brochure I'd been poring over for weeks. I used fake smiles, "I'm fines," and gigantic binges like other people used Kleenex. But now this man was treating my rant like a Chopin sonata.

"Celebrate?"

Dr. Rosen's eyes grew huge. "It's beautiful!"

"It's gross—"

"Says who?"

"The self-pity, for one thing—"

"I disagree—it's honest, authentic, and real. It's yours. And you shared it with me. Thank you." He rubbed his palm over his heart. "Welcome to your anger, *Mamaleh*. This is going to help you."

This was my first praise for the parts of me that were ugly, irrational, petty, reckless, spiteful, and spewing. I'd never heard of such a thing. If I were my therapist, I'd tell me to cut that shit out, but Dr. Rosen celebrated like it was Armistice Day with dance-in-the-streets, cancel-work jubilation.

"Don't worry," he said. "You're just getting started."

15

For the first time in over a year, I woke up after a whopping eight solid hours of sleep. I wasn't quite sure where I was, but I knew that there was a warm, buzzy feeling between my legs.

I'd had a sex dream. A graphic, steamy sex dream about R&B singer Luther Vandross. My main man Luther had caressed my face and kissed me deeply, his tongue filling my whole mouth. Then he did something with his tongue on my stomach—a circling-thrusting combo—that made me see beyond stars to other planets and galaxies. And when his soft lips circled between my legs, I mewled like a newborn kitten.

I woke up wet, hot, and satisfied.

On the train to group that morning, I hummed my favorite Luther Vandross song, "Here and Now." Oh yes, Luther, here and now indeed.

As the train lumbered past the darkened gay nightclubs and funky boutiques on Belmont, I felt buoyant—as if I could float up to the sky like an escaped balloon. I was not nearly as dead inside as I feared. The dream was also proof that whatever part of my subconscious had brought Mr. Vandross into my bed and let his tongue roam over my body was alive. And she was hungry. This sexual anorexic was working her way to the buffet table. I'd dreamed and felt sex that was hot, wild, noisy, wet, and completely focused on my pleasure. Sex with no inhibition, no nuns with their threats of hell, no disapproving parents who wanted sex linked to marriage, no worries about being pregnant or being fat or not "doing it right." There was my body, a gorgeous man, and pleasure.

Within the first ten minutes of group, I'd told them everything. "He was going down on me, and his back was smooth and muscular. I had an orgasm in my sleep."

"How long did it last?"

"Have you ever seen him in concert?"

"Is he the guy who sang that duet with Chaka Khan?"

Dr. Rosen, who had been silently taking in this conversation, finally spoke. "The dream's about me."

You could hear our necks swivel toward him.

"Come again, Freud?" I said, laughing. "No offense, but you bear zero resemblance to a smoking-hot black guy who's won a bunch of Grammys and is friends with Oprah. You're . . . well . . ." I gestured to his tufted head, his cable-knit brown sweater, and his thick-soled brown shoes. "I mean, look at you."

Dr. Rosen shook his head in that patronizing way. I scowled. If the dream was really about him, then why didn't Dustin Hoffman show up? Or maybe Adam Sandler?

"Uh-oh," Carlos said.

"What?" I asked.

Carlos and Rory exchanged a knowing glance. Then Carlos broke the news to me. "Don't you know that once you start psychotherapy all your sex dreams are about your therapist?"

Dr. Rosen nodded. "Van-de-Ross, sounds like 'Rosen.'"

"My god, they practically rhyme." I rolled my eyes. In no universe did my slim, balding, Jewish therapist resemble my new main man Luther. Dr. Rosen threw up his hands and shrugged. He wasn't going to try to convince me, which was the quickest way to get me to second-guess myself.

"Why do you have to make everything about you?" I murmured "creep" loud enough for him to hear. Then I ignored him as he rubbed his chest as if I'd said he was a stellar therapist. I refused to look at him, and the group moved on to another topic.

"Do you understand why that dream was possible?" Dr. Rosen turned to me with two minutes to go in the session. I shook my head. "Do you think it's a coincidence that you were able to express your rage directly to me two weeks ago, and then you had an orgasmic dream about me?"

I ignored the part where he connected my rage and sexual desire and bit on his insistence that the dream was about him.

"Why are you trying to ruin my dream?"

"Why would having sex with me ruin it?"

"You're my shrink." My face contorted at the thought.

"And?"

"What happened to Dr. Celebrate Everything?"

"I am celebrating. I'm not the one resisting."

"Resistant" was the one charge I couldn't ignore. It was the gravest therapeutic transgression, and I cringed when I saw it in my group mates. Dr. Rosen had been urging Rory to apply for jobs at higher-paying civil-rights organizations that would give her primo benefits, but she insisted that she could get hired only at legal clinics in Wisconsin that were run on a shoestring. With her credentials she could have worked anywhere in the Chicago area, but she continued to commute to Waupun, Wisconsin, and got pissed whenever we prodded her to reach for Something Better. Resistance—to change, to pleasure, to a shorter commute—was what held us back from what we really wanted. I would not commit that sin, even if I would rather punch Dr. Rosen in his smug little face than acknowledge my dream was about his saggy ass.

"Fine." I scooted to the edge of my seat and sat up straight. I gripped the arms of my chair and whispered in a singsong voice, "Dr. Rosen, I'd love to have your face in my crotch. I'm *dying* for you to put your tongue on me and slowly, slowly, slowly circle me until I come." I moaned a little for effect.

"Damn, girl," Carlos murmured.

The Colonel's eyes opened, cartoon-character wide. Rory blushed and cast her gaze to the window.

Dr. Rosen blinked twice. Then he said, "You're ready for another group."

Everyone waited for me to speak but I had no words, only sensations: hot Luther between my legs, annoyance at Dr. Rosen roiling in my belly, and the terror rising through my chest as I digested his words.

I mumbled the prayer at the end of group and walked out with Carlos in a haze. He put his arm around my shoulders. "I told you you'd get your chance for a second group."

Of course, now that I had it, I questioned it. Did I really want a whole other group? Coming downtown twice a week to excavate pinworm memories and pick up prescriptions to call group mates about my basic human functions? Why had I wanted this so badly? I thought it would make me feel like a favored child, like one of Rosen's Chosen, but now the invitation to a second group made me feel ashamed of how sick I must be.

The following week, I opened the session with my burning question: "Why now?" Dr. Rosen hadn't even taken his seat—he was futzing with the blinds across the room.

He took his seat and considered my question. "Your willingness to bring the dream into group, to be proud of it, and to discuss it means you're ready."

"For what?"

"For more."

"More what?"

"Heat. Intimacy. Intensity. Sex."

"Will it help me with relationships?"

"Guaranteed."

"Now group is like Best Buy?"

~~~

Sometimes I felt like Rosen-world was a cult. I'd begun to spot Rosen-patients out in the wild. In a 12-step meeting, I heard a woman say, "My name is Ginny, and my crazy therapist told me to tell you all that I'm bingeing on off-brand Oreos." Before she said another word, I realized I'd heard about her from Carlos: she was dating Chip from the men's group, and they almost broke up because he wouldn't go down on her. In another meeting, a woman sat in the middle of the circle taking superhuman bites of a Burger King Whopper. In the eleven years I'd been in recovery meetings for eating disorders, I'd never seen anyone eat so much as an oyster cracker during a meeting. Most meetings had an explicit rule that you weren't supposed to mention any specific foods by name because you could trigger someone's bingeing. So seeing someone devour a Whopper was shocking—like seeing the moon fall from the sky and land in your lap. Marnie leaned over and whispered: "She's got to be one of us." We later confirmed that Dr. Rosen had given her a prescription to gorge on fast food during meetings instead of in secret at home.

How would increasing my participation in Rosen-world mesh with my daily life as a seminormal person? As a law student, it was tricky to reconcile my public, professional trajectory with my, shall we say, unorthodox therapy life. Keeping Baby Jeremiah in my closet. Calling Rory and Marty every night. Telling the Smoker I'm a "cocktease." Part of me wanted to join the second group for the same reason I joined the first: I was curious. Curious about who would be in my group and how my life would change if I joined. My five current group mates and Dr. Rosen knew all the details of my eating, sleeping, and sex-dreaming. What would I do with *more* group?

As I mulled over the possibility of joining a second group, I surveyed the developments in my love life since starting the first. I'd been on one official date since the debacle with fifty-minute Sam and the fiasco with Andrew of the charred chicken breasts. Two weeks after I had sex with Andrew, I met Greg at a house party, and he asked for my number. He'd just gotten out of a yearlong medically induced coma. On the way out of a sushi restaurant on our first date, he forgot where he lived. I may not have been ready for a relationship, but he *definitely* wasn't.

Then there was Xavier, my ex-boyfriend from college—one of the decent guys I dumped because his steady loyalty nauseated me. I hooked up with him while visiting my family in Texas. We met in a darkened parking lot in a sketchy neighborhood near the DFW airport. When we started making out, I could see the faint outline of stars and galaxies. His lips on mine woke me up. His hand on my thigh was an unlocking, and I wanted to go further, all the way right there under the neon "Checks

Cashed" sign. Of course, I'd never felt this gut longing for him when we were together—I avoided sex with complaints about headaches and early morning shifts at my mall job.

As I hitched up my skirt, Xavier pulled away.

"Connie's flight is about to land," he said. I stared at him without blinking. "I know what you're thinking. But I'm not hooking up with you because I'm freaking out about getting serious with Connie."

My heart sunk. The word *fool* flashed in my mind. When I returned to Chicago a few days later, my group pointed out that Xavier was unavailable, which is precisely why I was attracted to him.

Now Xavier was engaged. So was my college roommate Kat, two of my law school friends, and two of my cousins. Dr. Rosen's new group felt like a rope I should probably grab.

"Okay, I'll do a second group."

"I suggest an all-women's group."

"Why?"

"It's what's next for you." My eye twitched.

He suggested the Tuesday-noon group. One hundred eighty minutes of therapy in a single day. Two round-trip train rides to Washington and Wabash on Tuesdays.

"That's insane." Plus, the noon group was Marnie's. I reminded him that we were friends. My eye twitched again.

"There are social risks for you." I squeezed my eyes shut and thought of Bianca and that table of girls in fifth grade. Since fifth grade, I'd been terrified that any group of women would eventually turn on me, and I'd end up taking my meals on the crapper. But would enduring some friendship friction be better than dying alone, unloved and untouched, heart as slick as an obsidian stone?

I said yes.

Part 2

16

I was cocky that first Tuesday. I already knew the drill. I'd tallied the minutes I'd spent doing group therapy over the past thirteen months: 5,265. My heart had a few score marks—shallow knicks, but grooves all the same—from all the work I'd done so far.

I wasn't planning to tell Clare, who wasn't a consumer of mental-health services, that I'd signed up for two groups in one day, but I'd blurted it out one afternoon on the walk home from family-law class. She paused and then smiled like she was proud of me. "Be sure to take a snack on Tuesdays because that's a long day, Tater." She loaned me her favorite Anthropologie sweater to wear on my first double-decker therapy day.

Thirty minutes before my second group session of the day, I strutted out of criminal procedure class, ready to slide like an egg into batter. I was seven minutes early, but I jabbed the group room button anyway, even though its purpose was to alert Dr. Rosen that a group member who arrived late wanted to be let in. *Guess who, Rosen? How you like me now? Two times in one day.* I took a seat and was soon joined by Emily, who was famous in Rosen-world because her father, a pill addict who lived in Kansas, was enraged when Emily started therapy, so he harassed and threatened Dr. Rosen through the mail and over the phone.

She and Marnie were close friends, and as we chitchatted before the session, I realized how weird it felt to intrude on "their" group. I dismissed the fear and greeted a tall woman wearing a straw hat. "I'm Mary," she said, taking the seat next to me. I'd heard about Mary from Marnie, but couldn't remember if she was the one Marnie loved or the one whose guts she professed to hate.

At noon, Dr. Rosen opened the door to the waiting room, offering each of us a smile. Before we were settled in our chairs in the group room, we were joined by an ample woman named Zenia, who had mulberry-colored hair and gigantic brown eyes stuck in the expression of *surprise!* She kicked us off with a story about her multi-orgasmic weekend, courtesy of an erotic online community for Dungeons & Dragons fans. She mentioned a girlfriend who lived in Croatia whom she'd never met in person.

I'd spent more than five thousand minutes in this room. Ninety of those minutes were three hours earlier. Everything looked the same: the swivel chairs, the bookshelf, the cheap mini-blinds, and the limp Easter lily hanging on for one more season. Yet it felt totally unfamiliar. Like a dream where you're in your house, but it's not really your house because the door is the wrong color and there are two stories instead of one. At the level of energy and particles, something was totally off.

Dr. Rosen looked like an unfriendly stranger: his lips were set in a stern line; his arms looked rigid and unnatural. There was nothing warm or familiar coursing between us, and my heart contracted with homesickness for Tuesday morning.

Zenia glowed as she discussed her relationship with Greta from Croatia—and the hours of sex they enjoyed online and how they were saving money to meet up for a convention in Brussels. Zenia smiled at me every few minutes, which I took as a generous welcome, and then segued seamlessly into a question for Dr. Rosen about how to treat one of her patients.

"Patients?" I said out loud.

"I'm a physician."

Dr. Rosen smirked at me. That fucker was laughing at me! Oh, look at the lonely prude sitting next to the successful doctor enjoying virtual sex with her girlfriend! I narrowed my eyes and scowled at him; his smile widened. I didn't expect him to coddle me, but I also didn't expect him to sit on his throne and laugh at me.

Mary shared that her abusive brother—the one who had threatened to kill her all through childhood—had called to ask for money. Regina, a massage therapist wrapped in what looked like two black shawls and a flowy nylon skirt, had come in during Zenia's sexalogue. She told Mary in a sympathetic, hushed tone that when her psychotic cousin pulled a knife on her, she filed a restraining order.

Dr. Rosen had misread my history. A fear-lump in my belly swelled as I realized this was the wrong group for me. I wanted to grab him by the crisp brown collar and remind him that yes, I'd suffered in the aftermath of Hawaii and battled an eating disorder, but there'd been no attempted murder. I'd turned out perfectionistic, frigid, and borderline asexual, but how could he think I belonged here? I was a lightweight, trifling thing, who was all *"boo-hoo* I wish I had a boyfriend"—I was absurd and garden-variety next to these women who were braver and more interesting and accomplished than I'd ever be.

Twenty minutes passed. Where was Marnie? She was supposed to be my swim buddy.

Marnie arrived thirty minutes into the session, dropped her orange leather bag unceremoniously on the floor, and fell heavily into her chair. I tried to catch her eye, but she wouldn't look at me. Her jaw was set tight and her brown eyes darted around the circle, looking for prey.

"I'm so fucking tired I want to die," she said. She'd given birth to a gorgeous baby girl six weeks earlier. "Pat's traveling every week, and the baby won't sleep. I can't—" Her hands were shaking as she pulled out a bottle of Voss. I'd talked to her earlier in the morning, but she hadn't expressed any of this anguish. Now she seemed to be pretending I wasn't in the room. That kind of studied avoidance could only mean one thing: she was angry at me. I could no longer hear anything because I was swept up into my own panic about how to stop Marnie's anger. I'd seen Marnie mad before. It wasn't pretty.

The door buzzed. A woman with a giant purse with leather tassels and a Styrofoam food container walked in, and all the molecules in the room shifted. It had to be Nan—Marnie had mentioned her, but had not told me she was so radiant, throwing off energy like light beams. Though I knew she was near retirement, Nan's skin glowed like a young woman's. When she smiled, two dimples appeared on either cheek. I couldn't tear my eyes away from her silver sandals, the ring of keys that jangled as she set her purse behind her chair, her sly smile at Dr. Rosen when she sat down, or her mouth as she mumbled under her breath while Marnie was talking. She acknowledged me with a quick nod of her head, and I smiled back.

"IN is having its way with me today," Nan said. "IN wants me dead."

I looked at Dr. Rosen. IN? He looked at me but offered nothing. If I wanted to know what Nan was talking about, I'd have to ask her.

Nan picked up her Styrofoam container and lifted its lid—one compartment was filled with mac and cheese, the kind with the near-orange sauce and elbow-shaped pasta. She kept talking as she took a bite. "I'm not even hungry." Her voice cracked. She looked at me and explained that the *I* stood for "inner" and the *N* stood for the racial slur that had oppressed her all her life. She made it clear that she—and only she—was allowed to say the full name of IN, and by God, I was not about to defy Nan. I nodded, grateful she had filled me in.

"Nan, I was talking," Marnie said. I knew that tone. Marnie used it with Pat right before the marital spat I'd witnessed. I curled further inward and found myself holding my breath. The air was sharp, flickering with the threat of violence. I didn't want to inhale it.

Nan pointed her fork at Marnie. "Hold. The. Fuck. Up." I sucked in a gulp of air and held it, suspended, in my lungs.

Marnie twisted the top of her water bottle. "Wait your fucking turn." It sounded like a warning, a hiss.

This was not like my other group, where Patrice snapped at Colonel Sanders or Carlos bickered with Rory about showing up on time. Between Marnie and Nan, I sensed something heavier, more corporeal and unstable. They were dragging their words from the depths of their bodies, not plucking them out of their heads. They were using their hands and arms. They were spitting. The air crackled with heat and something menacing.

Nan set her food down. I thought she was going to rise and roll up her sleeves, but she grabbed a napkin from her purse and wiped her mouth real slow, like a pissed-off sheriff in a Western. I let the air seep out of my lungs, tiny breath by tiny breath. They kept yelling—Marnie was a "skinny white bitch," and Nan was "a help-rejecting drama queen." Dr. Rosen looked alert but not alarmed. Then Nan pointed her fork at Dr. Rosen.

"You need to help me," she said quietly. Tears I hadn't noticed welling rolled down her cheeks. She bent her head low like she was addressing her leftovers. "Please help me." I wanted to cross the circle and put my arms around her. Instead, I picked the cuticle on my right thumb deep enough to draw blood and make my stomach seize.

"I'd love to," Dr. Rosen said, smiling and sitting up like an actor who'd been waiting for his big solo.

"This is all I know." She daubed her eyes with her napkin.

Nan turned to me and described a childhood filled with violence and addiction: an unstable stepfather who brandished a gun at her after gambling all night, a bipolar brother who punched the walls and broke family heirlooms. "Brute force—it's all I know."

Marnie scooted her chair toward Nan and touched her arm. "It's all I know too." Mary and Emily had tears in their eyes. Mine were stuck in my thumb, where I continued to dig at the exposed bright pink flesh. A drop of blood pooled in my nail bed.

In the five years I'd known her, Marnie had met every emotional situation with a hard-nosed defiance, a macho Italian "you talkin' to me?" bravado that I both feared and admired. I watched, mesmerized, as Nan and Marnie, two women I was sure were going to maim each other moments before, melted into a collage of mutual trauma and healing. Marnie held on to Nan's left arm.

I'd never seen two people fight—or make up—before. My thumb was throbbing, and I bit my lip to keep from bursting into tears. As the minutes ticked by, I fantasized about shrinking—losing skin, muscle, bone, cells—becoming nothing more than a heap of clothes in my frayed swivel chair.

The next time Dr. Rosen caught my eye, I mouthed, "Help me."

"What's that?" he said, cupping his ear with his hand.

No sound came out, but I kept mouthing, "Help me." Over and over. *Help. Me.*

The attention in the room shifted from Nan and Marnie to me. I couldn't look at any of the women, and I couldn't make any sound come out.

"What's your problem?" Marnie asked, finally giving me her full attention.

I shook my head, holding Dr. Rosen's gaze.

"Seriously? What's your fucking problem? If you're going to make it here"—she glanced over at Dr. Rosen and jutted out her chin—"and for the record, no one asked me how I felt about *her* joining *my* group—you have to speak up. We do deep work here."

My only thought was *I want to go home*—to the morning group, the people who knew and loved me.

I turned to Dr. Rosen. "Why did you bring me here? I don't fit here. Everyone has been on the other end of a knife or horrific violence. I just want some people in my life, maybe a boyfriend who isn't drinking himself to death or too depressed to have sex, but I feel disgusting—"

"Disgusting isn't a—"

"Yes, it is!" My whole body shook. I wrung my hands like I was trying to dry them. I wanted to shake the disgust off my skin, even though it was coming from inside.

"No."

"Fine. I feel shame for intruding on Marnie's group, scared of what I'm seeing and hearing, and mad at you for putting me here. I'm never going to have a place in this group. I never should have joined a second group!"

"Good!" Dr. Rosen stuck both of his thumbs up like my distress was a movie he'd just watched and was recommending to his audience. "It's already working."

"What's working?"

"This group." Cue million-watt smile. A sweep of his arm across the circle. Elfin joy.

"*Mamaleh*, one part of intimacy is learning to express anger. You've made huge progress in the morning group. But another part of intimacy is learning to tolerate other people's anger. This group will help you with that." He looked at Marnie, who stared him down without blinking. "It already has." In full Mister Rogers mode, he explained that my terror about other people's anger was yet another stumbling block to intimacy. Sure, I could now join my law school friends for lunch at the deli, book-end my baths, and yell at Dr. Rosen. But there was always more. Therapy was a Sisyphean trap.

"What do I do about Marnie?"

"You could celebrate her anger." I rolled my eyes. Then I asked how. "Look at Marnie," he directed. I swiveled my chair and stared into her angry eyes. "Tell her that you love her, and her anger is beautiful."

"Marnie, I love you, and your anger is beautiful."

"Now breathe." My words hovered over the circle. Every instinct pushed me to go off Dr. Rosen's script, throw myself at Marnie's feet, and promise to leave the group or stay up all night with her baby—*any*thing to stop her anger. But I kept breathing, each second pulling me away from my tired old impulses.

I broke my gaze to look at the clock, but Dr. Rosen told me to keep my eyes on Marnie. "Tell her that you welcome her anger and that you are available for more." I did. She didn't say anything.

"What are you feeling?" Dr. Rosen asked.

"Scared." My toes curled toward the floor.

"Good. If you can learn to tolerate that fear and let go of trying to fix her anger, you will be ready for an intimate relationship."

"I thought all I had to do was turn over my food to Rory. And book-end my bath. And take Baby Jeremiah. And tell the Smoker I was a cocktease."

"You definitely needed to do all of that. And this is the next thing."

The session was over. Dr. Rosen ended it in the familiar way. When the hugs began, I kept my eyes on Marnie, watching her embrace Emily, Mary, and Zenia. *Please hug me,* I wished from across the room. I heaved my backpack over my shoulder.

"Hey you," Marnie said, nudging my shoulder.

"Hey," I said, my eyes flitting to hers and then to the floor.

"You did good today." We both smiled.

"Doesn't feel good."

"I know."

She opened her arms, and I stepped forward into them. Marnie said something into my hair. "What?" I asked.

"I can be mad at you and still love you, you know."

No, actually, I didn't know that. I had no idea.

17

I slipped on one of Clare's black dresses and a new pair of black strappy sandals. Marnie was throwing a fortieth birthday party for Pat, and miraculously, I had a date. A date with someone I was attracted to. I'd met Jeremy a few years before law school at a party that was full of 12-step people. I was enchanted by his wire-rim glasses, gentle green eyes, and insightful comments. Turns out, he was also in Carlos's other Rosen group, so I heard tidbits about him from time to time. Like that he'd just broken up with his girlfriend.

The week before Pat's party I stood on the train platform at Fullerton and spotted Jeremy. He was absorbed in a thick, impressive tome— by Thucydides. His khaki pants were cuffed just so, and his blue fleece made his green eyes shine. I sidled his way. When a crush of people exited the next train, he looked up.

"Hey," he said, folding the top corner of his page and shutting his book.

"I thought that was you." I reached for the same train pole he was holding. He asked about law school, and I asked him about work and why he was reading Thucydides. "For fun," he said. His smile made me feel cozy, like we were sitting by a fire, not jammed into a rickety El train packed with short-tempered commuters.

"I've never seen you on this train," I said when I realized we lived two stops from each other.

He let out a short, unhappy laugh. "I used to stay at my girlfriend's in Bucktown. We broke up."

"I heard that." I smiled, wishing I could wink without looking stupid. He cocked his head. "I see Rosen. Tuesday morning with Carlos."

He leaned toward me, close enough that I could see specks of gold in his green eyes, and whispered, "I'd heard that."

"Touché." The whispers of the Rosen-grapevine echoed all around us.

We both laughed, and the sound of our voices rose over our heads and those of the people absorbed in their phones, books, and newspapers. Desire for this smiling, literate man flowed from my fingers twined around the steel pole, down my arm, and through my chest, belly, and between my legs.

Next thing I knew, the invitation for Pat's party flew out of my mouth, as if I was the sort of woman who routinely asked out philosophy-loving, newly single men. He agreed right away and wrote his address on a Post-it note he used as a bookmark. We touched hands when the train jerked its way to the Southport stop, and a fresh zing of desire shot through me.

He was waiting outside when I pulled up the following Friday night, dressed exactly the same as he was on the train, which put me at ease. Our first topic of conversation was Dr. Rosen. We joked about his unfortunate wardrobe choices, and his absurd optimism that group would cure absolutely any emotional impairment.

"He sure loves group," Jeremy said, laughing.

"He sure loves brown sweaters."

My limbs felt loose and relaxed as we ran through the common ground of our mutual therapy experiences. I had none of my usual first-date stiffness, no impulse to hold any part of myself back. I didn't have to: he saw Dr. Rosen.

By the time I pulled up to Marnie's house, I'd decided that the only thing Jeremy was missing in his life was the love of an emotionally available woman. By the time I'd found a sparkling water and a stuffed mushroom cap, I'd decided that would be me.

"Come here, I want to show you something." I led Jeremy upstairs to the nursery, where Marnie had hand-stenciled ducks on her daughter's buttery-yellow walls. Without any shame, I opened each drawer to fawn over Landyn's tiny diapers, impossibly minuscule socks, and a powder-pink sleep sack, soft as a snow owl.

"Cute," he said, when I held up a little bathrobe with an attached hood and bunny ears. Jeremy kept looking back toward the door like we were committing a crime. I offered him a baby cap to snuggle, and he stepped back. "Is this a prescription—to show me these clothes?" I shook my head and ran a cashmere sweater across my cheek. "Maybe we should head back to the party." Jeremy stepped into the hall and waited for me to put Landyn's clothes away.

Downstairs, he made conversation with Pat, Marnie, and their suburban friends. My limbs remained loose as I drove him home after eleven.

Whenever our conversation veered from Dr. Rosen, I noticed a few flags—not red exactly, but pinkish.

"I'm a bit of a loner," he said when I asked if he hung out with his group mates outside of sessions. I wondered if that might one day backfire on me. When I thought of the type of man I wanted to date, *loner* was nowhere on the list.

He also mentioned that his car wasn't working, and he couldn't afford the spare part. Money trouble gave me a touch of heartburn—Carlos had told me that Jeremy's breakup with his girlfriend had something to do with money he borrowed from her. I gripped the steering wheel and tried to stay loose. Would he resent my impending financial security? Was he anticapitalism? Was he, at the ripe age of thirty-six, still lost, professionally and financially? If so, how much did that matter to me?

A little, but he was so cute in those glasses.

"I don't think I know much about your work," I said, hoping a job description would ease the nub of tension at my neck.

"I run the front office for an industrial janitorial company. A small operation on the west side." The nub didn't budge. I'd had the impression he was an IT manager for a big company downtown. I adjusted my grip on the steering wheel again.

So we were different. Big deal. Lots of couples were famously different: Arnold Schwarzenegger and Maria Shriver. James Carville and Mary Matalin. Homer and Marge. Maybe we wouldn't make it to a silver anniversary celebration, but surely we could go on a second date.

When I pulled up to his building at the end of the night, I took my right hand off the steering wheel and let it fall to my side.

"There's a Polish movie playing Monday night that's getting rave reviews. Want to go?" I nodded, eager as a Yorkie. He gave me a not-entirely-chaste squeeze on my arm as he got out of the car.

A second date! I pumped my fist in the air. As I turned my car around to head home, I banked the curb with a jolt that snapped my neck and knocked my water bottle out of the drink holder, but I barely felt it. My joy hugged the border of hysteria.

~

"Tell me more about this Jeremy," Clare said the next night over dinner. She dropped her head into her open palm when I told her I gave him a tour of Landyn's nursery. "Tater! You don't show a man a nursery on your first date!"

But I felt no shame. "Don't worry. He sees Rosen. I don't have to play games with him. I can be myself." She cocked her head, skeptical.

"This sounds really promising, Tater. This is your reward for joining that second group!"

That night, I drew a line down the center of a piece of paper. No more haphazard romantic follies for me. I was in therapy now. I started with the "pro" column. He was undeniably intelligent. Who reads Thucydides for pleasure? He was sober, so he wouldn't piss on me in the middle of the night. He had a cat, so he knew how to take care of something. The glasses, the smile, the rapt listening. I wrote it all down. Then I wrote the biggest pro of all: *Sees Dr. Rosen.*

Dating a man who saw a therapist—any therapist—was ideal. Therapy made you more sensitive and self-aware. It gave you tools to navigate a relationship. Seeing a man who saw *my* therapist was a way to build a bulletproof relationship. After all, I trusted Dr. Rosen. Mostly. I knew his work. I *was* his work. Jeremy and I would have acres of common ground. We would never run out of things to say. Bonus: we'd have free couples counseling—we'd just see the therapist at different times and with other people.

On our second date, we sat on lumpy seats in the crowded Music Box Theatre reading the subtitles of a Polish film about two sad people walking through a city park. Jeremy elbowed me when I crossed my legs. "The great group no-no," he whispered, and we both laughed. He put his hand on top of mine and left it there until the end of the movie. Its warmth and heft felt like solid pleasure.

On the walk back to his place, we huddled together as the wind whipped all around us. We told each other our hardest prescriptions. I trotted out my cocktease prescription—not a story I ever pictured telling on a second date. He told me he hadn't done his hardest one yet. When I asked what it was, he looked away.

After a few steps, he said, "Rosen says I should ask my ex-girlfriend to forgive the loan she made me." He grimaced and looked down at his feet.

His living room featured a brown couch and matching coffee table. He'd positioned his desk and computer by the window in his kitchen, and his bathroom, while not exactly reeking of bleach and free of stray hairs, struck me as reasonably clean. I was impressed by his silver kettle and an array of teas.

A plump tabby with orange-and-white coloring purred at his feet. "This is Mr. Bourgeois."

"That's his name?"

He nodded and smiled.

"Looking at your bookshelf, I shouldn't be surprised." Machiavelli, Sartre, Plato, Socrates, Heidegger, Kant. The lightest read was Saint Augustine.

I slipped off my shoes and told him I hated my new group.

"Why?" he asked, sitting next to me on the couch. His knee touched mine.

"It's so raw and intense in there. Everyone screaming and eating, then crying and hugging. And Marnie isn't thrilled I'm there—"

"Why do you think Rosen put you in there?"

"Well."

"What?"

"He thinks it will help me open up to a relationship." I upended my teacup to hide how embarrassing it sounded.

He took my hand. "I hated my second group too. Every second of it."

"Why'd you stay?"

"I wanted to see what those feelings meant, where they came from." He shrugged his shoulders. "Now here I am." My heart lurched to the edge of my rib cage.

He leaned toward me.

"Is it okay if I kiss you?" he asked.

I felt a welling in my chest, the novel sensation of safety inching toward desire. I nodded, and our lips met. I tasted chamomile tea, and when he put his hand on my neck, I leaned into him and the chance he offered. I hadn't really tasted a man's lips in almost two years—with Andrew I was too busy dissociating to feel anything, and in the parking lot with Xavier all I could taste was my own neediness. Now, with Jeremy pressing his lips and tongue against mine, his goatee tickling my upper lip, I felt my libido flicker a few times and then ignite. The pressure between my legs was a mix of pleasure and pain, desire and ache, satisfaction and hunger. I was coming to life.

This is what I'd been waiting for.

18

"*No secrets,*" *Dr. Rosen advised when I showed up in group with* the epic news that I'd been on two dates with Jeremy. "Anything that happens between you and Jeremy—emotionally, romantically, sexually— bring it to both of your groups."

"Also financially," Carlos said, aware as he was of Jeremy's past issues.

Quick math: my two groups plus Jeremy's two equaled approximately twenty people who would know when we went dutch on dinner, gave each other house keys, or had sex during my period. I balked and held up my hands. "Whoa. Hold up. Won't weekly play-by-plays to every-goddamn-person take the *zing* out of the relationship."

"My suggestion is no secrets," Dr. Rosen repeated.

"Your suggestion sucks."

"How well has it worked to do it your way?"

On our third date, Jeremy and I babysat Marnie's daughter, Landyn, for a few hours so she and Pat could go out for an anniversary dinner. As the baby slept in my arms, Jeremy peeked in the cabinets, stared at Clare's dishes, and stood on the balcony admiring the view.

After Marnie and Pat retrieved Landyn, I suggested to Jeremy that we join Clare and Steven at a bar on Belmont for some live music. When he agreed, I was dumbstruck. Could it really be this easy? All I had to do was ask?

"Do you want to pack a bag so you can stay over?" he asked.

I couldn't hide my giddiness. I raced around the room stuffing contact lens solution and a fresh sweater into a bag.

The bar was not exactly Jeremy's scene—a cavern full of fraternity boys and aging Cubs fans sloshing drinks out of plastic cups. After the first set, Jeremy whispered that he was ready to go. My whole body trilled. I drove through red lights and rolled through stop signs. I couldn't wait to press my body against his.

I sat on his bed in the dark while he fed Mr. Bourgeois. When he sat next to me, I leaned into him. He pressed his lips against mine. "Is that okay?" he whispered. I nodded and pulled him toward me. I pressed my body against his, and he held me tight as he kissed me, harder and deeper.

He pushed me off gently and rolled onto his back. "I'm not ready for sex," he said. A simple admission—five words I'd never heard anyone, including myself, say. Was it a prescription?

"It's okay." And it was. What I wanted was a chance to be close to someone. It didn't have to be sex, not tonight.

As soon as he said sex was off the table, my body relaxed further into him, the bed, the moment. For tonight, kissing would be where it began and ended. He rolled toward me and held me close—chest to chest, belly to belly, thigh to thigh.

"Maybe we could just sleep," he said.

"Of course."

We settled into each other, our breathing deepened.

"Do you always sleep with this many clothes on?" he whispered into my neck.

I still had on my jeans and T-shirt. The only article I'd removed was a light wool sweater.

"Yes." I actually always slept in my bra. I had since ninth grade when my breasts exploded from buds to D's. I liked sleeping with my breasts bound, tucked into the underwire and lace. With past boyfriends, I would slip out of my bra when we were having sex, but when it was time to sleep, I put it back on. I'd never been with a man who noticed, or who was willing to ask me about it.

The next morning, shards of light sliced through the edge of Jeremy's blackout curtains, and Mr. Bourgeois sat on the edge of the bed considering me. I padded into the living room and found Jeremy at the little table in his darkened kitchen, typing on his computer.

"Hey." I stepped into the foot of space between the fridge and the metal shelves he used as a pantry. I crossed my arms and hugged myself.

An awkward silence gathered between us. I cleared my throat. "What are your plans for the day?" Would we brunch and walk down the street swaddled in the gauzy intimacy of the night before? Would we go back to bed?

He turned most of his body back to the computer. I crossed my right leg over my left.

"Catching up on stuff. AA meeting tonight. What about you?"

"Some reading for my cyber law class. Clare and I might see an early movie." I paused. Was I supposed to invite him? He looked at the computer screen, where a grid of pound signs, dots, and percentage symbols lit up a black background. "What's that?"

"It's an ASCII video game called NetHack." He blushed and looked at his feet. "It's a bit of a preoccupation."

Video game? Preoccupation?

"No judgment here." I smiled at him. But a frisson of warning shot through me. A grown-ass man sitting in a darkened room playing a video game? The claustrophobic image made my throat constrict.

"You say that now. But I literally might play this all day—" His green eyes were not filled with levity, but something shadowy I recognized. Shame.

"If it brings you joy, what's the harm?" My voice was shrill with false cheer. His face relaxed, but then I hugged myself tighter, aware of an urge to flee. "I think I'll get going soon."

When I pulled into my parking spot at home, I dialed Rory's number. "I'm not sure about him," I said.

"Honey, he just got out of a relationship. Bring it all to group."

On Tuesday morning, Patrice, Rory, Marty, Ed, and Dr. Rosen

cheered Jeremy for being explicit about his sexual boundaries. When I was with Jeremy, I'd felt comforted by his admission that he wasn't ready for sex, but now their cheers felt infantilizing—they were adults entitled to regular hot sex, and we were children who were stuck with kissing and cuddling. I hated their gaiety, and I hated myself for agreeing to disclose everything to my groups.

There were no pep rallies in the afternoon group. Marnie thought his sexual reticence signaled that he wasn't ready for a relationship. "I don't like it," she said, shaking her head. Nan and Emily wondered why he didn't offer me breakfast. Mary wondered why he didn't have a proper pantry. I shrugged my shoulders and swallowed lump after lump of shame.

"Dr. Rosen, morning group loves everything about this guy. After-noon group sees nothing but red flags. Which is it?" The sharpness of the afternoon group's critique scared me.

"The two groups reflect your own internal conflict. The split's in you—you don't know if Jeremy's pacing is a gift or if you are going to starve in this relationship. If he's a videogame addict or an introvert who likes computers."

"How do I find out which is true?"

"Keep showing up."

"Where?"

"Everywhere."

Dutifully, I reported to both groups with updates every session. All ten of my group members knew I paid for most of our meals with money I saved over the summer. That I drove us everywhere because his truck was still out of commission. That we mostly hung out at his place. They learned that the first time he touched my breasts, I shuddered with a pleasure that bordered on nausea—a cake too rich, a sunset too vibrant. "Is this okay?" Jeremy asked whenever he touched my body in a new way—a kiss on my belly, a hand on my upper thigh. My morning group loved his commit-ment to consent, but my afternoon group pronounced it "kinda lame."

As it happened, our slow sexual progress was indeed Dr. Rosen's doing. One night, while we were making out on his bed, Jeremy admitted that Dr. Rosen warned him not to rush. "He said I should take it slow or I would end up hating you like I hated my ex." Apparently, their relationship combusted not only because of unresolved financial conflicts, but also because the sexual progress of the relationship outpaced his emotional readiness.

I wrapped a blanket around my body. I felt exposed—I was the one who wanted more physically. It felt like rejection and made me want to hide my face from him, from Dr. Rosen, and from the twenty-odd people who knew I wanted to have sex with him.

A poll on the radio revealed that most couples go "all the way" by the third date. When I complained in my morning group about falling way behind the national norm, Dr. Rosen insisted that *we* weren't ready. I sensed a conflict of interest—because, really, it was Jeremy who wasn't ready. Dr. Rosen held his ground.

"What's your rush?" he asked.

"I've endured a lifetime of failed relationships and sexual repression."

"Then what's a little more time?"

Arguing with Dr. Rosen wouldn't work. I had to adjust my strategy if I wanted him to cosign intercourse. A few minutes later, I leaned toward Dr. Rosen and said in my most rational voice, "Can we talk about Jeremy? He's hiding out in video games. You should consider giving him a prescription to spend some time with his emotionally and sexually available girlfriend."

Cough. Cough. Cough. Dr. Rosen's theatrical throat-clear. Translation: *You're full of shit.* I ignored it.

"He exhibits classic signs of avoidance. He's afraid of intimacy—"

More coughing. Then a question: "And what about you, *Mamaleh*?"

"Me? I'm totally available." I stretched my arms out wide. Nothing to hide here. The whole room laughed.

"What's so funny?"

"Serious question?" Dr. Rosen said. I nodded. "How many bras are you wearing?"

"*Busted,*" Carlos said under his breath.

Confused, I looked at my shoulder, where three bra straps crisscrossed under my tank top. I'd run before group, and my chest was a double D. A single sports bra didn't keep my girls in place, so I wore two, sometimes three.

"Do you hate your breasts?" Dr. Rosen asked.

Of course I hated my breasts—they were bags of fat hanging on my clavicle. I associated them with being ungainly, not being sexual. And there was something scary about them—how important they were to other people (men) and how unwieldy they were. All my life I'd coveted a flat chest. Flat like the earth after a glacier scrapes by. Flat like a ballerina's, a model's, a little girl's.

"I don't love them."

"You're trying to make them small—"

"I was exercising, not trying to win a Playboy bunny contest."

"Do you think that hating your breasts might interfere with your sexual relationship?"

The correct answer was yes, but I couldn't bring myself to say it. I'd never discussed how I felt about my breasts with anyone before. I sat there shaking my head, trying not to cry. It had never struck me as sad that I hated my breasts.

"How does Jeremy feel about them?"

"I'm sure he thinks it's weird that I sleep in a bra."

Dr. Rosen's eyebrows disappeared into his scalp. Everyone else gasped as if I'd just confessed to murdering baby gorillas. The Colonel looked more animated than he'd been since the time Carlos mentioned lesbian porn.

"Are you curious about why you sleep in a bra?" Dr. Rosen asked.

A fist of anger filled my mouth. "I know what you're doing! This is where I'm supposed to remember something my dad or uncle or the skeevy gym teacher did or said. I don't have one of those things. Everything that's happened to me has been run-of-the-mill—"

"Nothing about Hawaii sounded run-of-the-mill," Rory said.

"That's insane! David's drowning isn't the reason that I'm wearing all these bras."

"Are you curious why you are?" Dr. Rosen repeated the question, steady and calm.

"There's no story. I was a young girl who wanted to be thin because everybody loves thin girl bodies. Because I was into ballet, an art form built on anorexia, and breasts are not thin. They are filled with fat. They make it hard to shop for tops at J.Crew and Anthropologie. They make me feel fat." I adjusted my tank top so all the bra straps were hidden. "Welcome to the female body in America, buddy."

"Do you want some help?" Dr. Rosen sat still as a bird of prey.

Why hadn't I picked a female therapist? I didn't believe that my male therapist could fathom my relationship to my breasts. Sure he was in recovery for an eating disorder, but he'd never been shopping with his grandmother in Waxahachie, Texas, and overheard the saleslady say that his breasts made him look much "fuller" than he was. He'd never had a ballet teacher advise him to go on an egg diet—three eggs for breakfast, lunch, and dinner and nothing else—when his breast buds appeared. He'd never walked by Hooters in downtown Houston and endured drunk men leering at his chest. Even if he had perfect scores in every subject at Harvard and a genius-like understanding of group dynamics, a man simply cannot know how it feels to walk the planet as a woman. But I nodded—*yes, I want some help*— because getting inadequate help from my male therapist was better than nothing.

"Get a henna tattoo on your belly that says 'I hate my breasts.'"

"Hate? I thought we were aiming for love and acceptance."

Dr. Rosen shook his head. "First accept the hate. Stop trying to outrun it." He gestured to my shoulders and the bras. "Take Jeremy with you."

19

*Jeremy and I pulled up to a crumbly industrial warehouse build-*ing on the corner of Racine and Grand. I pressed the buzzer that read Big Ernie. Big Ernie advertised himself in the *Chicago Reader* as a magician, dog walker, and henna tattoo artist. He buzzed us up, and we took the stairs to the second floor, where a man with a long black ponytail dressed in black genie pants greeted us from the doorway of his apartment. He could have been thirty or fifty years old—it was impossible to pinpoint. His warm smile soothed me, and the fifteen-foot ceilings in his loft made me feel like a prop in a dollhouse. The brick walls had been painted a lacquer white. He told us to take a seat in his living room while he prepared the henna. I took the couch and Jeremy crouched by the fireplace, where one hundred Pez dispensers were arranged in perfect order, like colorful, cartoon versions of white crosses in a military cemetery.

I'd called Big Ernie right after my second group the morning I made the mistake of wearing two bras to group. I'd told the ladies all about my prescription. They all nodded when I described my lifelong hatred of my breasts and shared their own stories. A man had recently grabbed Nan's breast while she shopped for lipstick at Marshall Field's. Zenia's dad had commented on her breasts all her life. Mary was ashamed her breasts were so small. Emily described a fight she'd had with her husband after he'd grabbed her breast playfully while they were watching *The Daily Show*. That was when I covered my mouth with my hands and started to cry.

ᒪᒪᕐ

I was sixteen. Junior prom. I wore a size-ten Laura Ashley strapless black dress that had a sweetheart neckline and a spray of giant pink gardenias across the front. I'd been going to the tanning salon every other day for four weeks, so my skin was an unnatural shade of brown-orange and tingled with almost-pain from staying too long in the coffin-shaped booth. My date, Matt, and I barely knew each other; we'd been thrown together after everyone else had coupled up. He was a few years from announcing he was gay. After the corsage-boutonniere exchange and dinner, a caravan of us stopped at a park to pound beers and wine coolers pilfered from parents' bars. The sweet fizziness of berry wine cooler sloshed in my stomach and made my head go fuzzy. The ground under my feet felt pleasantly unsteady, like trying to walk on a water bed. I remembered standing next to Jared Meechum's black Cherokee, surrounded by ten guys.

We were all laughing. Slurry clouds drifted by, hiding the moon every few minutes.

Jared approached me with a dare in his eye. My hands were at my sides—one clutched an empty Bartles & Jaymes bottle, one had gathered a handful of dress to keep me steady. I smelled the beer on his lips and saw the mound of dip bulging in his lower lip. I was midlaugh when he reached two fingers down the front of my dress between my breasts. I finished my laugh as if nothing happened, because I wasn't sure it had.

Had it? He'd stepped away quickly so it was easy to blame my sloshy stomach, my fuzzy brain. My breasts were so smushed into the dress that the sensation was muffled, and the memory easily dissolved.

I upended the bottle in my hand and licked the last drop from the rim.

Spencer was next. He did it quick-like and avoided my eyes. He had the decency to blush. But shame didn't stop him from whispering to P.J.

and Tad, both of whom seemed to tower over me as they slid their two fingers between my breasts. I watched the tops of the trees, swaying just so in the breeze even though the night was still and thick with late-spring humidity. My hands gripped harder at the dress and the bottle. There was nothing else to reach for.

The clouds continued to skate past the moon.

Where were the other girls? Where was my date? Why was I still laughing, acting like I was having the time of my life with these good Catholic boys I'd known all my life? I'd been longing for any of them to ask me on a date, to invite me to dance, to call me, kiss me, want me. Each of them was dating one of my friends. This was the first time any of them had ever touched me.

Jared appeared for a second time. On this pass, he stuck his whole hand between my breasts. Only then did I step back. Only then did I feel the crush of shame slamming through the buzz, the dress, the laughter. Only then did I let myself understand that they were laughing at me.

I continued to laugh.

Laughing, laughing, laughing. The sound of it covered so much—it covered the whole Texas sky with its false notes that disguised my terror.

My group sat quietly as I said the names of those tall Catholic boys and how their clammy hands felt down my dress.

⸻

Now Big Ernie's soft wet brush on my exposed belly tickled, but I wasn't laughing. I stared at the ceiling and squeezed Jeremy's hand. An expectant feeling tickled my throat. It was a cry or a scream—I couldn't tell which—but I wasn't letting whatever it was out in front of the Yogi Bear and Flintstones candy dispensers. I kept my eyes on the ceiling and never looked down.

Back at Jeremy's place, I stood in the bathroom and surveyed my tattoo, the top layer of which was a crust I peeled off. Smooth burnt-orange swirls and curlicues danced over my belly button and adorned the script: *I hate my breasts.* Honestly, it looked and felt hokey as hell. Still, I held my hand over it as I called Rory to report my food, and Marty for my affirmation.

I slipped off my bra before putting on Jeremy's soft black T-shirt with the words *Ars Technica* printed across the chest. He found me curled in his bed under the covers and asked if he could join me.

I scooted over to make room for him and unfurled my body. He shook off his jeans and got into bed with his boxers and T-shirt on. I rolled into his body with my arms still curled into my chest in a protective X. I took a deep breath. Then another. I relaxed my arms and let them rest at my side. Tears welled from the tender part of my chest where all that breast hatred had lived for so long.

"What is it?" he asked.

"I've been very afraid." He smoothed the back of my head with his palm.

"Me too."

"I don't know what I'm doing."

"Me either." He held me closer.

I kept crying, imagining the dye on my belly seeping through my skin and joining my bloodstream.

20

Jeremy waited for me in the lobby of the law library, head buried in a battered Nietzsche book. I slipped my hand into his. "Let's head up Michigan Avenue." I'd been dreaming of the two of us, hand in hand, walking down the strip of Michigan Avenue famously nicknamed "the Magnificent Mile" for its dazzling array of shops and restaurants. This time of year Christmas lights hung from every lamppost, and Salvation Army volunteers dressed as Santa rang bells in front of Neiman Marcus.

My fantasy was a nice dinner followed by sex at my place. I'd been holed up in the library all Saturday studying criminal procedure. It was early December. Finals time. My job at Skadden was locked down and everyone said that your third-year grades didn't matter, but I wanted to keep my class rank. My back ached from hunching over the textbook as I mastered the laws governing arrest and detention. I'd decided it was time to master my relationship. I was sick of Dr. Rosen controlling my love life. My relationship needed some leadership, and I was ready to step up. The kissing and light petting were gratifying, but I was hungry for more. Starving, really.

The wind off the lake hit my chest. I burrowed deeper into my coat and closer to Jeremy. The sidewalk was jammed with tourists carrying huge holiday bags from the Disney Store and Ralph Lauren. Jeremy got whacked in the thigh with an oversize Crate & Barrel bag. He scowled and pressed the pace. I lengthened my stride to keep up.

"Where are we going?"

"I can't take the crowds." He turned off Michigan Avenue.

I swallowed my disappointment in two gulps. My fantasy reel didn't include side streets—we were supposed to be on Michigan Avenue under the holiday lights and in the fray, where life was pulsing with energy and cheer.

Half a block up, he ducked into a California Pizza Kitchen. More gulps. My fantasy reel definitely didn't include a chain pizzeria packed with suburban teenagers.

"Want to share a pizza and a salad?" I said.

"Nah, I'm going to get a sausage calzone. I can polish it off on my own." I nodded hard. I ordered a California veggie personal pizza and a side salad with Italian vinaigrette.

He'd spent the day playing video games. I pushed down the bubble of contempt that my boyfriend, a grown-ass man within spitting distance of his fortieth birthday, spent his day trying to win the Amulet of Yendor. I'd run four miles, gone to a 12-step meeting, and studied for a criminal procedure exam for four hours.

Conversation stalled. When the food came, I wanted to mouth "help" to the waitress.

Telepathically, I informed her that I was drowning in the dead space between me and my boyfriend, who still wasn't ready for sex after almost two months.

Jeremy punctured his calzone and a puff of steam escaped. I moved the tomato slice from the high-noon spot on my plate to six thirty, and thought of things to say that would make him want to take me to bed.

"Want a bite of my salad?"

When we got back to my place, Clare and Steven were on their way to Lincoln Park to listen to live music. "Come with, you guys," Clare said, throwing her coat over her shoulders.

Before I could open my mouth to ask where, Jeremy said, "I'm going to hit the hay." He saluted Clare and Steven and beelined to my bedroom.

Clare whispered, "Get you some, Tater," and wiggled her eyebrows suggestively.

I played along. "Don't wake me in the morning!"

By the time I'd turned off the living room lights and walked into my bedroom, Jeremy was a snoring mound. I sat on the bed roughly, hoping to jostle him awake. I propped myself on a pillow and stared at a shadow on the wall. What exactly, I wondered, made me so different from Clare, whose boyfriend wanted to touch her and talk to her all night? Was it my years of bulimia? Was I subconsciously pushing Jeremy away? I knew I was attached to Dr. Rosen and my group mates. Why couldn't I do that with a man? I wasn't afraid of sex like Dr. Rosen insisted—I wanted to have it with Jeremy right then.

The clock glowed eight forty-five. Five minutes earlier than the end point of my abortive date with Sam. Disappointment and anger—at Jeremy, myself, Dr. Rosen, my groups, and this whole stupid night—rushed through me, making my fingers twitch. I sighed loudly. Jeremy didn't budge, so I climbed out of bed. In the cabinet under the kitchen sink, I found the box of mismatched plates and glass tumblers I'd brought from my old apartment. Clare and I kept an Ace Hardware hammer in the junk drawer for various home improvement projects that we never actually did. I took the box and the hammer and nudged open the balcony door with my elbow.

Hammer raised, chest heaving. *Smash.* Shattered bits of glass flew across the balcony. My bare knees scraped the concrete. *Smash. Smash. Smash.* My cheeks burned from effort, from the cold.

~

Rory and Carlos gasped.

"Did you protect your face?" Patrice asked.

I'd felt driven to smash. My body simply couldn't hold the impulses to bring the hammer down. I was brimming with rage. All I knew was that if I didn't destroy those dishes, I was going to turn that hammer on myself.

"Were you hoping to wake him up?" Patrice asked.

"I guess. But the breaking was purely physical, like sneezing or—"

"Vomiting," Dr. Rosen said.

"Yes! It was like having something in my body that felt—" What was the word?

"Toxic?"

"Exactly! Something that my body had to eject."

"Vomiting is your body preventing you from dying of food poisoning," Dr. Rosen said. "This anger is old. It's the anger you used to puke up, but it's still in there. By avoiding an intimate relationship, you've been able to avoid feeling this."

"I've been enraged with you. Remember when you marched us to your office to listen to my voice mail?"

"We're not sexually involved."

"Fair point." I understood the difference. To Jeremy I offered my body and I wanted his in return. But it wasn't working. "So what do I *do* now?"

The answer I would have accepted: break up with Jeremy. But Dr. Rosen suggested that I keep expressing my rage and invite Jeremy to join me. As if Jeremy would budge for me and my hammer.

"The question is whether you're willing to ask." What good would it do? I slumped down. Dr. Rosen seemed willfully blind to the obstacles.

"You honestly think I should stay in this relationship?"

"It's just getting good—"

"But it's totally dysfunctional."

"Not totally."

"Did you hear that story? I was on my twenty-eighth-floor balcony whacking at discounted stemware with a hammer in the middle of the night!"

"You said it was nine o'clock." The Colonel smirked across the circle.

My spittle flew in all directions when I told him to fuck off. I banged on the arms of the chair. "Help me!"

"I fully support your anger," Dr. Rosen said, smooth as a chalkboard.

"I want more from you. Give me something more."

"Buy safety goggles."

Three hours later, I stormed into the noon group and told Dr. Rosen to fuck off. The group leaned in as I told them about the dishes, and about Dr. Rosen and his safety goggles. Marnie side-eyed Dr. Rosen and accused him of not helping me. Emily suggested that Jeremy and I "take a break."

"I need more from you, Dr. Rosen." I was banging the same chair arms I'd abused that morning.

Dr. Rosen said nothing. He shifted his gaze around the room just like normal, letting me yell at him.

I slithered to the floor. I screamed into the carpet. Over and over, nonsense words of rage. Guttural sounds of exertion poured into the floor, shimmering over to the other women's feet. The more I yelled and beat the carpet with my coiled fists, the deeper I fell into a black hole of despair. Sweat rolled down my neck and my hair stuck to my forehead.

When I was in third or fourth grade, my parents planned a family beach vacation to Padre Island. My dad steered our cloud-blue station wagon, brimming with rafts, sunscreen, and beach towels, south toward the coast. Halfway through the eight-hour drive, the weather reports turned ominous: a hurricane had changed course and was zooming toward the curled tip of Texas, just miles from where we were headed. My parents said we wouldn't make it. Too dangerous. A new plan developed. We'd check in at a Holiday Inn in Houston and hang out with my mom's friend from high school. Maybe visit NASA. The next morning, in the hotel pool, my brother and sister splashed and frolicked while I moped in the shallow end. Come on, Christie. Get in the pool. Have some peanuts. Check out the ice machine down the hall. I wouldn't. Or couldn't. I'd had a picture in my mind of the moat I wanted to dig around my sand castle, and this stupid hotel pool in the middle of this humid, concrete city didn't fit in my imagination. Whatever skills my siblings had that allowed them to pivot, readjust, and find joy in the detour, I lacked. I could only seethe in silence, swallowed up by my internal gale-force fury and disappointment. My family, unsure of how to reach me, eventually let me be. No one had any tools to offer me then, or later when I didn't get ballet solos, or boyfriends broke up with me, or I didn't get into the graduate program I wanted. All I'd ever done with anger was swallow it or throw it up. Now it was pouring out, messy and loud.

et

Here, in this room in the middle of downtown Chicago, the side of my fists bearing streaks of bright pink carpet burn, I sat slumped on the floor and tried to calm my breath. Every single set of eyes on me was filled with compassion. Except Dr. Rosen's. His looked exactly the same: intense but impervious. Almost annoyed at his histrionic patient who was sinking, sinking, sinking.

"YOU! YOU! YOU!" I grabbed fistfuls of my hair with both hands and pulled as hard as I could. My scalp rang with pain, but I pulled again. And again.

Someone said something I couldn't hear. I sat up, still holding my hair as if for ransom.

"The poor baby," Nan said. Her voice wobbled. "Poor, poor baby." My body went slack in the lullaby of her voice. She scooted closer so she could pat my back. I let go of my hair and clambered to my seat. My scalp and hands throbbed with my heartbeat. Stray hairs twined between my fingers. I could not even look at Dr. Rosen. The women beamed me with love, but it stung like pity.

I had a boyfriend, ten group mates, and almost two years of Dr. Rosen under my belt. I felt as stuck as ever.

21

After the Night of the Broken Dishes, Dr. Rosen coached me on how to ask for what I wanted from Jeremy. Pretending to be me, Dr. Rosen would say, "Jeremy, my love, I want you to take me out to dinner tonight," or "I want us to take off our clothes and hold each other in bed." As me, Dr. Rosen sat up tall and smiled broadly. He made it look so easy, this asking for what I wanted.

When it was my turn to ask in real life, I sputtered like an old lawn mower. "I want—do you think we could—would you be open to, maybe—I don't know—leaving your apartment with me sometime?"

Jeremy smiled sweetly. "Where do you want to go?"

"The sushi place down the block?"

He hesitated and then said, "Sure."

One Tuesday morning I got a prescription: invite Jeremy over for the sole purpose of kissing me for five minutes straight. I was skeptical that Jeremy would make the effort for a five-minute kiss, but the point was whether I was willing to ask.

We giggled as I led him to my bedroom, where we stood on the strip of carpet between my closet and my bed. In the living room down the hall, the TV blared *Wheel of Fortune* while Steven and Clare cooked dinner. The night sky was a dark blanket over the window. Jeremy futzed with his watch. He stepped toward me with his finger over the button for the timer.

"Ready?"

I took a deep breath, and let out a shudder and a tiny squeal. Part of me wanted to break role, call this exercise stupid, and pick a fight. I pulled myself together, squeezed my eyes shut, and tapped into the other part of me: the one willing to have this kiss.

"Ready."

Beep.

He slid one arm around my waist and one behind my head and kissed me softly. I was stuck in my head—worried about the timer, whether to slip in some tongue, whether I was getting the most out of this prescription. Then I sent my mind to my lips. I inched closer to Jeremy. The tips of my toes touched his shoes and I pressed my body into his, testing. Could he bear my weight? He smelled like sweat, coffee, and mints. I pulled him closer to me for the final few seconds, knowing time was almost up.

Beep.

"That was cool," he said, fiddling with the button on his watch. He threaded his arm through his backpack, getting ready to go. I felt settled and calm, almost like a baby swaddled tightly and held close. When Jeremy hugged me good-bye, he held me for an extra beat. His body felt solid against mine, like he could hold me up for a long time. I stood at the front door until the elevator dinged and then watched him disappear behind the silver doors. The kiss had filled me up. I wanted it to be enough.

I stayed with Jeremy. I stayed with Dr. Rosen. I stayed with my two groups. I stayed because I believed the agony of staying was necessary to score my heart. I thought that leaving—wanting to leave *and* actually leaving—was proof I wasn't cut out for true intimacy. I had to prove to myself that I could endure whatever pain came up in my relationships. I could survive the heat without letting go. I could attach.

On Christmas morning, I left Jeremy sleeping to meet my friend Jill for coffee. As carols blared through a packed Starbucks, Jill cried about being single with no plans except to visit her abusive father, and

I teared up about the sexless state of my relationship. When I returned to Jeremy's apartment, he called me back to bed. "Take off your jeans," he said.

Merry Christmas!

I liked his initiative.

There was a condom on the pillow next to him, and my starving body heaved into him. An exhilarating openness overtook my body. He thrust once, and an orgasm seized my whole body in a split second.

I promptly burst into tears.

"What is it?" he said.

Underneath all the frustration and anger was an ocean of hurt and sadness. Waves of loneliness, just as Dr. Rosen had long ago predicted.

"Why is it so hard?" I said it over and over. Why, why, why? Was it that hard to love me and my body? Why couldn't we have this physical intimacy all the time? All those weeks I'd chased Jeremy's love and attention reinforced my fear that something wrong with the way that I loved and how I wanted to be loved. The neglect I experienced confirmed my defective capacity for attachment. I'd picked a boyfriend who doled out unsustaining portions of love and attention. And I'd picked him because he was all I could tolerate, even though I wanted so much more. I was like an anorexic who continued to eat rice cakes and celery even though she dreamed of filet mignon and a buttered baked potato.

As 2003 dawned, I sailed into my final semester of law school. Jeremy still needed more time apart than I did. He would occasionally shut down and roll over without any explanation, and his passion for his ASCII video games made me roll my eyes. But instead of breaking household items, I sent texts to Rory, Marty, and Carlos: *I'm so lonely. He's playing video games.* Between those blackout times when he drew the curtain between us, we inched forward, like Dr. Rosen promised we would.

But Dr. Rosen's conflict of interest was no small thing. Was he working for my welfare or Jeremy's?

One Thursday night, Jeremy returned from his men's group and asked if I would buy him a subscription to the *Financial Times* and a pair of running shoes. I could tell from the way he was asking—and because he'd just come from his group—that it was a prescription from Dr. Rosen.

"How dare you set me up to be his sugar mama!" I screamed at Dr. Rosen during my next group session. "You're supposed to be helping me, not using me to bankroll his hobbies."

"I *am* helping you."

"Bullshit."

"What are your two biggest complaints about Jeremy?"

I'd mentioned that Jeremy seemed stuck professionally. He was a member of Mensa and read Greek philosophers with names I could hardly pronounce, yet his job had no future and didn't cover his bills. He hated his boss and felt like he was wasting his potential. He once mentioned going to law school. I'd also expressed concern about his sedentary lifestyle, which I was afraid would negatively impact our nascent sex life.

"If he reads the *Financial Times*, might it help him focus his ambition? If he gets running shoes, he'll be more active. Maybe you can run together and then have sex."

Dr. Rosen, the great puppeteer, yanked the strings. He'd gotten Jeremy to ask, and he would get me to pay. He knew I had the money because the week before I'd brought the seven-thousand-dollar salary advance check that Skadden sent me. Dr. Rosen suggested I pass it around the circle. When it got to him, he held it above his head: *Baruch atah Adonai something-something.*

The rage that had brought me to my knees in group before Christmas surged—rage that Dr. Rosen couldn't truly help me, so he settled for using me to help Jeremy—but I stayed in my chair, pursed my lips, and let it fester. I didn't have words, just the sensation of anger heating my body.

The following weekend, Jeremy started receiving a daily copy of the pink-paged *Financial Times*, and we shopped for a pair of retro black New Balances. When I asked him if he wanted to run with me, he said, "Nah, you go ahead."

After he went after my money, it got worse. Dr. Rosen took aim at my vagina.

One late-winter evening, Jeremy swiveled away from his computer game and declared that March would be "going down on Christie" month.

"Where did this come from?" I said.

"I just decided."

We'd been dating for months, and there'd been little oral action on either of our parts. Now I was looking forward to the gifts that March would bring my way. But on the last Thursday in February, Jeremy returned home from his group with an announcement: "Dr. Rosen thinks it's a bad idea."

I dropped the law book I was holding. "Excuse me?"

"He thinks I'm trying to blow up the relationship."

So now my therapist, who had promised to get me into healthy relationships, including *sexual* relationships, was actively working *against* my pleasure. I excused myself and took the phone into the bathroom. I dialed Dr. Rosen's number, but got his voice mail. I hung up. No voice mails. I would gift him the full force of my anger in person.

"I hear your anger." Dr. Rosen answered with calm confidence when I confronted him in my morning group. I pounded fists on the arms of my chair. I called him a misogynist and a control freak.

"I hear you experience me exerting control."

"You told my boyfriend not to go down on me! What the fuck?" He smiled like *ooh, goody, she's really mad!* "Stop pulling the strings."

Dr. Rosen held up his hands and shook his head. "There're no strings. I don't control anyone's tongue."

"You make suggestions to people who pay you to tell them what to do."

"What do you want?"

"I want you to fuck right off." The anger was stuck halfway between my throat and my chest.

More stuckness. In my chair, in my body, in my relationship with my boyfriend and my therapist.

When Dr. Rosen put his hands together, it signaled the end of the session. I stood up with everyone else, but I didn't recite the Serenity Prayer, and when everyone split off in twos to hug, I took turns embracing Patrice, Rory, Marty, Carlos, and the Colonel. But I turned my back on Dr. Rosen. I wouldn't pretend everything was okay just because ninety minutes were up. I felt betrayed. His loyalty clearly belonged to Jeremy, and he brought all his Harvard expertise to bear in treating *his* sexual hangups. Dr. Rosen didn't have my interests or sexual pleasure in mind at all.

In the afternoon group, I refused to look at Dr. Rosen but explained to all the women how Dr. Rosen was interfering in my relationship by advising Jeremy not to pleasure me. Marnie narrowed her eyes and yelled at Dr. Rosen for using me to help Jeremy. Then she swiveled her chair toward me and scolded me for being so willing to starve in my relationship. "This isn't all Dr. Rosen," she said, pointing at me. "You're going along with all of this." I wasn't upset that she was yelling at me—I could hear that she loved me and wanted more for me. I did too.

22

That seven-thousand-dollar salary advance from Skadden made me bold. All my law school friends were planning post–bar exam trips with their beloveds. I dreamed of international travel with my boyfriend. I dreamed of us in Italy, holding hands on medieval bridges and feeding each other bites of pizza margherita, surrounded by languid rivers and soaring cathedrals. I dreamed of us laughing, touching, exploring, and loving. The man holding my hand in my daydreams bore little resemblance to Jeremy. But I set my sights on the trip and wouldn't back down. I'd worked hard in law school to earn a place at Skadden, which earned me seven thousand dollars in advance salary, and I worked hard in therapy to have a relationship. How hard could this be?

Negotiations were tense from the start. I would suggest Tuscany or the Cinque Terre, and Jeremy would shrug his shoulders and sigh heavily.

"We could do Greece, the birthplace of philosophy."

More shrugging.

"Can't we discuss this?"

"You get to control this because you have the money."

"So you pick." I threw up my hands. Honestly, I didn't care where we went so long as it was *together*.

After a long pause, he said, "Italy's fine."

Both of my groups and Dr. Rosen advised me to focus on myself and plan the trip I wanted to take. "He'll either come with you or he won't," Dr. Rosen said. So comforting. I pushed aside my brewing dread. I barreled ahead in the face of Jeremy's resistance because being a young woman alone in Italy was not a story I was willing to inhabit. Solo travel was not one of my heart's deep callings.

The temperature in Florence soared into the nineties, and BBC Radio reported seven heat-related deaths. Jeremy and I ate a breakfast of soft scrambled eggs, fresh strawberries, and toast with homemade orange marmalade on the sun-flooded second-floor terrace of the Hotel Silla. We moved our chairs to take cover under the shade of a fig tree. I could have stayed there all day, looking over the Arno River and listening to the pigeons coo, but I'd scheduled a bike tour that started at ten. The day before I'd taken a bus to Siena. By myself. Jeremy hadn't wanted to face the heat.

"Are you up for the bike tour?" I asked in my upbeat vacation voice, the voice of my heart holding on to hope.

"You go ahead. I'm going to study." He pulled out an LSAT workbook and his special black pen. He'd recently decided to apply to law school, which was an undeniably positive development given how much he hated his job. But his ironclad study schedule was not to be interrupted by the Florentine countryside, even though the LSAT was months away.

"Is there something else you would rather do? I can cancel the bike thing—"

"No, you go. I need to do a practice test."

Leading up to the trip, Dr. Rosen had encouraged me to accept Jeremy's introversion. Stop trying to change him. I understood the importance of acceptance, but when Jeremy said he wouldn't be joining me for the second day in a row, I wanted to flip the table and send his precious LSAT book flying into the cobblestone street. How small could I fold my desire so that Jeremy's rebuffs no longer stung? How could I make myself want less from this man who said he loved me, but who seemed to have so little desire to spend time with me?

He flicked his pen and started sketching out his answer to one of the questions.

I kissed him on the top of his head and set out for the bike tour, fuming. Who pays for her boyfriend to come to Italy and ignore her? My heart thrummed its familiar rhythm: alone, alone, alone.

A lanky expat named Sherry with a yoga teacher's posture showed me my bike. "Where's your partner?"

"Oh, he's—" Like the wife covering for an alcoholic husband who couldn't get out of bed, I lied. "Sick." I blamed the heat and jet lag.

The twelve other people in our group arrived in pairs. Honeymooners, fathers and daughters, college roommates, a couple celebrating thirty years of marriage. Our first stop was an old stone farmhouse, where a sunburned groundskeeper served us a morning snack. I sat on an ancient stone bench eating the salty cheese and buttery quail egg surrounded by strangers who were snapping pictures of each other.

"Want a picture?" a father from San Diego asked me. I wiped the sweat from my brow and stood by a fig tree, trying to look natural, even though I didn't know what to do with my hands. Clasp them in front of me? Put them on my hips? Steady myself on the stone wall?

The father whispered to his daughter, "It's so brave to travel alone in a foreign country." Believe me, buddy, I'm a lot of things, but brave comes well after desperate, foolish, lonely, depressed, sad, lost, humiliated, and starving.

When the other bicyclists headed back to Florence at the end of the tour, I broke away, pedaling so fast my quads burned. After I returned my bike, I followed the narrow streets back to the hotel but then stopped halfway there. Why rush? Jeremy wasn't pining for me. Would he even be happy to see me? I veered away from the hotel and toward the tourist strip by the Ponte Vecchio instead, where leather belts hung from stalls like slabs of meat. On a side street, I spotted a pay phone. I chucked coin after coin into the slot until I reached Chicago.

Dr. Rosen's voice mail picked up after three rings. At the beep, I let it out. "I just went on a bike tour, *alone*. Yesterday, I went to Siena, *alone*. I thought you said you could fix this—that you could fix me." I sobbed into the grimy Italian pay phone until a computerized voice cut me off.

After all the therapy sessions I'd sat through. The prescriptions I'd willingly done. The *feeling* of my feelings. Here I was, still so terribly alone. The loneliness was supposed to recede. I thought my progress in therapy would be a graph line that trended up and only up, but sitting alone in Florence, I felt that same desperate stirring I'd felt in Chicago before starting group. If I hadn't changed yet, when would I? Maybe it wasn't possible for me. I loved my group mates—and even Dr. Rosen—but they couldn't come to Italy with me. Dr. Rosen was right: I'd tasted the company and fellowship of sitting in group week after week, and now the loneliness was darker and more devastating than it had ever been.

When I returned to the room, Jeremy was asleep on the bed, his study guide tented on his stomach. He smiled when he opened his eyes. I lay down next to him, our bodies barely touching. In silence we watched the light fade from the window as the sun sank behind the Duomo.

That night after dinner, he clicked off the light and lay down on his back. Would we have sex? I breathed deep and commanded my body not to want. I folded my desire like a tiny origami crane and tucked it away.

"I'm going to masturbate before bed. You're welcome to join me." Jeremy slipped off his boxer shorts, and his busy elbow tapped my forearm with every stroke.

"Want me to do that?" I whispered, a strand of my desire shaking loose.

"I've got it."

I rested my hand on his shoulder, grateful he let me keep it there.

⟡

After Italy, I started working the long hours of a first-year associate at a big law firm, never leaving the office at night before seven. Suddenly I had a secretary, an expense account, and an office with a window overlooking the Chicago River. During my sixth week of work, I pulled my first all-nighter. My main task as a young lawyer was to review financial documents ten hours a day for a client whose beverages I grew up drinking. Skadden also sent me to the client's headquarters to interview the bigwigs who set up their sales strategy so we could defend them to the SEC. After a long day of back-to-back meetings with the all-male-except-me team and a long dinner, I would collapse on a hotel bed and call Jeremy, who was home playing his NetHack.

"You're doing great. I'm so proud of you," Jeremy would say.

While I was off learning how to be a Skadden lawyer, Jeremy slipped into a depression. He gained weight, stopped shaving, skipped AA meetings, and sat at his computer playing his game most of the hours he wasn't at work. Mr. Bourgeois puked up a hairball that languished in the middle of his living room for a week. The bathtub grew furry with hair and scum. When I spent the night over there, I held my pee as long as I could. I could almost make it eighteen hours. And we were *always* at his place these days. I understood he was unable to expend the energy to come all the way to my house.

In my spare time, I tried to pull him out of it by buying him groceries and suggesting he hit a meeting or call his sponsor. In group, I begged Dr. Rosen to help him. "Can't you see he's depressed?" Dr. Rosen's answer was always the same: "What are *you* feeling?"

The feedback from both of my groups was unanimous: "Concentrate on your new career."

"Focus on your new Skadden life. Maybe your tastes will change," Dr. Rosen said. It sounded like an offhand comment. My tastes?

I craved action. My boyfriend was not going to mentally deteriorate, or God forbid, relapse on alcohol, on my watch. I bought him a new comforter—a masculine plaid—took a bottle of bleach to the bathroom, and pulled globs of God knows what out of the drain. I scrapped cat puke out of the rug. I stocked his fridge with fresh fruit and lean proteins, his pantry with low-sugar cereals.

In my frenzy, I remained deaf to the one need he had expressed—to be left alone. Today, I have compassion for him and the illness that robbed him of joy and energy. I also have compassion for myself as his ex-girlfriend who thought she could cure his malaise with new linens and fresh pineapple. At the time, all I could manage was scrambling harder to "fix" him by fashioning him into the man I wanted him to be.

One night during this dark period, under the stiffness of Jeremy's new plaid comforter, I shimmied down to give him a blow job. I'd been working as a lawyer for six months. My standard of living had shifted from law student to Big Firm attorney. I occasionally let myself shop at Whole Foods. I bought a full-price skirt at J.Crew. My savings account swelled to two grand. During the daylight hours, I squared my shoulders and stood like a woman worthy of the thick white business cards Skadden printed with my name on them.

At night, I slumped and ached.

The blow job was my idea. An attempt to bridge the wide gulf between me and Jeremy. As my head bobbed between his sweaty thighs, I had a single thought: *I don't want to be doing this.* I violated myself by forcing the blow job and violated him by feigning desire and using oral sex to get him to pay attention to me and arrest his clinical depression. Jeremy hadn't showered in days—his body smelled sour with neglect and so many days' residue. I breathed out of my mouth, trying to ignore the stench of his body and the swells of my own disgust.

The following Tuesday morning I didn't mention the blow job because I was ashamed. Jeremy's unwashed body felt like something I should protect, even though Dr. Rosen advised me all along to bring *everything* to group. I was also ashamed that I forced a blow job I hadn't enjoyed. My relationship was a farce, and I continued to act dishonestly and against my own interest and pleasure. By the afternoon, everything I wasn't saying about my relationship was a loaded gun pointed at my throat. During a lull in the conversation, I spoke up.

"I don't want to suck dirty dick."

Everyone turned toward me.

"What did you just say?" Marnie said.

Nan's eyes grew wide as I described the blow job. "Hell no," she whispered.

When I finally looked at Dr. Rosen, I saw compassion in his eyes. "You don't have to suck dirty dick," he said.

My eyes teared up. He said it again very slowly. *You. Don't. Have. To. Suck. Dirty. Dick.* Then added: *ever again.* I nodded.

"I'm done," I said. My spine straightened in the truth of those two words.

Dr. Rosen held his arms out straight in front of him, palms turned up. Then he slowly turned his palms over. "This is how you let go."

I wasn't following. It looked like tai chi. My group mates put words to the gesture.

"Stop calling him."

"Stop trekking to that shithole apartment after work."

"Stop paying for everything."

If I just stopped—the chasing, planning, schlepping, conniving, cajoling, cleaning, shopping, pining, buying, and sucking—it would all be over. On his own, Jeremy wasn't going to pop over to my house. He wasn't going to make a dinner reservation or get tickets to see Wilco at the Riviera. If I let go, there would be nothing. I would be truly alone, but I would be free.

"So if I let go—" I said, grabbing Dr. Rosen's hairy forearm with both hands. I leaned toward him until our faces were less than a foot apart. I wanted him to finish the sentence. Whatever he said, I was going to hold him to it.

"You're going to find out what a real relationship feels like."

23

"Can you let yourself have an orgasm with him?"

Dr. Rosen and the morning group were waiting for an answer from me. I was three months out of my relationship with Jeremy and two weeks into a flirtatious fling with a Skadden intern who was in pursuit of a full-time job offer.

"Aren't there laws against this?" I asked. "I'm not supposed to bed the job aspirants."

"You're the lawyer," Nan said.

"I don't do sexual harassment."

"Apparently you do."

I'd met "the Intern" at a dinner the firm hosted at Japonais. Over a steady stream of raw tuna and unagi, I let him compliment my eyes and insinuate that his sexual prowess would blow my fucking mind. He was such a boy—cocky, loose-limbed, and unabashedly sexual in his designer jeans and hipster Adidas tennis shoes. He was six years younger than I was, but it felt like more. He grew up driving his dad's brand-new Lexus SUV and taking SAT prep classes. He'd never worked a full-time job. I accepted his offer to walk me home from the restaurant, thinking that a wiry thing like him would never be able to batter through the invisible fence that kept sexually alive men away from me. But he sailed over the fence, and in one smooth moment when he pressed his lips to mine under a busted streetlamp on Clark Street, I opened my mouth and received him. As his lips moved softly against mine, there was a zing between my legs, and my appetite for anything in the world other than his lips on mine vaporized in an instant.

The next day he tracked down my personal e-mail address. *That was some kiss*, he wrote. I didn't tell him I'd stayed awake all night thinking about it. I didn't tell him that every one of my limbs was thrumming with activity—still, after fifteen hours. I didn't tell him that I'd skipped breakfast and didn't have lunch until almost three because I was feasting on the memory of that kiss. What I told him was: *I've had better*. A delicious lie that drove him to promise me that he would be the best I ever had. *Prove it*, I demanded.

Dr. Rosen was impervious to sexual harassment laws. "So? Will you let yourself have an orgasm with him?"

Yes, I desperately wanted to bed the Intern and let him make good on all his promises. I wanted him to lick my honey until the sun rose over Chicago. But I also wanted a real relationship, a go-to-Costco-on-Sunday type of thing. And this boy-child didn't seem the type to appreciate a woman in her sweats, face dotted with zit cream after a sixteen-hour workday. In his third e-mail, he confessed to being both bi-curious and recently snorting cocaine in Miami.

"Nothing on his résumé screams 'suitable lifetime partner for a woman in recovery.'"

"You could fuck him and find out," Dr. Rosen said.

Toto, we are not in Catholic school anymore.

Our first date was on a Monday night, a few days after he accepted his offer from Skadden, so I was no longer in violation of harassment laws. He had classes all day Monday, so he pulled up to my office in his shiny black Lexus after his constitutional law seminar. He opened my door like a valet. The car was spotless—shiny black leather, clean cup holders, and a sound system that lit up the dashboard.

"My usual move is to take girls to Jane's in Bucktown and then to a neighborhood bar, but you're getting the deluxe treatment." His smile was sly. He'd already put more thought into this date than any man had ever put into planning time with me.

He drove to a bistro on Grand Street. I'd written him off as a smart-ass player, which he most definitely was, but underneath his relentless sexual swagger, he displayed a fascination with legal ethics and the contours of civil liberties. His face softened with genuine tenderness when he talked about holding his baby niece for the first time. He lost points for having voted for George Bush, but earned a few back when he mentioned his therapist.

"It's not Dr. Jonathan Rosen, is it?" He shook his head. Thank God.

By the end of the pumpkin soup course, I was ready to go full Luther Vandross with him. He brushed my calf with his foot, and I felt that heat between my legs again. As I sliced through my sea bass with the edge of my fork, I had only one thought: *Oh my God, I'm having sex tonight.*

When the check came, he pulled out his wallet and slipped a black American Express in the pocket of the leather folder. He scribbled a figure for a tip, signed his name with an illegible flourish, and stood up. "Let's get out of here." He held out his hand and I grabbed it. His suggestive smile told me that he had no intention of playing video games all night.

On the way back to his place, he asked me questions about Texas, as if it was an exotic region in outer space.

"It's flat, hot, and conservative."

"Any Jews there?"

"A few. My ballet teacher was a French Jew. Why?"

"We Jews are always thinking about our relative numbers." This was the first I'd heard of the Intern's religion. I could picture you-know-who's self-satisfied smile when he realized he'd instructed me to have an orgasm with a Jewish man. *Mamaleh, I'm so proud of you.*

As the elevator doors in his lobby closed on us, the Intern hooked his fingers into my belt loops and pulled me close. He smelled like clean laundry and something spicy, like cinnamon. He kissed me like he was starving for me, and I matched his intensity when I kissed him back.

When his hands cupped my breasts, I groaned with pleasure through my *one* bra.

I felt so free—like I could feel the air molecules dancing between us, celebrating my liberation. I slipped my hand under his shirt, and he moved closer to me. It felt like magic—a man moving closer to me, a man staying awake for me, a man hungry for me.

"You like that?" he whispered. Each time he touched me another layer melted away. He bit my lip playfully, and it was good-bye to the nuns who said French kissing was a sin because it mirrored the sex act. He touched the small of my back, and the grip of my mother's edict to save sex for marriage released its hold on my body. He held my face as he kissed me and washed away the stain of my relationship with Jeremy—the hairballs in the drain, the bad blow job, and the constant grinding of my flesh against the stone of his isolation.

When the doors opened with a ping, I tried to pull away, but he held me close. "Don't we need to get off?" I said. He flicked his tongue in my ear and whispered, "Oh, we're definitely going to do that."

We raced down the hall, him ahead of me, reaching back for my hand. Who was this guy who wanted to freebase pleasure and take me with him?

We barely made it to his apartment door before he had unhooked my bra. I'd never been kissed that deeply. Parts of me that had never stirred in the presence of someone else sprung to life. This, this, this, my body sang with pleasure. *More, more, more.*

He led me to his small, neat bedroom. The light was off, but I could make out a plain gray comforter on the bed, and some law books on the shelf next to a small clock with glowing red numbers. I opened my arms wide and belly-flopped onto his soft, clean bed.

There was nothing between us—no video games, no mental illness, no therapists. He reached for a condom and pulled off his pants. His forehead rested on mine, and I looked into his open, unafraid eyes. I pressed against him and shuddered into my prescription.

When I opened my eyes, his smirk offered a single message: *I told you I was good at this.* The waves of pleasure rose from between my legs and crested through my entire body. And then, I burst into tears.

"I don't know why I'm crying. I'm not sad." I tried to stuff the sobs back into my treacherous heart. The Intern kissed the tears as they slid down my cheeks. He asked what was wrong.

"You're just so—"

He raised his eyebrows and leaned closer, kissing my neck, chasing the tears that escaped. "What?"

"Clean." Tears continued to stream down my hot cheeks. "Oh my God," I whispered, covering my face with both hands.

"It's kind of hot, actually." He lifted my chin and kissed me on the lips. "What's your therapist going to say?"

"I did it, and then I cried." My afternoon group was rapt. I'd slept through my morning group for the first time in my therapeutic history. Finally. I'd waited three years to be too busy having sex to attend group.

Nan was incredulous. "What did that little white boy do to you?"

Dr. Rosen shook his head, his hands at his temples. "You let him pleasure you, and then you showed him all the feelings you had about it. Do you understand how intimate that was?" He gazed at me with amazement.

"I want to do it again."

"When's your next date?"

"Next week." Thumbs-up from the Good Doctor. "He's Jewish, by the way." Exactly as I suspected, Dr. Rosen gasped and held his hands to his heart. "I knew you'd do that."

"Why do you think I'm reacting like this?"

"So you can insist this is all about you. Like Luther." Dr. Rosen's head was bobbing maniacally, and he stuck up his thumbs like I'd gotten the right answer.

"You're so annoying," Marnie said to Dr. Rosen with a dismissive wave of her hand.

Dr. Rosen kept his gaze on me. "Do you understand?"

All I understood was that my therapist had a Freudian bug up his ass. Dr. Rosen accurately read my blank look as ignorance.

"If you attach to me—here, in treatment"—he pointed toward his dorky brown shoes—"then you will be able to attach to men out there." He gestured out the window. "Assuming we have a healthy attachment, you can use it as a foundation for your romantic relationships."

"Is it working?" I held my palms to my chest.

"Does a bear shit in the woods?"

⟨⟨⟩⟩

Once a week, the Intern picked me up in his shiny black car and whisked me away to a trendy bistro where we would pass innuendo back and forth like a basket of tortilla chips. It was hypercharged flirting—him bragging about how he could please me; me hinting I was far hungrier than he imagined. "I've been deprived a long time," I would say. "Nothing I can't handle," he would insist. Back at his place, he would hunch over his stereo, laboring over the perfect mood music. He favored Al Green and hip-hop. Watching him work so hard to set the mood was a huge turn-on.

The third night we were together, he pulled me into his bedroom with a puckish glint in his eye. "I have a surprise for you. Wait right here," he said, backing out of the room. When he returned, he handed me something blue and white that was folded like a flag.

"What the?" I giggled as I unfolded the heavy fabric and held up a giant football jersey with a number eighteen on it.

"It's Peyton Manning's jersey. I want you to wear it."

"Just because I'm from Texas doesn't mean football makes me hot."

"It'll be hot to sleep next to you if you are wearing that."

My body surrendered to the force of his easy freedom. I wanted to crawl into the jersey, into his body, into his world, where desire was naked and blatant and having sex was always on the table.

Both my groups loved the Intern. Both unanimously predicted that he was falling in love with me. Both pronounced me cured of whatever emotional injury or character defect led me to stay so long with Jeremy. Dr. Rosen beamed at me, session after session, praising my detailed disclosures of our intimate encounters, my joy, my surrender to pleasure.

I floated through my workdays. The glow of hot sex and a real, budding relationship softened the daily humiliations of being a junior female associate at a law firm. One Tuesday, when the partner asked me, the only female in the room, to take notes during a team meeting like I was a secretary, I bit my lip, but let it go when I saw an e-mail from the Intern pop up on my BlackBerry.

Two hours later, I handed Dr. Rosen a hard copy of the e-mail. "Read it," I said. "Start with the second paragraph."

"'It's imperative that I marry a Jewish woman.'" Dr. Rosen looked up.

"Why's he talking marriage? Y'all fucked, what, six times?" Nan said.

"Five."

"He's just scared," Marnie said. Emily and Regina agreed.

"White people are so weird." Nan laughed to herself, her golden hoop earrings catching the sunlight.

Panic coursed through me, making it hard to sit in my chair and hear what everyone was saying. How could they be so calm? The Intern was going to pack up all the pleasure and freedom and drive it away in his fancy black car.

"You don't know that," Dr. Rosen said.

"A lot of good dating Jewish men has done me! Thanks a lot, Dr. Rosen."

"It has done you a world of good. And you don't know what's going to happen next."

I knew the next time I walked into this stupid fourteen-by-fourteen room, I'd be sitting in a heap of my own heartache, kicking the tissue box away as tears streamed down my face.

When the Intern rolled up to my office for the last time a few days later, his smile looked fake and betrayed no hint of his trademark sass. His hug was the swift A-frame embrace you'd give your great-aunt Beatrice. Heat and the promise of sex no longer warmed the air between us.

He drove us to Sai Café in Lincoln Park, where we ordered separate sashimi rolls. I avoided the shrimp to prove what a good Jewess I could be. I called Rory from the bathroom where water softly trickled through a miniature rock garden. "I can feel a 'good-bye forever' coming." My stomach was at the top of a hill about to plunge into free fall. Rory told me to breathe and stay open to all possibilities. "Maybe he'll ask you to convert," she said.

"It's not going to work," he said as he pulled in front of my building at the end of the night.

I asked why we couldn't just keep hanging out. He shook his head, insisting it would be wrong to lead me on. I told him I'd consider conversion.

"You're Catholic."

"I haven't been to mass in years, and I'd be a wonderful Jew. I hate ham. I'll send my kids to shul. I'll blow the shofar." His lips turned up, but it wasn't a true smile. It was a pity smirk.

"I'm serious. I'm not talking about an Internet conversion course. I'll go to Anshe Emet or KAM Isaiah. I'll have a mikvah and a bar mitzvah—"

"Bat."

"I'll keep kosher, bake challah, circumcise—"

"I'm sorry."

I shut my mouth and stared straight ahead at the spot where he first kissed me, where my appetite shriveled, where this thing I called a "love affair" but would later downgrade to a "fling" had started.

"Can't you come up for one more night?"

"Let's not turn into caricatures of ourselves."

From my office the next morning, I begged Dr. Rosen to call me back. I couldn't wait until the next session. I needed him now. When he called, I cried into the phone, asking him to tell me why. Why didn't the Intern want to be with me? Why was I on the phone with him crying again? Why did I have to be raised Catholic? Why did my parents have to name me after Christ? I twisted the phone cord around my finger and listened for the hope in Dr. Rosen's answers. Nothing he said soothed me. He asked me if my life was getting better than it was before I started treatment. Yes, my life was better than it was before—I felt close to him and my group mates. Clare knew about my groups and my recovery. I was learning how to be who I really was in front of other people. But a relationship with a man felt as impossible as ever.

"I need more help. Something more. There must be something more. Maybe I've gone as far as I can with you, Dr. Rosen." I had no idea what I was asking him for. My thoughts were not coherent—I was babbling into the phone trying to beat back my sadness. My index finger turned white under the black phone cord.

"I have something in mind. We can talk about it in your groups tomorrow."

I took a ragged breath. "What're you thinking?" My heart lifted at the thought of a shortcut through the heartsickness.

"We can discuss it tomorrow." What was he planning? Individual sessions? Match.com for sexually anorexic women?

"Give me a hint."

"I'll see you tomorrow."

24

I showed up in the waiting room ten minutes early, my face tight and splotchy from crying. I slumped into a chair across from the particle board bookshelf and closed my eyes. When someone walked through the waiting room door, I opened one eye, expecting to see Carlos or Patrice, but it was a tall man in a gray business suit holding a brown leather briefcase. Total lawyer or finance type. Ten years or so older than me.

I'd forgotten that Dr. Rosen had announced we were getting a new member.

"I'm Reed," he said, sticking out his hand like he was at a cocktail party. I didn't stand up, but I offered my hand and felt something flicker in the air between us when our palms met. His salt-and-pepper hair was short on the sides and longer on the top, and his shoes were polished to such a high shine that I could see my sad, puffy face in them. Of course, I noted the gold band on his left hand and a dimple on his left cheek when he smiled. Seconds later, Dr. Rosen opened the door, and we filed into the group room. Carlos and Patrice arrived before we sat down.

"What's that?" Reed pointed to a purple terry-cloth hand towel in my lap. I'd been carrying it around with me since the Intern dropped me on the curb.

"This is my mourning rag. I just got dumped." I grabbed a thread between the fingernails of my index finger and thumb and yanked. I pulled another and then another. Soon individual purple threads criss-crossed my lap. A few drifted to the floor. As I yanked, hot tears rolled down my cheeks. Having something to do with my hands soothed me, and yanking threads out of the cloth helped me parcel out my anger in microdoses. Patrice scooted the box of tissues on the floor over to my chair. I kicked them away. "I don't do tissues."

Patrice ignored my outburst, rubbed my arm, and reminded me that the Intern was not marriage material.

Carlos took the lead on the interrogation of Reed and elicited the pertinent information: hotshot investment banker, married, twin girls, sober a few years, and then the jackpot:

"Why are you really here?" Carlos asked.

Reed's face reddened, and he looked at Dr. Rosen, who nodded encouragingly, like *tell them.*

"Out with it," Carlos said. When Reed hung his head, Carlos caught my eye and mouthed *he's so hot.* I nodded and yanked out another pur-ple thread.

"I'm struggling in my marriage." Ah, intimacy issues.

"Go on." Carlos raised his eyebrows.

"Oh, brother." Patrice sighed. She sensed what was coming—a tale of unfaithfulness, a long-suffering wife, a mistress who made him feel vital. Dr. Rosen's face wore his widest grin.

"I was at cocktail party for one of our funds a few weeks ago. There was a woman—" Reed looked around the room, unsure. Could he trust us? "She and I went back to her office, and she gave—"

"Oh my God, she sucked your cock!" Carlos clapped his hands.

Patrice asked if he'd told his wife. He hadn't; he hoped to save his marriage. Patrice and Rory praised Reed for his bravery in telling us.

I spread my towel out on my lap. I'd plucked a four-inch bald spot in the middle of it. I ran my hand over the sheared fabric. What would it be like to run my hand over Reed's lapel? His leg? This was the longest I'd gone without thinking about the Intern in a week. I felt something like hope bore its way into my rubble heap of a heart. I wished group was longer than ninety minutes.

Before group closed, I gathered my purple threads and lobbed a burning question. "Do y'all think I'll ever have sex again?" Reed's mouth curled into a half smile.

"If you want to," Dr. Rosen said.

"I do. Really soon." My body hurt from missing the Intern and the pleasure he offered.

"You're open to suggestions?"

"I'll do *anything*." Our fidelity-challenged, hot new group member had made me forget that Dr. Rosen was going to suggest something to me. "What'd you have in mind?" I dropped the towel into my lap and opened my palms.

"I suggest you join the Monday/Thursday group."

I sucked in a sharp breath and grabbed the towel with both fists.

"You cannot be serious. Another group? *Twice* a week?" Did he know I had a full-time job? Did he know that lawyers have to bill forty hours a week? I shook my head and pursed my lips. I picked up the towel and yanked hard at a thread on the border of the bald spot.

"This group is different. It's the same members twice a week, which creates additional intensity. Every member is a long-term patient—"

"I need to come here four times a week to get into a real relationship? How fucked up am I?"

"You're very fucked up." Dr. Rosen smiled.

"Nice sales pitch."

Dr. Rosen suggested I stay in the Tuesday-morning group, but drop the afternoon one to make room for this Monday/Thursday group. Where was this offer a year ago when I would have rather shaved my head than return to the group where Nan and Marnie almost came to blows? Now I felt a pang of sadness. Those women carried me through my Jeremy days and all through my fling with the Intern. Nan had held me that day I tried to pull my hair out. Zenia had taught me about fan fiction and long-distance lesbian sex. Was I ready to leave them behind?

"I'll think about it."

When we stood up for the closing, I let my sheared towel and all the plucked threads fall to the floor.

Here I was again, debating whether to join *another* Rosen-group. I'd said yes twice and now my life was filled with people who knew me well. Intimately. Rory knew about every drop of food I put into my mouth. Marty offered my nightly affirmations. My groups knew about the dirty dick I'd sucked, my pinworms, my temper tantrums. Wasn't that what I'd always wanted? People to fully know me and all my stories while also sharing theirs with me. That was definitely part of it and now I wanted more. I wanted a family of my own, one like Marnie's, Patrice's, Rory's, and Nan's. I was grateful for what I had but new desires bloomed: To have a family of my own with a partner. To become a mother. To settle romantically. To find my power at Skadden. I believed Dr. Rosen could get me there, though it stung that it would take three sessions, as in two hundred seventy minutes, of group each week.

I'd heard of the Monday/Thursday group. It was the only Rosen-group that met more than once a week. It was known as the "advanced" group. There was some pride at being invited. And there was also sus-picion that Dr. Rosen just wanted my money—I was vulnerable and making six figures. He could be offering me a way to get where I wanted to go or using me as a cash cow to finance a sailboat. How could I know which it was?

And yet, of course I said yes. With three days a week of group, surely I would have everything I wanted in a less than a year.

Part 3

25

The temperature was well below freezing the third Monday in January, but I was too nervous to feel the burn of the wind on my face. When my feet went out from under me, I skidded on the fresh layer of ice blanketing the sidewalk, ass on concrete, two blocks from Dr. Rosen's office. Was joining this new group a horrible idea? My throbbing hip-bone suggested yes.

"What have you heard about us?" Max asked. He had tousled blond hair and perfect posture, and wore a blue blazer with the gold buttons. Midforties. Very country club. I'd heard of Max. The word on the Rosen-grapevine was that he had come to Dr. Rosen years earlier strung out on drugs and living in his car. I'd heard something about felony charges. But he'd cleaned up and risen through the ranks of a pharmaceutical company. Now he was a hotshot exec, served on the board of his daughters' fancy private school, and summered in Snowmass. Something in his raised eyebrows and smirk told me he knew I'd heard the rumors.

"Nothing much." My skin felt too tight.

"You're lying." Max stared at me. My eyes darted away from his. I glimpsed Dr. Rosen, who offered nothing but his goofball smile.

"Well." I took a deep breath. "I heard you're a recovering addict."

"And?" My too-tight skin turning red.

"You used to party pretty hard."

Max didn't look away. He knew exactly what I wasn't saying. It was a test, and I'd failed.

Here, there was no plum-headed Zenia describing her fan-fiction sex. No one was eating or screaming or bawling. Everyone had a briefcase or a dignified leather purse tucked beside their chair. "We're the advanced group." Max was clearly the spokesperson for this highly composed and civilized group of people.

Patrice from Tuesday morning was there. She'd graduated to this "advanced" group a year earlier, but hadn't said much about it, other than that Max could be a handful. This morning, she smiled warmly but did not offer any tips on how to survive the next eighty-five minutes. The bruise on my hip pulsed with my heartbeat, but if I winced or rubbed it, I would draw attention to myself. No thank you.

Lorne was another familiar face. He was midforties and slightly disheveled—wrinkled khaki pants and frayed maroon sweater—but had an open smile that felt like a welcome. I'd met Lorne at his wedding, which I had attended as Jeremy's date. Jeremy and Lorne were in the men's group together. My left foot jangled as I considered what that meant.

"We've heard about you," Brad said, as if he had read my mind. Brad was slightly older than Lorne, tall and thin like Ichabod Crane with salt-and-pepper hair. The only thing I'd heard about him was that he was obsessed with money.

"What'd you hear?"

He and Max exchanged a look. Both smiled.

"That you had anal sex with Blake," Brad said with only a hint of sheepishness. Not what I was expecting, a memory from a relationship before I started group. My mouth twisted into a scowl. Whatever, Brad. I could own my sexual history.

"With Jeremy too, actually," I said.

"I'd heard that too," Brad said.

My stomach heaved with anxiety. Was I going to throw up? What was I doing, letting men I didn't know quiz me about my sex life? This was the first moment in my three and a half years with Dr. Rosen that

I wished desperately for confidentiality. All these years, I admired Dr. Rosen's insistence that secrets were toxic. Now I saw the murky downside: I'd just joined a group full of people who knew everything there was to know about my anal sex résumé.

The group let me stew in my discomfort and went on to discuss Lorne's unhinged ex-wife and Brad's upcoming job interview for a position that would increase his base salary by 20 percent. When there was a lull in the conversation, I caught Dr. Rosen's eye. "What makes this the advanced group?" I asked. Before he could answer, a woman with shoulder-length silver hair wearing a navy polyester pantsuit jumped in.

"Max and I are charter members of this group. Going back to the late eighties. I'm Maggie, by the way." She was sitting right next to Dr. Rosen. "We knew Dr. Rosen back when—" She paused.

"When what?" I said.

Maggie rolled her eyes. "Let's just say Dr. Rosen used to have very different boundaries."

"What does that mean?" I asked.

"Max once had lunch at his house—"

"He served me a ham sandwich," Max said. Ham? Dr. *Baruch Attah Adonai* served *tref* to a patient? "He used to be less Jewish. His über-Jew thing started when he married his second wife."

Maggie leaned over and told me she was once "very close" with Dr. Rosen's ex-wife, who was anorexic and cheated on Dr. Rosen with a man she met at the Checkerboard Lounge. "I think it was a Black man."

"Guess that explains your reaction to my Luther Vandross dream," I said to Dr. Rosen. He clutched his belly and laughed.

Max mentioned that Dr. Rosen took an extended leave of absence in the early nineties for an undisclosed reason. Brad and Lorne debated whether it was treatment for sex addiction or codependence.

With each revelation, my stomach clenched tighter. The shiny Dr. Rosen who lived in my imagination, to whom I gave the power over my deepest desires, was splattered with mud with each new divulgence. I curled my lips over my teeth and pressed down hard.

Max turned to Dr. Rosen and slapped his forearm. "Remember when you had diarrhea for months? When was that? Eighty-nine?

Ninety-one?" The rest of the group called out different years. Why did they know about Dr. Rosen's bowels?

I wanted to vaporize and float out of the room and out of treatment. Max and Maggie were fire hydrants gushing story after story about Dr. Rosen dating back to the first Reagan administration—when I was still in junior high. *That time his dog ran away. That summer he wore seersucker. That time he had to physically restrain Maggie from attacking Max and broke one of her ribs.* In fifteen minutes I learned more about my therapist than I had in the past three-plus years. The blank slate was slathered in muck.

Dr. Rosen smiled in his usual unguarded way. He wasn't embarrassed by these disclosures. I looked around the room—no one else was alarmed. Their bodies were loose in their chairs. These stories were like family lore shared around the Thanksgiving table year after year. If Max stopped in the middle of a story, then Maggie or Brad would keep going. So many stories. So much history. So many layers of shit slathered on my Dr. Rosen.

Until this moment, I'd admired what an iconoclast Dr. Rosen was, even when my friends who saw other therapists raised their eyebrows when I told them about Baby Jeremiah, the cocktease prescription, my nightly calls to Rory and Marty. I believed Dr. Rosen was courageous, smart, and gifted at treating addicts like me. But now I worried that he was something else: deeply flawed and possibly negligent. Maybe even dangerous.

The longer I sat and listened to my new group mates laugh about the past, the more nauseated I felt. They all had marriages, children, and careers. Maggie was a grandmother. None of them were desperate for something like I was, though Brad definitely fixated on increasing his net worth. None of them needed Dr. Rosen to be the powerful Oz and not an ordinary con man as much as I did.

Dr. Rosen cocked his head toward me and smirked. "Yes?"

"I have nothing to add to this trip down memory lane."

"Did you want to share something? You were mumbling under your breath?" Maggie said through her innocent-as-Grandma smile.

Everyone stared at me. My hands were shaking as if I'd stepped up to a podium to address hundreds of people, not a circle of six. "Look, I'm here to get into healthy relationships and start a family of my own. I don't want to know about Dr. Rosen's fecal history." I turned to Dr. Rosen and asked my favorite question: "How is this going to help me?"

Before he could answer, Max did. "How do you know it's not helping you?"

"Listening to stories about his history as a shrink with bad boundaries is helping me?"

"Why not?"

Max knew nothing about me. I glanced at the clock again. Why couldn't I make my feet move to the door? Why was I putting myself through this? This group—all of this therapy—might never lead to any of the things I wanted. I might come here faithfully twice a week, pay my seventy bucks a session, and still die alone.

Grandma Maggie held up her left hand and pointed at her wedding band. "Dr. Rosen is really good at getting women like you married. You'll see. I got married two years ago." Maggie was easily in her midsixties and had been with Dr. Rosen since George H. W. Bush was vice-president. It was hardly consoling to think I had decades to go before settling down and starting a family.

"Six months," I said. "If my life isn't better by July, then I'm leaving." Never mind the five-year timeline I started with at my first appointment. I'd been in treatment with Dr. Rosen for three and a half years, had now signed up to come three sessions a week and spend eight hundred dollars a month on therapy. The stakes had risen. I wanted results.

"Threatening to leave is an interesting way to build trust and intimacy." Max smirked.

"I come here three times a week—"

"So do I," Lorne said.

"Me too," said Patrice.

"This really is a cult." Everyone laughed. "Six months."

"Would you leave Tuesday-morning group too?" Dr. Rosen asked.

"Yes. All or nothing. Six months."

That evening, I sat in my office as the sun slunk below the horizon. I typed a search into Google: "Therapists in Chicago." A list of links appeared. A psychologist named Linda, an analyst named Francis, who was in the same building as Dr. Rosen. I imagined calling Linda or Francis, but it felt impossible. It took too much energy to fill someone new in. The apples. The worms. Jeremy. The Intern. Dr. Rosen and my first two groups had taught me to eat, sleep, and have sex. I'd miss Dr. Rosen and his goofy-ass laugh. I'd miss my Tuesday-morning crew. The first session in the "advanced" group was not exactly life-altering, but I owed it to myself to give it some time. Just in case, I bookmarked the website with Linda's and Francis's contact information.

My new life with three group sessions per week: I went to group before work on Monday and Tuesday; on Thursdays I went in the middle of the day. "Long lunch," I called it. I worked from nine thirty in the morning until seven at night, unless there was a project that required me to stay late. At night, I'd log off and walk home to my new apartment across the street from Clare, who'd recently gotten engaged to Steven. Instead of entrenching myself as their third-wheel roommate, I'd rented a one-bedroom in a high-rise on Clark and Maple from Kathryn, a Rosen-patient in the Friday women's group. While I missed Clare's company, it felt good to spread out into all corners of my new space and to watch the sunset from my western windows. Dr. Rosen viewed this move to a place of my own as evidence that I was making space for a romantic relationship. I narrowed my eyes when he said that, afraid to abandon my skepticism, solid as shale, for flimsy, see-through hope. On the weekends, I'd go to 12-step meetings and spend at least half a day at the office, reviewing documents and proving (to myself) that I deserved to be at Skadden. Behind the regular hum of my life, I waited for Something Big to happen. I waited for the "advanced" group, which I imagined as a blowtorch aimed straight at my heart, to work its magic on me. But there was no magic, no sparks flying from a naked flame, no fast-tracking my ability to attach to other people. There was sitting in the circle and talking, listening, feeling—the same things I'd been doing since I started with Rosen.

The six-month clock ticked on.

There were a few changes. The first thing was that I contracted severe constipation. My bowels would release only every eight days, so I
walked around for seven days with a dull throbbing in my lower belly. It
hurt to bend down. It hurt to run. It hurt to sneeze. I felt fatter than my
fattest PMS day. My digestive system had turned off as soon as I started
the new group. Nothing was moving through me. If this was the only
gift of the new group, then I didn't want it. To console myself, I would
flip the calendar to July like a kid counting the days until Christmas,
except instead of anticipating a jolly man in a red suit with presents, I
imagined how I would terminate my relationship with my elfin therapist who promised I wouldn't die alone. When I complained in Monday
group about my constipation, it spurred Max to remind Dr. Rosen of his
legendary diarrhea in the late eighties. When I asked what I should do
about the constipation, Max would bark, "Maybe if you didn't have a
six-month deadline, you wouldn't be so full of shit."

On Tuesday mornings, I told my original group that I had no idea
what to do in the new group. I tried to describe how it felt to have no
idea what to do with my hands or my voice for ninety minutes straight.
Patrice shook her head. "She's doing just fine in there."

"It doesn't feel like group therapy. No one except Lorne comes in
with any issues. They chitchat like old friends. No one knows about my
pinworm or my eating disorder or how I debased myself with Jeremy.
They don't seem to care about anything but what's right in front of
them."

"And the problem is . . . ?" Dr. Rosen asked.

The problem was that I sat through two hundred seventy minutes of
therapy per week and didn't feel any better.

During Monday/Thursday sessions, I felt like a stranger who wandered into someone else's family reunion. Pulsing through each conversation were layers of history, memory, story, and relationships that
I couldn't access. When Max or Lorne asked me how I was doing, I
voiced my heart's most immediate desire.

"Seriously, how can I get rid of this constipation?"

"Lots of water," Dr. Rosen said. "You could also try psyllium husk.
That's the active ingredient in Metamucil." Apparently, I was now

paying eight hundred forty dollars per month to learn about the active ingredient in a laxative.

In Monday/Thursday group, Dr. Rosen didn't give prescriptions. Nobody called anyone else to get to sleep or to discuss their after-dinner fruit binges. For ninety minutes twice a week, we sat in the circle and pinged off each other. Brad would talk about getting cheated out of a commission at work, and Max would call him out for being pathologically obsessed with money. Patrice would complain about the partners in her practice, and Dr. Rosen would confront her on not owning her authority as the most senior member of her practice. If I was quiet for too long, Max would turn to me and ask how many months until I quit. I'd ignore him and ask Dr. Rosen how this was helping.

"Of course it's helping you." Max sighed with annoyance.

"But nothing's changed except my bowels."

"That's bullshit. And you know what?" Max said, his voice raised. "Stop trying to convince us you're pathetic. Just stop. It's annoying."

No one could shame like Max. When he shook his head and sighed with disgust, I felt chastened. When I looked to Dr. Rosen for guidance or comfort, I saw only his inscrutable smile, so I shifted my gaze to a blotch in the carpet shaped like Australia.

A few minutes later, Dr. Rosen turned to me. "Why don't you ask Max to tell you all the reasons you aren't pathetic?"

My chest constricted. In the split second before I took Dr. Rosen's suggestion, I imagined Max repeating the same messages that thundered through my head: *It's your own fault you're alone. You're untreatable. You* are *pathetic!* Planting my feet on the ground, I looked directly at Max.

"So, how come I'm not pathetic?"

Max looked at Dr. Rosen and said, "I have to do all the work around here." Then he sighed and turned to me. "You're this brilliant attorney who's working at one of the most high-powered firms in the city. You've graduated to this advanced group. You're working hard to figure out how you're fucked up and what you should do about it. You're not pathetic—you're pissed that you haven't gotten all the things you're working hard for, which is better than this 'poor me' thing you do." He paused for a beat, and I held my breath, thinking he'd saved a zinger for his closing salvo. "Don't fucking do that."

I knew I was supposed to keep looking at Max and breathe, but I couldn't. Who would I be if I saw myself the way that Max did?

One March afternoon, I sat at my desk eating a box of raisins—still working on that constipation—when my work e-mail dinged. *Would you like to go for drinks?* It was from Alex, who lived four floors above me. I'd chatted with him in the elevator a few mornings earlier when we were both on the way to the gym and learned that, like me, he was a junior associate at a huge law firm. He'd chosen a treadmill close to mine. In the mirror, I watched his lean legs turn round and round. Zero body fat, perfect form, easy breathing despite his six-minute-mile pace. His physical beauty was so distracting I had to move to the bikes.

I covered my mouth with my hands to conceal my joy at this invitation, this potentially Big Thing.

26

We met at an Irish pub on Clark Street the following Monday after work. And even better: I was no longer constipated. Less than an hour after receiving Alex's e-mail, my bowels cranked back to life.

Alex and I compared notes on our budding legal careers—"so much document review"—and split the shepherd's pie for dinner. I hesitated for only a millisecond when the dish arrived covered in a layer of browned mashed potatoes with mystery brown lumps floating underneath. I could do this: I could eat stew from another country with this beautiful man.

From the bathroom, I called Rory to tell her I was on a date with a neighbor who looked like Brad Pitt, only cleaner and taller.

"Gay?" she asked.

"Possibly." He was raised by a single mom and had two sisters, so it made some sense he was not bursting with machismo. What hidden thing in this physically beautiful man's heart could hurt me later?

Alex and I e-mailed throughout the week, and I put my best Christie forward. Witty responses. Jokes about law firm life and pop culture. I waited a few hours before responding to his e-mails, even though I prepared my responses within seconds. I curated a Christie I imagined would appeal to him. My best guess about what a man as beautiful and put together as Alex might like: Lighthearted humor. Intelligence and ambition. Independence. And based on his BMI, a commitment to physical fitness. I had all of those things, and I shined them up for Alex and served them in balanced doses in each missive. As for all my emotional ups and downs, I sequestered those in group.

Two days after our first date, he asked me out for a second: Italian food and then live jazz.

The darkened club was packed with couples who looked at least a decade older than we were. Alex and I sat against a far wall beneath a picture of a young Billie Holiday. A round-top table big enough for only our two drinks separated us from the aisle, where harried waiters brought mixed drinks to the tables crammed all around us. As a trio played a set, Alex held my hand, his thumb tapping to the beat against my palm.

When the band took a break between sets, he asked follow-up questions to the getting-to-know-you ones he'd asked at our first dinner.

"You think you'd ever move back to Texas?"

"No way." When he asked why, I paused. There were multiple answers. I could tell him that I didn't like the heat or the conservative politics. Or that I felt like I had to make it on my own in the city I'd adopted and that moving back home would smack of defeat. Or that I'd failed to secure any attachments to any of my friends who still lived in Texas, so I wasn't itching to return. Those were true, but when I looked at the curve of his lips and his perfect jawline, I felt emboldened to give him the real reason. "I'm pretty attached to my therapist." And once I trotted out Dr. Rosen, I decided to go all the way. "And I do group therapy, so I'm attached to all of my group mates too." No need to tell him it was two groups and three sessions a week. I stared at the image of Billie Holiday singing into an old-fashioned silver microphone. Oh God, what have I done? Was I subconsciously trying to scare Alex away by hinting I was crazy?

"That's cool," Alex said. He smiled in a curious way. Like he was surprised that I'd revealed something so vulnerable. He inched closer. "Would you like me to join you out on that limb?"

I smiled. "Sure."

"I told you my parents got divorced, right?" I nodded. "What I didn't mention is that after their divorce, they remarried. Each other. And then divorced again." He shifted his gaze to the vacant stage. Then he turned back to me. "So, that's complicated."

"Sounds like it."

What I wanted to say was "thank you." Thank you for understanding vulnerability. For meeting me on the limb. For showing me it wasn't disastrous to mention therapy on our second date.

As the band shuffled back on the stage, Alex scooted his chair closer to mine. In the darkened club, we sat hand in hand, knees touching, letting the music seep into our bones. I recognized the familiar feeling of warmth and safety that settled after the rush of emotional risk. This was how I felt in group after sharing something difficult and then hearing my group members say "same here" or "I relate to that." Like the time I told the women's group about my breast hatred and each one of them offered me a story about her own tortured relationship to her breasts.

My turn, your turn. Back and forth.

So this was how it happened. This was how you built an intimate relationship. Word by word. Story by story. Revelation by revelation.

Just like group.

He invited me up to his apartment after the jazz club. "I want to show you the view from my southern balcony." He put one arm around me as he pointed out the Big Dipper. With the stars as our witness, we shared our first kiss. When he pressed his perfect lips against mine, I swallowed starlight, and my heart began to glow. He walked me up to my place. "There will be more," he said, kissing me again.

If this was the gift of the advanced group, I'd stay forever.

✐

Alex was wonderful. Our dates were the stuff of my deepest longing. I could hardly believe how much I enjoyed being with him. The only downside was the low-grade anxiety I felt all the time about how to make it last. I agonized about how and when the relationship would sour or fizzle or implode.

I brought my anxiety to group. "This can't last," I insisted. "Tell me what to do to keep this thing going."

"Can you let go of your need to control it?" Dr. Rosen said.

"No." Dr. Rosen didn't understand. Alex's body was near perfect, he smelled like fresh sport deodorant, and I could see my sexual prime on the horizon. If I gave in to this relationship and let myself believe it was something real, then what if it failed? Would that destroy me?

"Can you let go of your expectation of failure?"

"I'll try."

Life with Alex, who had signed up for two triathlons for later in the summer and a marathon in the fall, meant early morning runs and bike rides before work, followed by swims at the gym or in Lake Michigan after work. Within a month of dating, he began inviting me to join him most mornings and evenings. One Saturday, he knocked on my door at six in the morning. He had a race bib pinned to his fleece jacket and his hands stuffed into thin black gloves. He fastened my bib to my shirt and handed me a water bottle. At the starting line of the ten-mile race he signed us up for, he rubbed my shoulders when he noticed I was shaking from the cold. Patches of snow still clung to the ground by the running path, and only several hundred runners had showed up for the lakefront race, where the wind promised to slap our exposed faces. I'd never run a ten-mile race, but my body had taken on a new buoyancy since dating Alex, which was part anxiety, part joy. A loopy willingness to try anything, including this freezing-cold road race, made me say yes to whatever he was offering.

Each time we walked to dinner after work or ran on the lake, a featherweight optimism knocked on my heart, inviting me to let go of projecting the failure of the relationship. Maybe every relationship wouldn't end with me huddled in the group room crying into a rag. Maybe every relationship wouldn't end at all. Maybe it would last.

After the race, my hamstrings ached and my shoulder stung where my sports bra strap dug into it. But with Alex, the pain gave way to pure joy.

ler

Dr. Rosen held up a picture for everyone to see one Monday morning. Patrice slipped on her reading glasses and Max leaned forward. "This is what it means to get unblocked," Dr. Rosen said. It was a picture of me and Alex: I wore a pink cocktail dress, and Alex wore a tux. We'd gone to a gala for the Joffrey Ballet. In the darkened theater, the dancers twirled in brilliant tulle and Alex held my hand in both of his. I inched closer to him in my red velvet seat, until our legs were touching. During dinner in the giant, gilded Hilton ballroom, he rubbed my back and played with the clasp of my necklace. On the dance floor, he held me close as the band covered Otis Redding. Later, he kissed me again on his balcony. "It feels like you're my girlfriend," he said. I leaned into him and exhaled.

Grandma Maggie pointed at the picture and then tapped her wedding ring. "You're next, kiddo."

Alex, who was so comfortable in his skin, made me feel like I could be too. With complete ease, he talked about all the things we would do in the future. A boat trip on the Chicago River with his firm in June. A sprint distance triathlon in July. A trip to visit his sister in Iowa at some point over the summer. A comedy show, a concert, a trip to the zoo. He acted as if we had a future, and I slowly let myself imagine us being a couple for more than a few months.

"Seriously, what's the catch?" I asked my group mates and Dr. Rosen.

"You tell us," Max said.

I shook my head. The situation with his parents sounded tricky, but he didn't come across as secretly hobbled by trauma or afraid of a relationship. His workout schedule bordered on obsessive, but it never depleted him to the point he was too exhausted to hang out or have sex with me. His taste in books struck me as a tad immature, but plenty of people loved Harry Potter—that wasn't a valid reason to discount someone as wonderful as Alex. I was just afraid.

One morning, Alex and I stopped at Corner Bakery for breakfast before work. We sat in a booth by the window feeding each other bites of muffin and acting like the kind of couple I would have scorned when I was single or struggling with Jeremy. At one point, I got up to get some napkins, and Alex called my cell phone, buried in my purse right next to him. The voice mail I heard later melted my anxious, defended heart: "Hello, pretty lady in the café. This is your boyfriend calling. He thinks you are quite lovely." I played it again and again, thinking, *It's going to suck when this falls apart.*

Dr. Rosen became a broken record. "Trust it, *Mamaleh*. Trust."

As the weeks went on, traces of anxiety remained, but my constipation eased, my joy soared. Both groups cheered my weekly check-ins.

"Stability suits you," Dr. Rosen said.

"I hope you're giving us credit for this relationship," Max said. "In those other groups, you sucked dirty dick and got dumped for being a shiksa. You're welcome."

Lorne gave me a thumbs-up, and Brad calculated mine and Alex's combined net worth given our high-paying legal jobs. Grandma Maggie patted my hand, whispering, "I knew it."

I beamed and floated. On the July morning that marked my six-month anniversary in the Monday/Thursday group, I announced I was staying. Forever.

"Oh, goody," Max said in mock annoyance.

"You can stay," Lorne said, "but I'm not dressing up for your wedding. If I can't come in jeans, I'm not coming." He winked from across the circle.

I beamed at them all, my advanced group members. Alex and I had a solid, healthy, sexual relationship, and I gave them most of the credit for that.

ccv

"Mom," I said during a Sunday-afternoon check-in call. "I've met someone. He's great. Really great. We ran a 10K together this weekend." I danced around my apartment as I told her the news. I'd stepped into the new reality of Christie as a woman who enjoyed her highly hygienic, functional, attentive boyfriend. Christie as a woman worth spending time with and paying attention to. I could leave my dysfunctional past where it belonged: behind me.

"How wonderful, honey. You sound so happy."

"Come up for some chili," Alex said one night. He browned ground beef and emptied canned tomatoes into a small Dutch oven. The smell of cumin wafted through the air. I wrapped my arms around him from behind. He kept stirring.

"Do you know what the secret ingredient is?" he asked. I shook my head.

"You really don't know?" His shoulders slumped, and his face registered confusion bordering on hurt.

Had I forgotten an inside joke about chili? Did Harry Potter love chili? I didn't want to let him down, but the only thing coming to mind was a tasteless fart joke.

"Tell me."

"Love," he said. "The secret ingredient is love."

I ate two bowls.

"Oh my God," Lorne said when I bragged in group about the love in Alex's chili. "He's so cheesy."

I swiveled my chair toward Lorne and kicked the air between us. "Don't ruin it! It was so sweet."

"Cheesy."

"You're just jealous."

"Of Alex's stupid chili?"

"You had to buy Renee a giant ring from Cartier, and all Alex had to do was serve me chili."

"Can you hear yourself?"

One Sunday, Alex and I woke up at five, before the sun glinted across the lake, to ride thirty miles up and down Lake Shore Drive. We wore bike shorts and pounded Gatorade. When we slipped off our bikes for a late breakfast of eggs and English muffins, our backs were stiff, and our gaits were unsteady.

"Come upstairs," he said.

We kissed on his brass bed, our tired bodies heavy from the early morning and the hours of pedaling. He pulled off my shorts. The noonday sun streamed brazenly across his clean white sheets. His skin tasted like salt, and I wanted to gulp. He filled me up. I came and came again.

This sweet boy-man who cried through *Les Mis*. Who showed me how brilliant the sunrise over Lake Michigan could be from a bicycle. Who filled his food with love and offered it to me. This man-boy with no sharp edges that could hurt me. My heart and body leaned into him. In my mind, Alex and my new group formed a double helix that wove around my grooved heart.

"This guy is 'The One,'" Marnie said after she met me and Alex one night for sushi. Clare said the same thing. So did Patrice and Dr. Rosen.

"I really like him," I told my groups and my friends. I said it over and over; I shined my teeth with it. I slept deeply.

In mid-July we attended the wedding of my friend Kathryn, the Rosen-patient who rented me her apartment in Alex's building. Kathryn married Jacob, a man she'd met in a Rosen-group. Across the room at table four, Dr. Rosen and his wife ate their steak and smiled as patients streamed by to say a shy hello. By the chocolate fountain, I introduced Alex to Dr. Rosen. As they shook hands, I watched Dr. Rosen's face fill with warmth and welcome. A swell of wholeness flooded my chest. I'd never been so full. *Christie*, they said. I heard love and claimed it as mine. An insistent joy spun inside me like cotton candy.

That night, in my darkened bedroom, Alex slipped my white cotton nightgown over my head. It felt like falling and being caught over and over. He leaned back.

"You're so beautiful," he said.

"I'm so happy," he said.

"I love you," I said, holding his beautiful head in my hands.

I sat tall in my Monday-morning group, letting the summer sun bathe my arms from the western window. I wore the million-watt smile. "I told him I loved him."

"Did he say it back?" Lorne asked.

"Not in so many words." Brad and Max shared a quick look across the circle. Grandma Maggie gazed down at her hands. I chased away the fleeting worry by sinking into my body. I remembered our skin against skin. Of course that was love.

⟋⟋⟋

In late July, I traveled to St. Petersburg with Patrice and her family for a vacation planned before I started dating Alex. Our apartment off Nevsky Prospekt was infested with mosquitoes that left angry red marks up and down my legs and arms. I ached for Alex at night as I stared at the moon and scratched the welts. During the day, I stole into cyber cafés to check my e-mail. My stomach twisted when there was nothing from Alex after two days, three days, four days. By then, I could hardly eat a full meal I was so distressed. Why wouldn't he write? Weren't we attached? Wasn't it love?

"He's gone," I cried to Patrice outside the Hermitage. She wrapped her arm around my shoulders and told me to enjoy the view: a street performer with a boom box coaxing a chained black bear to dance to Cyndi Lauper's "Girls Just Want to Have Fun."

"I can't. My stomach hurts." I bent low to scratch at a cluster of bites on my ankle. "I hate Russia, its dumb domes, its mosquitoes, its dancing bears." In Russia, I was cold, nauseated, and so far away. Lonely and forgotten. I scratched until my ankles bled. My blood and skin mingled under my fingernails. Patrice rubbed my back in a circle and offered me a piece of dark chocolate. I closed my eyes and missed group, where I could cry, gnash, and let all the feeling pour of me.

⟋⟋⟋

"I had some time to think while you were in Russia." Alex and I were walking down Dearborn after a 5K race for the Legal Aid Society. My body was spinning in space, somewhere between Russia and Chicago, throbbing through the jet lag that made me feel drunk.

"The thing is, I know you're not the one." He marched down Dearborn without breaking his stride or looking at me.

No, no, no. I breathed through my nose to smooth out my voice. "What are you talking about?"

"I just know. You're not the person I'm supposed to be with."

My arms shook in the humid August air. I tasted the postrace banana I'd swallowed four blocks back. Sweat on my neck turned icy cold.

In the lobby he stopped to check his mail, while I shivered like a stray cat by the elevators. Did he really need to get his Visa bill and the grocery store circular at this moment?

When the elevator opened, I shuffled in, but he stepped back to wait for the next one.

I brought the shards of all the dishes I broke that night to my Monday-morning group and dumped them in the center of the circle. Pieces of a ceramic Thanksgiving platter I bought at Walgreens, the IKEA glasses, the pale blue fruit bowl from the Tag outlet that I bought with Carlos. I'd shoveled them into a double-ply Macy's shopping bag, which I hooked on my arm as I walked the mile from my apartment to group. The jagged edge of a dinner plate pierced the bag and tore the skin on my calf as I crossed Chicago Avenue. A stream of blood ran down my leg and into my black ballet flats.

"He's gone," I said to this group that brought Alex into my life. Now I needed them to catch me because I was really falling. "I'm not 'the one.'" Tears fell, soft and incessant. Patrice got out of her chair and pulled me to my feet. She wrapped her arms around me. "I'm so sorry."

Dr. Rosen leaned toward me as if he was telling me a secret. "*Mamaleh*, he just got scared when you left for Russia."

No, he was gone for good. That bomb I'd once imagined beneath his smooth skin and beautiful ribs had detonated. I was in pieces.

"Aren't y'all disappointed in me? Y'all thought Alex was my person." I looked at the faces around the circle. Max's concerned stare. Lorne's and Brad's attentive gazes. Grandma Maggie, who was always flashing me her wedding ring and calling me "kiddo," now shaking her head with pity. Patrice, who was yet again spending her group time consoling me. And of course Dr. Rosen, who still believed in his little

Mamaleh, even though she'd broken all of her dishes (again) and carved up her leg on the walk to group.

"We don't know that he's not."

Dr. Rosen, eternal optimist or raving lunatic?

As I walked out of group after the prayer and the hugs, Lorne, Brad, and Max invited me to breakfast with them. "But you can't bring that insane bag of broken dishes," Max said, so I left them in the group room. I ate eggs while they drank coffee. We talked shit about Dr. Rosen's wardrobe, speculated about his marriage to the stylish Mrs. Rosen, who we sometimes saw walking down the hall after our Thursday group. When I stared off into the middle distance, thinking about Alex, his chili, and his brass bed, Lorne snapped his fingers in front of my face. "Come back, Christie! Eat your eggs. Tell us what you think of Dr. Rosen's wife!"

At ten o'clock, I rose from the table. "I have a conference call in thirty minutes," I said, grabbing a napkin in case I cried on the walk to work. All three of them stood up to hug me. Lorne reminded me that Alex was "cheesy as hell." Max told me to order new dishes for express delivery. Brad, who'd paid for my eggs, offered to walk me to my office across the Loop. He carried my work bag all six blocks and assured me at every stoplight that I would find love again. He stayed by my side even when I openly wept on LaSalle Street.

At work, there were no group members to distract or comfort me, so I cried without bothering to shut my door. My coworker Raj stopped by several times to see if I was still blubbering. If I was, he shut the door and speculated about the partners' sex lives until I let a smile break through. I had a small CD player under my desk that played *Riverdance* on a constant loop. Billable hours passed as I sat listening to the haunting Celtic songs that matched my mood. I pressed the brass tip of a letter opener into the pad of my left index finger. The skin didn't break, but the prick of pain soothed me. I *could* break the skin if I needed to.

I cried through Tuesday group, barely uttering a coherent sentence. On Thursday, I sat directly to the right of Dr. Rosen with my purse in my lap so I could secretly press the top of the letter opener into the pads of my index finger. Of course, hiding was impossible in that fourteen-by-fourteen room. The entire point of group was to be witnessed, to come out of hiding.

Dr. Rosen extended his right hand to me, palm flat and open. "I want your weapon." I shook my head. "I want you to give it to me."

I surrendered the blade because I didn't really want to hurt myself. Dr. Rosen took the letter opener and continued to hold my hand. I let him because I wanted him to save me from myself, from my attraction to sharp objects that made me bleed, from men who didn't love me, from my mental illness, whatever it was. I wanted him to save my heart, which would never be scored deep enough for lasting attachment. I would die like this: paying someone to hold my hand while my life slipped away. The thing that had always been wrong with me felt worse than ever. I couldn't meet anyone's eyes, only their shoes. Max's expensive broughams, Lorne's scuffed brown Eccos, Grandma Maggie's thick-soled white shoes, Brad's gray New Balance tennis shoes, Patrice's navy flats. It was the only view I could take in.

"Do not cry alone. Be with your group members, as much as you can," Dr. Rosen said. My gaze lingered on their shoes.

"Renee is being induced this weekend. Come to the hospital," Lorne said.

"Come over for dinner on Saturday night," Patrice said. "You can spend the night."

"I've got tickets to the opera, and William doesn't want to go," Grandma Maggie said.

I cried in the grocery store. I cried at work. On the train. In group. At home. On Marnie's couch. On Patrice's couch. On the phone with Marnie, Marty, Patrice, and Rory. I went to the hospital to meet Lorne's baby boy and cried up and down the maternity ward, frightening the nurses on call. I went to the gynecologist for a checkup and cried when she asked me if I needed contraception. Concerned, Dr. Spring put down her pen and offered a referral to a therapist.

Every morning I startled awake with a violent stomach cramp. Diarrhea. One morning I didn't make it to the bathroom and shit in my favorite cornflower-blue cotton pajamas in the middle of the living room.

Dr. Rosen promised it wouldn't last forever—the crying, the shitting. I believed him one second, but not the next. Shame consumed me. Shame that I was coming undone over a five-month relationship. Shame that I was literally losing my shit over a beautiful man I'd slept with twenty-seven times. Shame that after nearly 380 therapy sessions—more than 34,000 minutes of therapy with an Ivy League–educated therapist—my heart was still defective, could not attach.

27

"Is your passport up-to-date?" Jack, a middle-aged partner with thick glasses and a friendly chortle, stuck his head in my office, where I was drafting a memo on my beverage-company case. I paused *Riverdance* and sat up straight. It was August 2005, and my two-year anniversary with Skadden was two days away.

"Good until 2014."

"Do you speak German?"

"*Nyet?*"

"That's Russian."

"Then, no."

"Doesn't matter. We've got a new matter. The Department of Justice is involved, so we have to move fast. Can you leave Sunday?"

"For Germany? Absolutely." This was the best news I'd ever heard. I'd let my career simmer for months while I biked, ran, and ate chili. Jack was a rainmaker—his star protégée was about to make partner. If I impressed him, I could end up on the partner track. A glow in my chest: I'd been chosen. Never mind that years ago I'd called Dr. Rosen with the express purpose of building a life filled with relationships, not billable work.

"At the partner meeting, we discussed which associates had no commitments—no spouses or children—and your name popped up first."

"Excellent." My face froze in a smile.

I showed up at Thursday group two days later, smiling for the first time in days.

"I don't recognize you without all the tears and sharp objects," Max said.

"My firm is sending me to Germany. I'll be flying there every other week for the next few months. Maybe longer."

Everyone nodded, impressed. No doubt they were picturing me scaling stone steps to a stately German high court building during the day and raising a stein in the Hofbräuhaus at night.

"You're getting an opportunity to work on your professional life." Dr. Rosen nodded approvingly. "Now you can stop pretending you're not interested in making partner and admit that you want success in both work—"

I covered my ears. "I *hate* it when you do that." Professionally, I was successful and would always be successful because I knew how to work my ass off and get shit done. I'd risen to first in my class before I ever stepped foot in Rosen-world. I'd learned to kiss partners' asses and knew how to treat the support staff like human beings who deserved my respect. I knew how to laugh with colleagues at happy hour and how to hold clients' hands when the SEC threatened legal action. Personal relationships housed my stack of failures. "Focus on my personal life, buddy. Eyes on the ball."

That night, I called my mom out of the blue. We usually spoke once or twice a month, usually on Sunday after she and Dad returned from mass. I wanted to tell her about Germany, but the first thing out of my mouth was that I was terrified there was something seriously wrong with me, something that would keep me from having a family of my own.

"I'm so alone," I said, bursting into tears with my mom for the first time in my adult life. We'd never discussed my isolation from the family or my fears about ending up alone. My plan had been to have Dr. Rosen fix me so I could present myself as the daughter who wasn't fucked up after all. But we'd both be dead at the rate I was going.

"Honey, I felt the same way."

I sat up on the couch and wiped my nose on my sleeve. As far as I knew, my parents met at a volleyball party and the rest—three kids and a redbrick ranch house on 6644 Thackeray—was history. It was impossible to picture my mother—with her late-1960s bob and postcollege job as a bank teller in Dallas—curled under a blanket, worried she would die alone.

"I was just like you. All my friends were married and had babies on the way, and I never thought it would happen for me. I was still single at twenty-six, which in 1970 was pretty ancient. It felt like nobody wanted me."

This was genetic? I felt strangely exhilarated—maybe this wasn't all my fault. Maybe it wasn't a failure of imagination or feminism or will. This state of believing that something was wrong with me around relationships was something I shared with my mother like brown eyes and a mortal fear of dental procedures. Maybe I could stop trying to outrun it. Maybe I didn't have to hide my grief and confusion from her anymore. I wasn't ready to tell her I was back in therapy to the tune of *three* group sessions a week, but it was a relief to share some emotional truth.

"Do you want me to come to Chicago?"

Her offer made me cry harder. I needed her mothering, but I couldn't stomach her flying all the way Chicago. It was enough that she asked and that I no longer had to hide my greatest fears from her.

I never saw the Autobahn. Or a German courtroom. What I saw day after day in Germany was a giant, un-air-conditioned room in a nondescript four-story office building in the middle of a field outside Augsburg. The low sound of cows' mooing greeted me in moments of unexpected silence. The sharp smell of dung also made its way into the second-story work space, where lawyers and paralegals from Germany, Chicago, and Atlanta worked elbow to elbow on long tables. The office was stingy with toilet paper, so you had to go before three in the afternoon if you wanted to wipe.

The high point of the day was lunch in the staff cafeteria, where the main food group was brown gravy. It appeared on absolutely everything: main dishes, side dishes, salads. Brown, viscous, fatty, and flavorless.

I hated Germany. I hated my work. I hated my life.

I was grateful to be busy, but in the downtime between tasks, I'd stare at the clock and compute the time back in Chicago. One Tuesday afternoon, I used the office phone to call Rory's cell while she was in group. She didn't pick up.

That night, alone in my German hotel, I collapsed on the bed. I'd been expecting fancy four-star digs, but instead, we stayed at the German version of a La Quinta, minus the friendly staff and Denny's next door. In the shower, the temperature hovered at lukewarm. I missed home, where at least the water was scalding hot.

The only thing on TV was the brewing destruction of Hurricane Katrina—startling images of surging brown water and displaced people crammed into the Superdome in New Orleans—and violent German porn. Room service was my last hope. The "pizza" I ordered arrived as a hunk of semimelted white cheese on a plain pita swimming atop a smear of ketchup. I crawled under the covers, still shivering from my tepid shower. Sleep mercifully delivered me from consciousness.

The clinking of glasses and muffled laughter woke me less than an hour later. I lifted the window shade and saw that directly below me was the pool, an open bar, and a dozen people eating appetizers and having drinks, buck naked. My room was just above the *Schwaben Quellen*, which apparently means "eating schnitzels and drinking Heineken in your birthday suit."

I dialed the international operator and gave her Dr. Rosen's number. Across the Atlantic, Dr. Rosen sat in his final group of the day and would check his office voice mail soon.

Beep.

"There are naked people cocktailing outside my room. I can't do this. Please call me. Please." I left the number where he could reach me.

At two in the morning German time—seven back home in Chicago—I accepted the truth: Dr. Rosen wasn't going to call me. I rolled myself up in the scratchy comforter and closed my eyes. *How dare he abandon me.* I unrolled myself and asked the international operator to connect me again.

Beep.

"Show me the goddamned *JAMA* article that says doctors can't help patients across international lines! How could you possibly withhold five minutes of your time to assure me that you're still there? I would have paid you back for the charges, you know. Asshole!" I slammed the phone down. Fuck him. After all the money, time, and trust I'd willingly given him—he had nothing for me?

On Friday, in the Augsburg conference room, Jack asked for a show of hands: Who wants to go home? Those who flew home would brief the team back in Chicago and return the following week. Most associates wanted to stay for weekend jaunts to beer gardens and the Black Forest. Oktoberfest was days away. My hand shot up, high and tall. *Send me home.*

I arrived at the airport three hours early, but the Augsburg-to-Frankfurt leg of my flight was canceled. An officious woman at the United counter offered me a flight the following day. I shook my head. No. I bought a train ticket to Frankfurt; I booked a later flight to Chicago. If I had to crawl across Germany, I was going home.

An hour later, I handed the train conductor my ticket without looking up. I'd made a decision: when I returned to group, I would break up with Dr. Rosen. My hurt and anger wasn't hot and fiery. It was cold and sharp. A decision made. A contract signed. A door locked. If I was sinking all the way down, then let my feet hit the bottom. Dr. Rosen proved he couldn't tend to me when I needed him most, so I didn't want to be in his care. I'd look up Linda or Francis. Get myself a real therapist. One who gave a shit about me.

I curled toward the window, not seeing the German countryside zooming by. I was supposed to be better by now. No one else had made so little progress after so many years of treatment. Other group members came in and got better. Their careers shot off in promising new directions. They paid off debts. Their kids graduated and went to liberal arts colleges. They moved in with their boyfriends. They got married. They had babies.

And then there was me. Relationships kept slipping through my hands no matter how many groups I joined. What a damn fool. Maybe Dr. Rosen was mad at me because I ruined his track record. I was the quarter horse who was expected to win but couldn't make a clean lap around the course. Someone should shoot me. I was back to where I was before I ever called Dr. Rosen, except this was worse because I'd learned to *feel* so much more. All those one- and two-syllable words: Angry. Hurt. Lonely. Ashamed.

I pulled out my BlackBerry so I could let someone know I would be arriving in Chicago six hours later than expected. But who? I could tell my parents that I was now on a train instead of a plane, but that made me feel like a thirty-three-year-old loser. Who cared where I was at this very minute? No one. Absolutely no one.

I typed a message to Dr. Rosen: *I'm so sorry. I really tried. I swear I did.*

On Monday morning in group, I did not say a single word for the first hour and twenty-five minutes of the ninety-minute session. Everyone seemed to sense I needed space. I felt Max and Grandma Maggie staring at me, but they said nothing. I lacked the energy to break up with Dr. Rosen. It would take too many words, spawn too much discussion. For now, I would float until my head went under.

"I won't be here next week," Patrice said at five minutes to nine. "Conference in San Francisco." Dr. Rosen pulled out the blue appointment book he kept in his pocket—his customary practice for when someone announced they would be gone from group. I once asked why he always wrote our absences down in his little book, and he'd said it was because he cared where we were. I remembered when I believed that.

He looked at me, his pen poised, waiting for me to announce when I'd be back in Germany—so he could write my initials in the Monday, Tuesday, Thursday squares. I said nothing. My head slipped below the waterline.

Dr. Rosen clipped his pen to his book and cleared his throat. "I need to turn something over to the group." His lips were a straight line, his eyes blazed serious. I felt him looking at me, but my gaze bored into Brad's New Balances.

"When I got your last e-mail, Christie, for the first time ever"—he paused and looked around the room—"I feared for your safety."

I'd scared the impervious Dr. Rosen? The guy who thought everything was hilarious, useful fodder for emotional growth?

"Normally, you're full of passion and fury." He waved his hands spastically and bobbed his head back and forth, imitating me. "You're screaming and frothing and outraged. This was different. Scary."

It couldn't be good to scare your therapist.

A memory flashed into my head: two summers earlier, I hunkered down with bar exam study guides seven days a week, and in my off-hours, dug my claws into my dwindling relationship with Jeremy.

"Can I borrow one of those?" I pointed at the motley stash of stuffed animals that Dr. Rosen kept in the group room. "I could sleep with it at Jeremy's house when he's too busy playing video games to sleep with me." Dr. Rosen opened his palms like *go ahead*, and Carlos tossed me a careworn brown teddy bear. I tucked it under my chin and pretended to snooze. "Perfect."

One Sunday night that summer, my youngest cousin—the one whose diapers I'd changed growing up—called to tell me that she and her fiancé had signed a contract on a house in Houston. When I got off the phone, I burned with shame. I hadn't even known my cousin was engaged. I also burned with envy at her forward momentum, while my boyfriend couldn't be bothered to swivel away from his computer screen. Now, couples composed my entire family tree. It was only I who still dangled alone on a branch by myself.

When Jeremy fell asleep that night, I sat in his darkened living room, mentally decorating my cousin's new house: a Mission-style dining room table, a sleigh bed in the master. As I dreamed up her perfect life, a streetlight glared through the window, emitting just enough buttery light to see a pair of orange-handled scissors on Jeremy's desk. I grabbed them and hacked at the teddy bear's right arm with the scissors. The following Tuesday, I tossed the dismembered bear and the Ziploc bag full of its arm stuffing onto the floor in the middle of group.

Dr. Rosen stared hard.

"My baby cousin's buying a house. It's two stories." The group was used to my outbursts by then, but Dr. Rosen sat still as poured concrete.

"He looks mad." Rory sounded anxious.

"Why is his jaw twitching?" Carlos said.

The Colonel grabbed the one-armed bear carcass. Pieces of white fluffy stuffing rained to the floor.

"Why are you acting so weird?" I asked Dr. Rosen. He was definitely not beaming with pride. He sighed, started to speak, and then shifted in his seat again. I imagined him opening his mouth and hissing: *You're in trouble, trouble, trouble.*

"You destroyed something that belongs to me. What does that mean to you?"

"It means I'm an isolated loser next to my entire family tree! Every last one of them is on the way to joint tenancy—"

"And the bear?" I searched my body for the feeling Dr. Rosen insisted should be there. I knew I was in trouble. Shame churned in my belly.

"I grabbed the first thing I saw."

Dr. Rosen didn't blink or soften. "The bear represents me and the group." He gestured around the circle. "Are you willing to look at what it means to take scissors to that?"

"But I hammered all those dishes on my balcony—" My hands began to shake.

"Those didn't belong to me."

Why wasn't he smiling? Why were my eyes filling with tears? I picked up the bear and placed it in my lap. I ran my finger along the hole where the arm had been attached, trying to feel something. What I found under the shame of being in trouble was a cold lump of fear. It scared me that I didn't understand my subconscious mind. Why, since starting group, did my response to jealousy and disappointment involve sharp objects?

"How can I fix this?"

Dr. Rosen's jaw softened slightly. "Ask the group for help."

Marty met my gaze. "Come to my office this afternoon. I'll suture the arm." Before settling on psychiatry, Marty had dreamed of being a surgeon. He looked excited about the prospect of getting out his needle and thread.

In Marty's tiny Uptown office, I stuffed as much of the polyester filling back into the bear as possible, and then gathered the edges of the wound for Marty to stitch. "Like this," he said, pulling the thick thread through the bear's fur. I sewed the last few stiches, and then held it up for him to inspect. With the arm sewn up, the white stuffing had no way to escape.

m

When I'd hacked up his teddy bear, Dr. Rosen seemed angry. Now, in the wake of my e-mail from Germany, he seemed afraid and sad. I knew better than to ask for a quick fix. Those didn't exist in Rosen-world. It was nine o'clock. Group was over. We all stood up, and I offered my open hands to Lorne and Patrice, but it was only muscle memory, not a genuine gesture of connection. Their warm palms against mine did nothing to thaw the chill. When each of them hugged me, I went through the motions of hugging them back. More muscle memory. None of it reached the frozen center of my being. And I didn't join Brad, Max, and Lorne for breakfast. I didn't let Brad walk me to my office. I rejected their concerned joviality and refused to watch them take turns keeping me afloat with jokes and affirmations. I wanted to be alone. I wanted them to let me sink all the way down. I walked back to my office, shut the door, turned on *Riverdance*, and drafted memos all day until the sky darkened at eight fifteen, and I went home.

28

I had to get off the German case.

I'd returned for my second stint in Augsburg and found myself in a room overlooking the naked schnitzel nibblers. Again I'd fantasized, briefly, about swallowing a bottle of Aleve. When I got back to Chicago that second time, Dr. Rosen suggested that I tell Jack that personal matters would prevent me from traveling to Germany for the near future. I e-mailed Jack saying I needed to discuss a personal matter. He responded right away. *Let's have lunch!*

He was an important partner and a decent person. He'd invited me to lunch; he'd used exclamation points. Maybe I could do a few more weeks in Germany? I thought of the hotel, the naked happy hour, and those long lonely nights. My whole body howled *No.* If I was ruining my legal career by turning down this plum assignment, so be it.

Jack and I walked to One North and sat at a table on the terrace, surrounded mostly by other people in power suits eating power lunches. I took a few deep breaths while Jack ordered a chopped salad, feeling the seconds drag me closer to my confession.

"So what's up?" Jack's face was so open that I almost lost my nerve. I flexed my fingers under the table and leaned forward.

"I can't travel to Germany—there's a personal matter—"

Jack held up his hand. "Say no more. There's plenty for you to do here. I'll let the partners know." He picked up his BlackBerry and typed a new message. I stared out at Wacker Drive, praying I had not completely derailed my career.

✑

Twice, I ran into Alex in the elevator, and both times he was with a blond woman wearing Duke University spirit-wear and running shoes. Both times we ignored each other. Both times I held my breath and stared straight ahead, but as soon as they disappeared down the street, I dialed Rory to cry about Alex's new no-fat girlfriend.

"You should buy a place in another building," Max said.

"With your income, you could afford a three-bedroom," Brad said.

"A woman in your position should definitely own property," Grandma Maggie said.

When Dr. Rosen asked about my resistance to buying a condo, I told the truth: "I don't want to do it by myself." Buying a condo alone would cement my status as a successful but single, alone-in-the-world woman. How depressing to visit empty homes and dream of the future with only a real estate agent at my side. How lonely to embark on a massive financial transaction by myself. Buying the condo might be a win for feminism, but it felt like the exact future I had hoped Dr. Rosen would help me avoid.

"It couldn't hurt to look," Max said on the way out of group.

✑

On a Thursday in late January, I sat on the tenth floor of a title company in a navy-blue suit signing a stack of documents. I wasn't totally alone: a lawyer I hired sat on my right and Lorne's wife, Renee, sat on my left. I signed my name dozens of times under the line that read: *Christie O. Tate, Unmarried Woman, Spinster.* "Wow," I whispered.

"Some of the standard real estate documents have retained rather antiquated language," my lawyer said with a chuckle.

"Ha-ha," Renee said sarcastically. "Maybe someone should update them." She rubbed my back in a circular motion as I signed page after page.

When I got to group, a few minutes late, I pressed the group room button with my right index finger, and with my left, I twirled the keys to my condo, amazed that I now owned, along with the bank, a fifth-floor loft in River North. Two bedrooms. I felt high on progress and my ability to put 10 percent down on a piece of real estate. What good fortune, what a blessing. Everyone congratulated me as I took my seat, but as the session wore on, the high drained away, leaving me with one thought: Christie Tate, Spinster.

I interrupted Max. I can't remember what he was saying, but I sliced into his story with my panic. "Y'all, I'm not sure about this condo." All those papers. All that official evidence of my spinsterhood under the Illinois state seal. I had to fill those empty, echoing rooms all by myself.

Annoyed at my intrusion, Max huffed. "It's fine. You'll be fine. You did the right thing." Then, he returned to his story. I sat quietly as long as I could, but the anger at Max and panic about the condo were too intense to stifle for long. My hands clenched, and I pitched forward, about to scream.

"Oh, here we go," Max said. I wasn't looking at him, but I heard the eye roll in his tone.

Fuck him. I slipped my feet out of my shoes—pink Uggs for the snowy streets—and threw one of them in Max's direction. I swear I aimed for the wall above him, not his face. And I didn't hit him, but I got close. As my shearling-lined shoe sailed across the circle, my "FUCK YOU" traveled with it. I stared directly at smug-ass Max. "I'm sick of being intimidated by you. Sick of your sighs. Your telling me what is and is not fine. You never had to buy—"

Max grabbed the shoe I threw and strode right over to my chair, pointing it at me like a gun. He stopped in front of me, and I rose to meet him.

"Fuck you too!" he yelled in my face.

"No, fuck you!"

We stood so close I could feel the brass buttons on his coat brush against my abs. My fury unfurled into his mouth, and his rage blew straight into mine. In his eyes, I saw flecks of gold and pure hatred. For me. And I hoped he saw my ferocity and hatred for him and every other

person in the circle—in the world—who never had to buy a condo alone
or date in their thirties or swim through thousands of hours of therapy
to end up at the exact place she'd hoped to avoid. *Christie Tate, Spinster.*

"You don't fucking know me, Max!"

"Yes I do! Of course I do! Why do you say such stupid things?"

"I'm not stupid!"

"Then stop acting like it!"

All I knew is that I would scream into his face as long as he would
scream into mine. I would not crumple into my chair, breaking the spell
with pitiful tears. I would stand my ground and scream as long and
loudly as he did. I would hold my power in my own body. He couldn't
have it.

Then we were silent. Still inches from each other. Fury still pulsing
between us. He backed away and sat down. Only then did I take my
seat.

Dr. Rosen didn't make a grand pronouncement after the fight.
There was no *This means you're willing to be intimate.* No leading
questions like *Have you ever had a fight like that with a man? With
anyone? Do you understand what this means,* Mamaleh? I wouldn't
have heard it anyway with my heartbeat galloping in my ears. And for
the first time in all my hours of group therapy, I wasn't secretly hoping
that Dr. Rosen would turn his attention to me and praise me for all the
deep work I was doing. For the first time, I didn't need his affirmation
to prove I was moving forward and doing the hard things to become
the person I wanted to be. I had keys to a new condo in River North
in my purse. I'd thrown my shoe at Max and stood my ground in a
highly charged confrontation. It was undeniably life altering to buy real
estate, but I'd sat through enough group therapy sessions to recognize
that my willingness to fight full out with Max might be an even bigger
indication of transformation than a new address on Ontario Street. My
body buzzed with adrenaline that was sure to wear off, but in those
dizzy moments after the shouting match, there was a solid, still part of
me that knew: I was moving forward in my own messy, noisy, fright-
ened way.

At the end of the session, I stood up, unsure if my shaky legs would hold me up. I wasn't ashamed exactly, but I wasn't sure how to deal with Max during the hugs or on the walk to the elevators. It was he who approached me after he hugged Dr. Rosen. For the second time in thirty minutes, he stood a few inches in front of me. This time, he opened his arms wide. I opened mine too. Neither of us said a word, but we held on to each other tightly.

29

I hung my red trench coat on the back of my office door, took a seat at my desk, and pressed the start button on my computer. It was still booting up when the phone rang. I checked the number on the curled business card clutched in my damp hand. Yes, it was him, just as he promised.

"Christie Tate speaking," I said to sound official, to steady my nerves, to prop up the sham that this was a business call. Reed, the new man in my Tuesday group, had been running deals—or whatever hedge fund managers do—for two decades. I'd been a lawyer for two years. He didn't need my legal advice. When he laughed on the other end of the line, I could picture his dimples because I'd just seen them in group when we'd laughed at something Rory said about her dad.

"You sound like a real lawyer," he said.

"That's because I am a real lawyer." My body temperature rose. I fanned myself with the card he'd pressed into my hand.

"Did you think I would call?"

Would truth function here—in the untamed, unsupervised space outside of group—like it did in there? Would it rescue me from the cliché I saw myself diving into like a shimmering pool in a 1970s night-time drama like *Dynasty* or *Dallas*? What did I think would happen between me and this married older man with the ropy forearms and lean neck with a hairline like the seashore? The married man who joined my therapy group because he couldn't stop getting blow jobs from other women?

"I wasn't sure." But I hoped he would, was glad he did. "How can I help you?"

"Do you know anyone who does M&A work?"

My turn to laugh. Skadden was internationally famous for mergers and acquisitions work. I sat one floor away from thirty M&A lawyers. "I can give you the name of the head of the department."

"I'll take a name and a number."

I gave him the name and number of the partner with the snow-white hair who wore custom-made pinstriped suits and closed deals that ended up on the front page of the *Wall Street Journal.*

There was a pause. I flicked the corner of Reed's business card, and then pinned it to the bulletin board behind my phone, even though I'd already memorized his number.

There was another pause. Then another.

"So," he said, and I could hear his smirk and picture the glint in his eye. "If I keep you on the phone, are we going to need a chaperone?"

"What for?" I wanted to make him say it.

"For all the things we are going to say and do to each other."

When I hung up the phone, still smiling, still warmed and thrumming from my thighs to my scalp, I stood up and wrung my hands, trying to break the spell, the heat, the throbbing, the pleasure of having Reed's attention. I relived each beat of our conversation, thrilled that he'd punctured the pretense that our conversation was work related.

I cracked my neck and arched my back, but my body begged for release, so I pressed in the metal lock on my door. Pushed back my chair and lay on the floor. I slid my hands between my legs. My jaw tightened as I touched myself, thinking of Reed's dimples, his strong hands, and his crisp collars. His voice on the phone. Those delicious pauses. I came with such force that I bumped my head on the edge of my computer tower. My whole body pulsed—fingertips, triceps, lips, belly, Achilles' heel, toes.

I was still breathing hard when I sat in my chair, straightened my sweater, and began to answer e-mails from Jack and the team in Germany.

From group, I knew that Reed viewed his marriage as a stalemate. He was the guilty, straying husband; his wife Miranda's rage simmered just below boiling. Their communication was limited to terse exchanges about the logistics of getting their girls to gymnastics and tutoring. They slept with their backs to each other.

I also knew it was cliché for me to run headfirst into a relationship with him while I was still reeling from Alex. And yet I sprinted.

The following Thursday and Monday sessions, I didn't mention Reed, an omission I justified because he was in my Tuesday group, so I should talk about him then. On Tuesday, I set my alarm fifteen minutes early so I could take extra time getting dressed. My stomach somersaulted when the train pulled into the Washington stop. *I get to be with him for ninety minutes.*

Reed arrived a few minutes late. He put his briefcase next to my chair, and as he sat down, he scooted several inches closer to me. Could they all feel the heat rising between us? My heart was pounding. Surely Dr. Rosen and everyone else could hear it.

During the session, I stared at the dark indigo of Reed's slacks, the fine hair on his wrists. When he talked, I watched his lips move; when he brushed his hand through his hair in frustration, I couldn't make myself look away. But I also watched the clock obsessively, because at nine o'clock, group would end, and Reed would head north to his office and I would head west to mine, where my gray life of document review and *Riverdance* awaited me. But in group, less than a foot away from Reed, my life shimmered with color and promise because I could watch him challenge the Colonel, brush his foot with mine, listen to his laugh.

And this: my feelings for Reed were undeniably of a sexual nature, which meant I should share them with the group. The pressure to disclose pressed against my lips, but Reed beat me to it.

"I think about Christie all the time. When I get in bed with Miranda,

I wish she was Christie. At the girls' soccer games, I wish Christie was with me. We talked on the phone the other day, and it was really—" Reed looked at me as if for permission. I nodded. "It was really nice."

Everyone looked at me, waiting for my half of the confession. I admitted that I enjoyed talking to him. I didn't mention how I shut my door and touched myself in my office after our first conversation. What words matched the sensations in my body? The constant thrumming, the woozy feeling like I'd pounded shots or snorted laughing gas. The only words I could imagine were ridiculous. I couldn't tell them I was falling in love.

At the same time, I wasn't a woman who stole another woman's husband. I'd taken women's studies classes. I'd read MacKinnon, Chodorow, and Cixous. Plus, I knew better than to believe that married Reed would leave his colonial in the suburbs. I hadn't sat through hundreds of therapy sessions to dive into the cliché of the lonely girl who falls for the unhappily married man *from her therapy group*. I'd already tried dating a man who saw Dr. Rosen, and it hadn't worked. I remembered Monica Lewinsky—the public scorn and the rescinding of her Revlon job offer when the blow-job scandal broke. Given the loose boundaries of Rosen-world, I too could end up publicly shamed, not to mention I was jeopardizing my therapeutic home base.

"What do you want?" Dr. Rosen asked me.

"I don't know how to answer that."

"Why not?"

"I don't know what I'm allowed to have." I stared back at Dr. Rosen and believed he knew the answer: I wanted Reed.

Each morning my cell rattled on my bedside table. Reed on his way to work before dawn. Stock market hours. He always called my office mid-morning to say hello, and then again when the market closed. At night he called on his walk from his office to the train. I could hear his shoes clicking on the sidewalk. Sometimes we talked from the moment he left his office, all through his train ride and walk to his front door when he'd put his key in the lock and whispered that he had to go. He showed me how to send PIN messages on my BlackBerry—messages that bypassed our firms' servers and allegedly left no record. When my BlackBerry light glowed with a blinking red light, I knew it was a PIN from Reed and my body responded with a jolt.

He told me I could ask him anything, so I asked about Miranda. Maybe then she would be real to me, and I would back off. What did she smell like? (Clean) How thin was she? (Size four) What was his favorite thing about her? (Her devotion to the children) When was the last time they slept together? (Couldn't recall) Why did he marry her? (It felt like I was supposed to) Why hadn't he left her? (The girls) I drew a picture of her in my head: a woman my height in a plum-colored dress with silver sandals with perfect sun-kissed highlights in her mostly blond hair and a coldness that I associated with super-thin wealthy women who didn't have to work. I imagined she had a signature lipstick shade and nibbled at her food. I dreamed her as flawless but cold; self-possessed but starving; perfectly manicured but brittle. My body had more flesh, more warmth, more vitality, more youth, more power.

I felt guilty. I was a fake feminist after all. A husband stealer. A cliché.

And yet: I'd never felt so alive.

"I have to go to my noon AA meeting. Meet me there," Reed said one morning.

Jack was expecting me for a meeting in ten minutes. After he'd supported my German travel ban, I was loath to cause any trouble. How much would I risk for Reed?

I e-mailed Jack: *Something has come up. Can we meet at 1:30?*

The AA meeting was four blocks from my office, and I raced over in my heels with no coat, even though it was thirty degrees. I had no wallet, no money, no fucking sense in my head. All I had was the force of Reed's voice inviting me to be with him and my reckless yes. Across the Chicago Loop, I bobbed and weaved between pedestrians and stepped into traffic so I could get to Reed sooner, so I could flee my gray, loveless life that turned vivid in his presence. Yes, I sprinted to an AA meeting:

Even though I wasn't technically an alcoholic.

Even though I had to push back a meeting with the largest rain-maker in my department.

Even though Reed was a married man with well-documented fidelity issues.

I sat next to him in the back at the end of a row. He pressed his shiny black lace-up shoe against my black wedge heel. My breath hitched. I leaned back in my chair and snuck my hand into the space between his elbow and his rib cage. The throbbing in my fingertips was my own pulse, but it felt like his. The chairperson of the meeting passed around a flyer for a 12-step retreat, and when I passed it to Reed, I let my fingers rest on his palm. Skin to skin. Everything disappeared. The white-walled room packed with sober lawyers, secretaries, traders, and a massage therapist. The serenity coins. The stackable chairs. The woman in a security officer uniform eating her Chipotle burrito in the far corner. It was all gone and with it, the Loop, the El train, the traffic on Wacker.

There was only my fingertips and Reed's palm.

And that throbbing through my body.

He walked me back to my office. I matched his long stride so that every few steps our hands would brush. Each time, we pulled our hands away quickly as if shocked. Or busted. We wore goofy smiles.

Oldest fucking story in the book. Older successful guy and his younger mistress. The end of this story would find me huddled some-where bawling, leaving messages for Dr. Rosen, shaking my fist at my stupid-ass decisions. But this moment on corner of Wacker and Ran-dolph with Reed's hand centimeters from mine and my body bursting with unexpressed longing was all that mattered. It was enough.

"I want you to know everything about me," he said as we stood before the great glass revolving door that would churn me back into my office.

"Like what?" Thanks to group, I already knew his dad was a pre-scription pill addict who pressured Reed into an MBA program even though he wanted to be an architect. I'd heard the story about the track coach who got him drunk and molested him at an out-of-town meet during middle school. I'd been privy to the sessions where he described who he was when he drank every day, and of course that blow job that brought him to group. And the other extramarital shenanigans that fissured his marriage. I knew things. Knowledge was power that felt like love.

"Everything. How I open a bottle of water. How I hold the steering wheel or swim laps in the pool. Stuff I can't show you in group or on the street." He leaned over and whispered in my ear: "I want you to know what I look like when I tell you that I love you."

ur

"I did something yesterday," I announced in Monday-morning group, where it was easier to disclose because Reed wasn't in that group. For weeks, I'd come right up to the line of committing a sin with Reed. I rationalized each near transgression as harmless because nothing overtly sexual happened. Grazing his palm at an AA meeting wasn't an affair. Neither was meeting him for lunch in a dark bar hidden under the El tracks or talking to him late at night after his family had gone to bed. We hadn't even kissed. I lied to myself that I was blameless, though deep down I suspected what I was doing with Reed was like secretly eating a dozen apples but professing to have recovered from an eating disorder.

"What happened?" Lorne said. He'd predicted for weeks that my "friendship" with Reed might get too friendly. His wife, Renee, had been in group with Reed years earlier, and they'd come close to having an affair, which should have given me pause. It didn't.

"We were talking on the phone yesterday—and things got—out of hand."

"What does that mean?" Patrice's brow furrowed with motherly concern. Grandma Maggie clucked as if she knew what was coming.

"He called from the grocery store." On the weekends, Reed and I patched together a series of guerrilla phone calls whenever he was able to sneak away from his family. I was glued to my phone at all times. "He said things—he was in the frozen foods aisle—"

"Jesus, we don't care about frozen peas!" Lorne sniped.

"Fine. We had phone sex."

"While he was buying food for his wife and kids," Patrice mentioned helpfully.

"He did this with Renee, you know," Lorne said. "Did he tell you how special you are? That he loved you?"

I told myself the same things every woman in my position tells herself: I was different. But a braided knot in my stomach—one strand for Reed's wife and each of the girls—tightened. I pressed my lips together and looked at Dr. Rosen, who prompted me to say more, so I described how I'd touched myself on the floor of my closet while Reed told me to imagine him inside me. He'd told me that he loved me, that he'd do anything for me. When I'd heard the cashier ask if he wanted paper or plastic, I tried to hang up, but he wanted me to stay on the line until he got into his car.

"Why the closet?" Max always with the relevant questions.

When the conversation with Reed had turned racy, I'd been standing in my closet looking for a sweater. Next thing I knew, I was on the floor, fingers between my legs, phone cradled to my ear, staring up at the hems of my pants and skirts.

Dr. Rosen spoke up. "Where better to hide sexuality than the closet? It's an obvious choice." Unable to meet his eyes, I stared at the outline of Dr. Rosen's chin. He asked what I was feeling. There was only one answer: Shame. Shame. Shame. All the throbbing excitement turned to liquid shame, sloshing through my body.

"I'm a fucking cliché. I should be better than this. I'm moving backward." A married recovering alcoholic with teenage children was a trapdoor in the space I'd previously labeled "the bottom." There was no way Dr. Rosen could convince me that moving from single-but-not-in-love-with-me Alex to married Reed was progress in the right direction. Dr. Rosen insisted I was moving forward. "I want my *own* husband and my *own* children, not someone else's! I want more than phone sex on my ballet flats."

"What if this is exactly what you need to do to get where you want to go?"

"You can't mean that."

"When was the last time you let yourself be adored by a man who wanted to fuck you?"

"The Intern—"

Dr. Rosen shook his head.

"You should be warning me, raising a red fucking flag right under my nose." It would never happen. Dr. Rosen was die-hard about letting us find our way without judging us. If I, as a so-called sexual anorexic, needed to have an affair with a married man to finally hit bottom with unavailable men, then so be it. To me, Reed was a category-six hurricane about to make landfall, and I wanted Dr. Rosen to pick me up and carry me to higher ground. But that wasn't what Dr. Rosen did. He was a witness, not the National Guard.

Patrice balked at Dr. Rosen's laissez-faire approach. "Maybe you shouldn't talk to him outside of group, Christie."

I nodded, knowing I should heed her advice, but positive I would stay the course, following the immortal words of Martin Luther: *Be a sinner and sin boldly*—though Luther wasn't referring to getting off in the closet to the murmurs of a married group mate.

"How is this going to get me where I want to go?" I asked.

"We'll find out." Dr. Rosen shrugged—not an inspiring gesture as I headed toward inevitable devastation.

"Max, help," I said.

Ever since our showdown, I sensed that I could trust Max more than anyone else in the circle. When you scream into someone's face, you learn something about how solid they are. Max was a goddamn redwood whose roots ran deeper and wider than anyone else's in the circle. If he told me to run from Reed, I'd consider lacing up my shoes.

"I think you have to play this out." Though the serious look on Max's face scared me, I also heard his blessing for my folly.

But Dr. Rosen was the authority figure, the doctor, the Harvard alum. He should make a decree or recommendation. "Isn't it malpractice for you to bless this affair?"

"You think driving this underground and making it *more secretive* would be helpful for you? Come on."

30

When my group mates considered Reed's potential as a mate for me, they stopped at the solid-gold band on his left ring finger. I wasn't ignoring that detail—even when he hinted that I'd be a great stepmother and that he could move into my new condo. Instead, I focused on how much better he was than the other men I'd dated. He told me he loved me every time I talked to him, so he was the anti-Alex. He didn't care about religion, so he was the anti-intern. He answered my e-mails within thirty seconds and asked me to lunch every other day, so he was the anti-Jeremy. I rationalized that it was good practice to bask in Reed's love and attention. Eventually, I would transfer my attention to a man who was just like him, except without that gold band.

As soon as Reed sat down in group on Tuesdays, he would extend his hand toward me. I'd held a lot of hands in group: Patrice, Marty, Nan, Emily, Mary, Marnie, Max, Grandma Maggie, Lorne, and Dr. Rosen. Sometimes those hands supported me, and sometimes my palm served as someone else's ballast. But this was different. Holding Reed's hand didn't feel like a gesture of therapeutic support. It felt like foreplay.

The first time we held hands in group, Rory and Marty both gasped. Patrice sighed in frustration. Carlos whispered, "Girl, please." Dr. Rosen made a show of seeing our hands together, fingers like a lattice to each other's body, but said nothing. When I caught Dr. Rosen's eye, the seed of fear and frustration would blossom into protest.

"What's your plan, Dr. Rosen?" I held up my hand still knitted to Reed's.

"Plan? I'm not God."

"What about Reed's wife? Don't you care about her?"

"She's not my patient. You are."

He asked me what I was feeling. My answer was always the same: shame and hunger. Dr. Rosen asked me what I wanted. "Reed. I want Reed. Are you helping me? I came here for help with relationships—"

"I *am* helping you."

"The sum total of your therapeutic advice for me is come here, feel feelings, and disclose everything?" As I confronted Dr. Rosen, Reed held my hand, his thumb tracing a circle across my palm.

"Yes."

Did Dr. Rosen think that Reed and I should be together? *Together* together? I stared hard at Dr. Rosen—his unblinking eyes and straight neck, the slight hunch of his shoulders, his shoes planted on the floor. When he peered into the future, what did he see for me? A life with Reed and his girls? A life with someone like Reed, but whom I could have all to myself?

Patrice and Grandma Maggie begged me to cut it off. Lorne trotted out Renee's history with Reed as a cautionary tale. Max continued to say I had to play this out and that the mysterious alchemy of the advanced group would somehow immunize me from total destruction. Rory, Marty, Carlos, and the Colonel looked to Dr. Rosen, who smiled inscrutably and held his palms open. In the elevator one Tuesday morning, Rory, in a quiet voice, said, "I don't know what Dr. Rosen is doing with you." Her eyes darted from my gaze in fear.

In late February, Steven threw a party for Clare's birthday and invited all of our law school friends. When I stepped into the dark restaurant, I spotted Clare decked out in a silk top and skinny jeans. I felt like I'd just returned from a long trip to a faraway country. My relationship with Reed had so consumed me that I'd forgotten there was a big wide world beyond my three-inch BlackBerry screen, where I read and re-read Reed's messages while waiting for him to break from his family and call me.

All through dinner, my BlackBerry buzzed. Each time it vibrated, I pretended to search my purse for lip gloss or gum or a pen so I could read the message from Reed: *I miss you.* Two minutes later: *When are you going to be home?* Ten minutes later: *I have a second to talk. Can you pick up? Where are you?* Five minutes after that: *We are driving home soon. I won't be online for about an hour.*

"Tater, what on earth are you expecting on that BlackBerry?" Clare cornered me in the line to the bathroom.

I told her I was involved with someone, and she wanted to know why he wasn't with me. My mouth froze in a smile as I realized with perfect clarity: Clare would never meet Reed. I was a secret, a *mistress.* Having to look Clare in the eye and tell her I was with a man who was currently at his niece's ballet recital with his wife of nineteen years was a sickening jolt of reality. I mentioned that he was "sort of attached," and she understood instantly.

"Are you in love with each other?"

I pulled out the Valentine's Day card Reed gave me that I kept in my purse. She opened it and read aloud. "*'I love you, Reed.'*"

"How'd you meet him?" Clare knew all about group therapy, but the truth stuck in my throat. The words vibrated with sheer insanity as I said, "Group therapy."

"Well, he clearly loves you!" She waved the card in the air and hugged me again. I absorbed her genuine good cheer for my counterfeit relationship.

Hours later when I climbed into bed, my BlackBerry glowed red with a new PIN message. I typed in my passcode, but stopped myself from clicking on his message. The look on Clare's face when I told her Reed was married made me want to curl my legs into my body and groan out loud. Reed was never going to leave Miranda and his girls. And if he did, would we even be attracted to each other anymore? How could I ever trust him given his history? And what if the real draw to the relationship was the illicitness, the secrecy, the current of shame that animated our connection? Wasn't this covered in the most basic of Lifetime movies?

I hurled my BlackBerry into the closet. The pain of not connecting with Reed before falling asleep was physical—a stomach cramp that felt like something scrambled in my guts. Reed might love me, but he wasn't available. Didn't I want something real? How did screwing around with a married man make me a real person if the whole thing was a secret? I rocked back and forth. I stuffed a corner of my pillow in my mouth and bit down hard. The red blinking light on my BlackBerry flickered like a heartbeat.

31

I ducked into a Starbucks in Logan Square on a Friday night at six thirty. Commuters were rushing home, and darkness had chased the weak winter sun well below the horizon. Reed's call was ten minutes late. My resolution from the night of Clare's party had dissolved the next day, and we resumed our daily phone calls. There was also a week-night trip to a suburban mall where I helped him shop for a winter coat—when the mall closed, we groped in his minivan by the light of the Cheesecake Factory. Ours was a very classy romance.

When my phone finally buzzed, I moved to a quiet stool away from the espresso machine. Reed's breath swallowed his voice. It sounded like he was running down the street. I pictured him sprinting down Madison so he could get home. To his family. *I want him to run to me.* Something cold and sharp in his voice made me sit up taller. He always swore he had no secrets from me, that I could ask him anything. Now it took all my courage ask: "Where're you going?"

"I'm taking the girls out for pizza." *Girls* undoubtedly included his wife. The lump in my throat held the shape of her in that plum dress and those Hollywood highlights. "It'll be an early night. We're headed back to Iowa tomorrow." Miranda's father had recently been diagnosed with terminal liver cancer. I was sure the diagnosis would bring Reed and his wife closer together, but so far, he reported she was shutting him out more than ever.

"Are you okay?" I rocked back and forth on the stool, one hand on the phone, one on my chest.

"Nervous about the trip." That cold thing in his voice was sharper still.

"I'm here if you need me—" The espresso machine grinded and whirred, drowning out all other sounds.

"I've got to go."

For the first time ever, he hung up without saying *I love you*. The noisy Starbucks counter spun in my vision as genuine panic set it. I'd felt this before. Reed was loosening his grip on me. Now he would slide under the water and disappear, just like all the others, just as I always knew he would.

Reed's PIN message popped up just after eleven that night. *Sorry,* he wrote.

I wasn't about to interrogate him. I was the anti-Miranda—never suspicious, never prying, never difficult. I wrote back: *No need to apologize! I love you! Let's talk tomorrow.* I certainly didn't ask why it took four hours to eat pizza "with the girls."

"I lied to you." It was six the next morning. I'd been up since four, wandering around my apartment and swigging skim milk from the carton, trying to calm my stomach.

"Dude, I already know about the wife and kids." I forced a laugh; he was silent.

"Last night, Miranda and I went out for our"—I sucked in my breath, mouthing the word before he said it—"anniversary."

I pressed my back against my bedroom wall and slid down.

Anniversary. Such a beautiful word, now turned bitter in my mouth. The truth of his lie settled in my belly. My body craved expulsion: vomit, tears, screaming. But I sat against the wall, my body perpendicular to my legs.

He hadn't said a word about his anniversary in group. In all the therapy sessions we sat through together—holding hands—I got the impression that there was insufficient civility between Reed and Miranda to sustain them through a meal without the girls. Now I couldn't get the picture of them sitting down to fillets and flourless chocolate cake out of my head. I saw candlelight, apologetic caresses, and a softening of all the hard hurt between them.

I shook and shook and shook.

"I love you. Please don't doubt I love you," Reed pleaded. "Say something. Please."

"This is boring." I'd been smart enough to know we'd never last but dumb enough to hope for a different ending.

Still gripping the phone, I crawled to the bathroom and peered over the toilet seat, a comforting view I'd known so well as a teenager. Nothing came out because I hadn't been able to eat any dinner, unlike Reed, who'd had a lovely anniversary meal *with his wife of twenty years.*

"I'm hanging up now." I flipped my phone shut and threw it as hard I could against the bathroom mirror. It clattered to a stop by the bathtub. I turned off my BlackBerry and locked it in the trunk of my car.

No more PIN messages.

No more phone sex.

No more secret thrills.

The fury in my body—at myself, at Reed, at Dr. Rosen for calling this "progress"—made it impossible to stand still. I was also mad at Max for encouraging me to "play this out." At Rory, Patrice, and Grandma Maggie for being right all along. I laced up my running shoes and ran ten miles on the Lake. I pounded past groups of runners and clumps of tourists taking pictures of Navy Pier. I pulled my hat low over my brow and didn't make eye contact with a soul. My music was set to the highest volume, and I let it drown every thought about Reed and what a fool I was. When I was done, I still felt pumped and jittery. I could have run ten more miles. I could have run until I shredded every muscle in my legs, scorched my lungs, and made bloody stumps of my toes.

But what I really needed was to cry.

I sat through a 12-step meeting without hearing or saying a single word. Several people approached me afterward asking if I was okay, and I shook my head no. I leaned into the white of my knuckles. No, I'm not okay.

I sat in my car after the meeting, unsure where to drive. Sunlight streamed in on all sides, and laughing DePaul students and clusters of suburban tourists wandered down the street. The world beyond my car was too noisy and scary.

I called Patrice. "I've shut off my BlackBerry. I'm done."

"I've been so worried about you. You shouldn't be alone right now."

I drove to Lorne's house and cried into his throw pillows and fought the urge to unlock my trunk and grab my BlackBerry to check in with Reed. Lorne's wife, Renee, patted my head, telling of the nights she too cried over Reed once she realized he would never leave his wife. Lorne and Renee's son, Roman, toddled on the floor at my feet, making sweet baby sounds.

The crush of grief worked me over, and I kept landing on the absurd notion that I was unfairly abandoning him. "His father-in-law is dying. Maybe I should break up with him this summer."

Lorne and Renee shook their heads.

"Dr. Rosen is going to be so proud of you," Lorne said. Tears sprung to my eyes. What must Dr. Rosen have thought as he watched me holding hands with Reed, describing our silly trip to the mall, our closeted sex life? He'd kept a poker face all these weeks in group, but surely he shook his head back in his office, wondering when his fool of a patient would come to her senses.

"I have an idea. Follow me." Renee led me to her desk and sat me before her computer. She pressed a few keys, and the screen filled with the smiling faces of a young couple. In the background, blurry images of people holding sparklers surrounded the couple. The words on the screen read, *Discover where Jewish relationships begin. Start browsing now.*

"JDate?"

"These guys are single—"

"And looking for *Jewish* women. I'm literally named after Christ."

"Trust me. They're going to love you. We'll call you 'Texas Girl.' Once they meet you, they won't care if you're a nun."

I hesitated, but she gave me a look: *Are you willing or not?* She'd built a happy life with Lorne, a nice Jewish boy, shortly after she broke off her relationship with Reed. Now she had a beautiful son, throw pillows, and farm-fresh eggs in her fridge. She seemed so sure this could work for me. On day one of treatment, Dr. Rosen suggested I could get well if I let him and the group into my decisions. Surely, this counted as not "going it alone."

Renee coached me through the questions on the profile form. No, I was not Ashkenazi. No, I didn't attend shul every week. Renee insisted I check the box indicating I kept kosher because I hated ham. I had sparse hope that the men on JDate would embrace me, but Renee had me laughing. She sent me home with leftover challah from their Shabbat dinner. "Shalom," I said as I shut the door behind me.

Lakeshore Drive heading downtown from the north side on a clear, late-winter night is one of the most gorgeous scenes imaginable—the stony Drake Hotel looms like a castle and the Hancock building grazes the stars. As messed up as I was about Reed, I couldn't look at the city and feel anything other than awe. It was my third night as an aspiring Jewess on JDate, and I was driving home from a recovery meeting. I knew my apartment would be cold and empty, but I preferred the harsh punch of loneliness to the electric, buzzy instability of trying to build a life around Reed. So far I hadn't broken any dishes or palmed a letter opener.

I dialed Dr. Rosen, who'd been out of town for a conference and didn't know about the lie and the anniversary dinner. "I let go of Reed. I won't have any contact with him outside of group," I told his voice mail.

I took a deep breath. There was so much more to say. For weeks, I'd wondered how Dr. Rosen could live with himself as he stood watch over my affair with Reed. Group members had repeatedly confronted Dr. Rosen on my behalf: *Why aren't you doing something about this? Christie's going to get hurt. This is totally unethical.* Dr. Rosen met each confrontation with a neutral expression, asking what, exactly, he should do to stop me.

During my tenure in Rosen-land, various group members had referred to Dr. Rosen as *brilliant*. I'd seen him speak fluent German to the Colonel and Max; I'd watched Hebrew blessings roll off his tongue. He made deep connections between seemingly disparate events in group members' lives. Pet ferrets and the Holocaust. Guitar lessons and cyanide pills. Pinworm and credit card debt. He was sharp, but was that brilliance? Maybe.

What I valued most in Dr. Rosen were his balls of steel. He trusted himself enough to allow two group members to have an affair literally on his watch. He watched me make one questionable choice after another, patiently waiting for me to come to my God-given senses. If I would have killed myself over this, surely he would have found himself before a licensing board. But he trusted himself—and he trusted me. Waiting for me to wise up must have felt like having teeth removed without Novocain. I could never stand to watch someone I cared about make such questionable decisions.

I was grateful that he could.

32

I was naked, shivering, holding my arms across my chest like a V, which was inadequate to the task of hiding my breasts. Sort of silly given that I'd just had sex with him. My clothes were across the room on the radiator. The only light was the glowing isosceles triangle from the closet. Sade crooned in her timeless voice.

I stood there for several minutes watching Brandon, who had already buttoned himself into his matching pajama set. He made hospital corners with the bedsheets and folded the comforter just so after pulling it tight. He didn't acknowledge me, standing there shivering; he was in another world, a fugue state composed of sheets, blankets, comforters, flat lines, and surfaces with no ripples. My arms shivered against my breasts and goose bumps rose on my belly as my mind tried and failed to return to the moments before Brandon's vision tunneled to his linens.

Brandon stepped back, hands on his hips, and surveyed the bed. He nodded and mumbled something to himself. He strode to his side of the bed and peeled back the covers gingerly. He shimmied his body down carefully so as to not disturb that hard-won smoothness. With his head on his pillow, he turned to me with a wide, unguarded smile.

"Coming to bed?"

After Renee set up my JDate profile, a series of men who were seeking Jewish partners rejected me upon discovering that "Texas Girl" was actually a shiksa named after the savior of the New Testament. Aaron and Oren seemed offended that my profile had been designed to dupe them, while Daniel, Eric, and Marc were amused at my claims to a kosher diet. Jerry, who must have been sixty-two years old, offered to take me to Manny's deli and then show me his Jewish sausage. I let my JDate membership lapse and moved on to eharmony.com.

Brandon's first e-mail charmed me immediately. He asked if I liked to eat breakfast cereal for dinner, which launched a lively debate about the merits of Frosted Flakes versus granola. From his missives, I gathered that he was experienced at dating because he knew how to flirt over e-mail. I also assumed he was well educated, because he knew when to employ a semicolon.

Brandon met my sole criterion for a date: he wasn't a married man in my therapy group. He had the settled air of a man in his late thirties who now wanted a steady plus-one. On our first date we met for lunch at the East Bank Club, Chicago's version of a country club that boasted the membership of Oprah and the Obamas. He wore a blue blazer and smiled with kind eyes. He stood an inch taller than I was, and his hair was longer than it was in his profile picture. He looked boyish and approachable, like a Beatle preparing for his first gig on *The Ed Sullivan Show*. For our second date we saw a play called *Love Song* at the Steppenwolf, followed by dinner at Boku on Halsted. Brandon was the type of guy who ordered off the specials menu and wore pressed khaki pants on weekend nights. He always paid, always held the door open, always insisted on sharing dessert. His college, the same place he went to medical school, was famous for educating dozens of presidents and Supreme Court justices. When he laughed, he held his hand over his mouth shyly. He'd recently taken up rock climbing to force himself to learn something that didn't come naturally to him. His hygiene was impeccable—he brushed his teeth before and after we made out, and showered twice a day. He never cursed, didn't drink, and never lost his cool. I was 90 percent sure he was Republican, but he had yet to demonstrate any misogyny, racism, or classism, so I let myself be wooed by his blue-blooded manners and kind demeanor.

With Brandon, there were no spontaneous jolts of desire that propelled me to the floor of my office in search of orgasmic relief. During our first kiss on my couch after the play at Steppenwolf, I felt pleasant, if not particularly turned on. And that was mostly fine by me. The loss of appetite around the Intern and the illicit charge from my relationship with Reed had left me wrung out. With Brandon, my body was a calm lake on a quiet June morning.

Sometimes, in group, I whispered that I was almost bored.

"Good," Max said. "The hallmark of a healthy relationship is boredom."

"It's true, kiddo," Grandma Maggie said, beaming her smile my direction. "It's part of every marriage."

Dr. Rosen agreed: If I was bored, I was doing something right. But when I listened to other people talk about their early days with their beloveds—Clare or Marnie or Renee—they mentioned not sleeping, not eating, not being able to concentrate. No one described a rippleless lake. Part of me missed the excitement that crashed through me with my previous lovers, even as I recognized that it hadn't served me. Now, when I pictured my heart, I saw that it was grooved from Reed, gouged a few times by Alex and the Intern, nicked by Jeremy. Of course each group member and Dr. Rosen had left their marks. I tried to imagine attaching to Brandon. Once, at dinner, I stared at his starched white shirt, imagining the surface of his heart. Did his grooves match mine?

And now I'd watched Brandon straighten his sheets like someone in a sketch routine about OCD. What, I wondered, did his obsessive bed-making ritual portend? I could only imagine that some unspeakable childhood trauma led him to demand such order from his bedsheets. I wanted to ask, but his eyes were already heavy with sleep. He looked so youthful with the sheets tucked around his shoulders—I felt like I should offer him a glass of milk and a graham cracker.

The sex was weird. We'd walked home from his favorite Thai restaurant, hand in hand. Back at his place, Brandon put on Sade. He led me to his darkened bedroom, where we kissed on his bed for the first time. The calm lake of my belly rippled slightly as he pulled off his shirt and then mine. When all of our clothes were removed, he sat up on the edge of the bed and rolled the condom on. He crawled over to me and straddled my hips with his legs. It was less foreplay than I'd imagined or wanted, but he hadn't had a girlfriend since medical school fifteen years earlier. I didn't fault him for being rusty, and I hadn't been willing to speak up.

Instead of the standard missionary-style sex I'd expected, Brandon put his right palm under my left shoulder and flipped me over in one swift motion. Everything went black as I face-planted into the pillow. Before I could lift my head or say anything, Brandon hoisted my hips up and entered me. Brandon's thrusts were swift and clinical, though not unpleasant. I was stuck in my head: surprised and mildly titillated that someone who seemed so straitlaced, so possibly Republican, was into sex from behind.

But I didn't want my face jammed into a pillow. I wanted to see him, to hear the music, to breathe freely. The words to get myself flipped back over—*Wait. Hold up. Stop. Flip me back. This isn't what I'm into*—wouldn't come out of my mouth. As I lay there trying to sort out how I would tell my group about this flip, Brandon's fingers reached between my legs and my mind went blank as the pleasure rose through me, quick and hot. My back arched, and then my face hit the pillow with a muddled thud. When I rolled over to look at him, he was putting his arms through his pajamas.

Thoughts swallowed every bodily sensation as if my body rolled up into my brain like a window shade: *What's with the pajamas? Did I enjoy that? Where had Sade gone?*

And this: *What happened to my voice?*

From the moment we entered his bedroom, we'd been totally silent. There was no moaning, no panting, no oohing, and no aahing. There was no conversation—no "What do you like?" or "How does that feel?" It was neat and tidy, just like the stack of old-fashioned pajamas lined up in his impeccable linen closet.

As Brandon slept, I replayed the whole scene, from the flip sex to the hospital corners. None of it turned me off, exactly. He wasn't mean or inattentive or checked out. I diagnosed him as phobic about face-to-face sex and psychotic about sheets. But we all had our baggage. I could bring all my judgments, insecurities, fears, delusions, and feelings about everything that just happened to group. They would help me sort through it.

⁓

"You're dating Dr. Flipper," Lorne joked, "but he's better than Reed."

Max said it wasn't clear if the sheets thing was endearing or a sign that he was rigid and unyielding. "You'll probably have to get him into therapy," Max suggested.

I told them we hadn't discussed therapy yet, and Max raised his eyebrows at me. "I'm not hiding it, it just hasn't come up."

"You're waiting for him to ask you if you come to group three times a week?" Max smirked.

The rule was to tell Dr. Rosen and my groups everything, not to tell my potential love interests everything about my therapy. "I'm not sure if I like him. My body doesn't really respond to him."

"Did you have an orgasm?" Lorne asked.

"Yes."

Dr. Rosen beamed like a full moon hanging in a cloudless sky.

⁓

On my thirty-fourth birthday, Brandon stood in my kitchen while I packed my overnight bag. We always spent the night at his penthouse overlooking Navy Pier because it had imported furniture, a surround-sound stereo, and, of course, his pajamas.

"Who's this?" Brandon pointed at a picture stuck to my fridge, every surface of which was plastered with pictures, 10K-race bibs, and ticket stubs. Of the dozens of faces he could have pointed to, he zeroed in on the one I didn't want to discuss. Were we really going to do this on my birthday?

"That's my—" I paused.

He cocked his head like *well?* and kept his finger pinned to the picture.

"My mentor."

Brandon leaned in close and studied the picture. "Really?" It was a

close-up picture of Dr. Rosen's face from Kathryn's wedding right before I'd introduced him and Alex. "What kind of mentor?"

I didn't want to tell Brandon about Dr. Rosen because I had no idea
what he thought about mental-health treatment. When, a few weeks
earlier, I'd told him I was in a 12-step program for an eating disorder, he
scrunched his face and said, "I don't get why you need all those people
or why anyone can't stop eating when they're full."

"Well, actually"—fuck it—"he's my therapist."

He leaned toward the picture and gave it a good hard look. "Therapist? How'd you get this picture of him?"

"From a wedding. Two of his patients married each other—I'm
friends with the bride."

A flicker of alarm in Brandon's eyes. "Two patients married *each
other*? What, they passed each other in the waiting room and then fell
in love?" I explained about group and how Dr. Rosen didn't forbid out-
of-session consortium. Brandon's lips settled into a tense line. He paced
the floor and asked a dozen questions about how group worked, where
my group mates came from, how it all worked. I assured him it was like
regular therapy just more crowded. He wanted to know if I ever talked
about him, and when I nodded, he stuffed his hands in his pockets. The
temperature in the room seemed to drop several degrees.

Back at his place, the sex was even quicker and more perfunctory
than usual: he flipped me, and we were tucked in within twenty minutes. Afterward, I laid my head on his chest, but I could feel him staring
at the ceiling. I sat up.

"What's going on?" I asked.

Brandon's gaze didn't waver from the crown molding. "Please don't
talk about me in your group."

"What?" Did he know how therapy worked?

"Don't mention my name." I'd yet to tell him that my "group" was
actually *two groups* and that I went three times a week.

"They already know I'm dating you." They knew *everything*. One
Monday after group, Max and Brad googled Brandon and discovered
that his apartment was worth more than a million dollars and that his
mother was a major donor to Catholic Charities.

"Do they know my name?"

I nodded, and I felt my face burn red. I wasn't supposed to say his name?

"Please"—he turned to face me—"just leave me out of it."

I nodded—not because I agreed, but because I understood what he was asking. He took my silent nodding as assent, leaned over to kiss me on the cheek, and settled back on his pillow.

33

"How was the birthday?" Max said.

I praised the salmon and the black truffle panna cotta at Custom House.

"Did he give you a present, like looking at your face while he fucked you?" Lorne asked. I gifted Lorne my middle fingers.

"Can we move on?" I asked.

Max narrowed his eyes. "You're usually such a blabbermouth—what he said, how he kissed you, whether he was in denial about his OCD—"

"How he flipped you—" Lorne said, and I gave him two more middle fingers.

"Now you're acting like it's none of our business." Max said.

I looked at Dr. Rosen. "Can you help me?"

Dr. Rosen and I had spoken on the phone the morning after my birthday. He said he would not force me to talk about Brandon in group, but he strongly suggested that I let the group know what Brandon had asked of me. Now he gestured for me to go ahead. I took a deep breath and explained Brandon's request and my tacit agreement not to discuss him in group.

Everyone asked the same question: Why would he jeopardize my treatment? I pursed my lips. They were so dramatic. Brandon simply wanted privacy. Just because I was comfortable telling my groups what I ate and how I fucked didn't mean he was. What was the harm in trying it Brandon's way? If I returned to suicidal ideation and apple binges, I could always change course.

The group lobbed more questions at me. Grandma Maggie wanted to know how I would get help with the relationship. Lorne wanted to know if Brandon knew his nickname was "Flipper." Max's question landed hardest: Was this relationship worth the sacrifice I'd agreed to make?

Dr. Rosen sat silently as I fielded questions. I looked over at him several times. In one moment, I would see approval for my decision to be open to Brandon's request. When I looked again, I'd see the straight line of his lips and detect a wariness that made my spine stiffen. I wanted to press my palms to my ears and scream. Why did every one of my relationships have to be such a goddamned production? When would this get easier?

By the end of the session, I'd struck a bargain with the group: I would not bring in stories about Brandon, but when I needed help with the relationship, I would leave a message for Dr. Rosen, who would counsel me outside of group. Then I would disclose to the group, not the substance of the conversation with Dr. Rosen, but simply the fact he gave me feedback outside of group.

"This is never going to work," Lorne said. I saluted him with my middle fingers once again. But even as I acted confident about the bargain I'd struck, worry tugged at me. I'd spent five years learning to bare myself to Dr. Rosen and my groups, learning to "let them in." What would be the cost now of shutting them out?

"Christie," Max said in his most serious voice. "Seriously. What's this about? Why can't you talk about him in your therapy?"

I figured there was some ancient family secret he was protecting out of allegiance to his bloodline. My best guess was a family history of something he was ashamed of, like addiction, mental illness, or a pregnancy out of wedlock. I knew that his dad died when Brandon was young, and I sensed both pain and shame woven through that story, which Brandon had alluded to only once. In time, Brandon would learn from me that secrets were toxic and that disclosure was the route to freedom and intimacy.

That night over sushi, I told Brandon that I was willing to sequester him from my group as long as I could tell Dr. Rosen anything I wanted. He said he could live with that. I rose from my chair and walked around to his side of the table so I could give him a hug. He blushed at the public display. We ordered a lemon tart with two forks. The mood was celebratory.

The next few weeks in group were awkward. Before Brandon's edict, I had a place in the hot center of the action every session, talking about who I was sleeping with, who just dumped me. I tore up rags, tore out my hair, and demanded to know how group would help me. They had taught me to laugh at myself and look at my relationships from multiple angles. Now I curled into myself when sex or relationships came up, pressing my lips together to remind myself and all of them that I would not be sharing anything.

After every date with Brandon, I left data-filled messages on Dr. Rosen's voice mail ("we had dinner with his college roommate" or "I slept at his house Friday, Saturday, and Sunday!"). I wasn't committing the cardinal sin of *going it alone*. I still called Rory every night to tell her what I ate.

Brandon and I sat side by side at his custom-made oak table, eating steel-cut oatmeal on a Thursday morning. He was in his monogrammed robe, and I was dressed for work. We'd been dating over three months and had a comfortable rapport on weekday mornings. The *New York Times* was filleted on the table, and we each had a section: Business for him, front page for me.

"I have to get going," I said, folding up the paper. "Conference call with a client in an hour."

"What time is it?" he asked.

"Eight thirty."

He turned back to his paper. "My appointment's not until ten."

I assumed he was referring to a patient. When I leaned down to kiss him good-bye, he said, "I'm meeting with Dietrich—" He waited a beat, then: "my shrink."

"Your *what*?"

He laughed, grabbing his stomach right where his robe was tied around his waist.

"My shrink."

He continued to laugh. I suddenly saw Brandon not as eccentric or inexperienced and brainy, but calculating and cruel. I took a deep breath and shifted my bag from the right shoulder to the left.

"How long have you been seeing him?" He pretended to count on his fingers, still chuckling to himself. "Brandon. How long?"

"He's an analyst, actually."

"How long?"

"It's not group. I don't know how you do that—sitting around, listening to other people's problems—" He was chuckling and folding the paper with studied precision. "The group thing would never work for me." He followed me to the door. "Why are you so mad?" He talked to my back as I fumed toward the elevator.

"You're making fun of me." I stabbed the down button. Brandon followed me with a contrite look on his face.

The elevator dinged.

I stepped inside.

As the doors shut, I heard, "Nine years."

I'd thought Brandon was a good person—quirky and a little repressed, but fundamentally good. The mixture of his smile, soft-spokenness, and impeccable manners left me with the impression that he was a gentle soul who, like me, was finding his way. Despite his wealth and privilege, he treated everyone with a quiet respect. He tipped well. When I told him I loved *King Lear*, he got tickets to see a production at the Goodman. Even when I learned about his weirdo bedroom habits, they didn't seem like latent sociopathy. He was just socially awkward, like Justice Souter or Bill Gates. Or me.

But this was too much. He'd asked too much of me—to stop discussing him in therapy—without even telling me that he had a therapist. Not okay. If I could survive the other guys, the ones who made my body zing to life, I would survive him too. I fantasized about calling him later to say, "Have a nice life. Enjoy your penthouse and your money."

But I didn't think I was allowed to let go. That was literally the word in my head: *allowed.* I'd been bellowing about relationships for years. I'd invested thousands of dollars in therapy. I'd joined J-fucking-Date even though I was named after Jesus Christ. I'd recently been involved with a married man. Therefore, I wasn't *allowed* to walk away from Brandon. He was single, solvent, and mostly kind. As the cab roared down Wacker and made a whiplash-inducing turn right in front of my office, I knew I wouldn't break up with him. The urge to flee was overpowered by my need to prove I was willing to do the hard work I was sure intimate relationships required. I'd learned to hold anger, to face it head-on. I'd had too much therapy to simply cut and run. But now I faced a true dilemma: Should I tell my group what just happened?

I had four and a half hours to decide.

"Nine years?" Max said. Technically, I didn't break my promise to Brandon because I'd said, "The man I slept with last night told me he's been seeing a therapist for nine years."

"Yes, almost a decade. Asshole."

Dr. Rosen held up his hand. "Can we slow down?"

I pointed at Dr. Rosen. "He's known about you for months. You should have seen him laughing at me. And his secrets—"

"It's not a secret. He told you about it." Dr. Rosen spoke in his calming voice, which only made me angrier.

"Don't you want *more* for me?"

Dr. Rosen raised his eyebrows. "What do you mean, more?"

"He cut me off from the group and didn't tell me about his own therapy. This relationship is another dead end. My specialty."

Dr. Rosen wore his thinking face and stared at me. He rubbed his chin and started to speak a few times. Finally he offered his sage wisdom: "I don't know."

But I didn't pay him eight hundred forty dollars every month to *not* know. I paid him to use his fancy degrees to transform my life by teaching me relationship skills so I could use them in healthy relationships. I asked if it was time to break up.

"Why would you break up with him?" Dr. Rosen looked as if I'd announced a plan to steal Brandon's silver.

"He lied by omission for weeks. I'm going to end up right back where I started. For all I know, he has a wife and kids in Peoria."

"That's impossible," Dr. Rosen said.

"Why?"

"Because Peoria sucks," Lorne said.

Dr. Rosen leaned toward me theatrically as if he was going to tell me a secret. "Pssst. Confidential to Christie. This is the best relationship you've ever had."

I wanted to knock his half-bald noggin off his scrawny neck. *This was my best?* "Fuck you, Dr. Rosen."

"It's true," Patrice said. Grandma Maggie nodded along.

"Reed would never have kept his therapy a secret from me."

"He lied to you plenty," Brad said.

"Fine. But Alex—we did sunrise bike rides and had sex twenty—"

Max let out an exasperated sigh. "He didn't love you, remember? Remember the letter opener and that sack of broken dishes." Everyone jumped in with reasons Brandon was my best so far. Dr. Rosen broke into a self-satisfied grin. I quit arguing. I'd sacrificed the jolt in my belly I had with Reed and Alex so I could have a so-called real relationship with an available man. But that available man had some deep-seated issues that scared me.

"You're sexually attracted to the prospect of being abandoned," Dr. Rosen said.

I wanted to argue with him, but how could I? In every previous relationship, at least half of the attraction was the inherent dare to overcome the obstacles—the Intern's religion, Reed's wife, Alex's ambivalence about me.

"Brandon's not going anywhere," Dr. Rosen said. In the silence that followed, I swear I heard him say, "Neither are you."

Brandon showed up at my office with a *please forgive me* smile that night. "It's hard for me to get close to people," he said. All my breakup bravado slipped away. Instead of saying, "This isn't working for me," I said, "What should we do for dinner?" Later that night, when he flipped me, I detected urgency in his thrusts, and I imagined that he'd been afraid of losing me. It bothered me that we never talked about our sex life—the flipping, the weird silence we slipped into once we were being intimate. I drifted off with a single question in my mind: Could I honestly make a family with this man? Was this better than being alone?

34

I tested Brandon. Would I have done it if I'd been free to talk about him in group? Probably not. I wanted to know if he thought he could love me. If he saw a future with me. If he cared about me as much as he cared about those hospital corners on his bed. It felt easier to test him than to come right out and ask him directly.

The first test: when John, a tall, introverted corporate attorney from work, asked me out to dinner, I said yes. All I knew about John was that he liked golf, didn't own a TV, and had a long-winded way of telling a story. I said yes to John because a date with another guy was just the thing to force a *so where's this going?* conversation with Brandon.

When I told Brandon about dinner with John, he didn't even look up from the newspaper. "Sounds fun," he said. The next day, I canceled on John.

One night, Brandon and I ate prosciutto sandwiches and black olives on a ledge overlooking North Avenue Beach after the sun went down. He put his arm around me as we stared at Lake Michigan quietly lapping the sand. He kissed me in the shadow of the trees by the chess pavilion, and I imagined something deep stirring in me. Not the zing or thrill of lust. Something more substantial. Was this how functional adults fell in love? When he pulled away, he stared at me. "You may not know this, but I usually spend the winters in London," he said. He reached for my hand. "This year, I want to stay here. To see where this goes."

Later, when we had sex, he didn't flip me.

On a Monday night a few weeks later, Brandon called from the sidewalk in front of my condo. Did I want to go for a walk? Outside, Brandon was typing something on his phone with a distressed look on his face. He started walking without saying a word, and I followed and waited for him to speak. He stopped abruptly at LaSalle Street. A bus whisked by.

"I want to tell you something, but you can't tell anyone. Including Dr. Rosen. This is just between us."

I stared at the red letters that spelled out *Sports Authority*. Now *I* was being tested. Why was he asking this of me? Worse, why would I agree?

In five years, I'd never shifted my allegiance from Dr. Rosen to one of my boyfriends. Would cutting my dependence on Dr. Rosen help me move forward? Maybe it was necessary to draw a circle around something and keep Dr. Rosen out. But should I really put my mental health in the hands of a guy who gazed more lovingly at his thousand-thread-count sheets than at me? Would saying yes score my heart? Or would saying no?

Yes. In the time it took for a light to turn green, I officially jettisoned my treatment so I could sequester Brandon's deepest secret inside me and let it wedge me apart from Dr. Rosen, who was legally obligated to keep any secret I told him.

Brandon admitted: "I don't have a libido."

I burst out laughing. A real Rosen laugh where I grabbed my belly and folded forward. One, because I already knew that. Two, because who cared if Dr. Rosen knew about his libido? No one expected Brandon to fuck like Mick Jagger circa 1975. Relief coursed through me, and I felt warm and powerful. We could work through this.

He shook his head. "It might not ever change."

"What does Dietrich say?"

"That I have intimacy issues." Huh.

"Anything else?"

"Not really."

Lights from the two-story McDonald's lit the sidewalk ahead of us. The traffic on Clark Street jammed up by Portillo's drive-thru. Libido was not a deal breaker. If we stayed together and worked on this—him with Dietrich and me with, well, I had just promised to do it alone— then who knew where we could end up? I wasn't giving up over his big "revelation."

"I should want to tear your clothes off, but I don't." He touched my arm and said he'd never felt like that about anyone, ever. His eyes told the story of his self-torture. I knew that story. My whole life I lived in a story that there was something deeply broken in me. I'd searched for years to find solutions to my own troubles. I'd battled who I was sup- posed to be as a girl, a dancer, a Texan, a student, and a girlfriend, and that battle led me to the toilet for years. Like me, Brandon had always exceled at academics and then rose through the ranks in medicine. But his personal life—how he felt about himself, how he coped with the early loss of his father, and how he interacted with other people, espe- cially women—had been neglected for years. How could I turn my back on Brandon when he was finding his way through the same thicket I was? He requested emotional safety, and I loved him enough to try it his way. At least for a while.

When I showed up for group the next day, I was skittish as a squir- rel. I felt an urge to cross my legs every ten minutes. Fragments of my conversation with Brandon swam in my head, but I said nothing. In ninety minutes, I barely said a word.

Two days later, the same thing happened in Thursday group. Lorne asked what was going on with Dr. Flipper, and Patrice asked if I was okay. When I refused to give any meaningful answers, everyone left me alone until right before group ended, when Max asked if I thought the secret-keeping thing was working. Patrice said she was wondering the same thing.

Dr. Rosen started to say something and then stopped. "What?" I asked. I'd left him a message explaining that I'd agreed to keep a secret for Brandon, but I gave no details.

"Can I say something about the message you left?" Dr. Rosen said.

"Go ahead."

"I won't tell your secret, but—"

"Secret?" Lorne asked.

"Christie," Max said, drawing out both syllables in a low voice. "What are you up to?"

Dr. Rosen assured me that I didn't have to tell Brandon's secret, but he wanted to be sure I understood how secrets work. "When you agree to keep someone's secret, you hold their shame." I already knew this was Dr. Rosen's philosophy. What I didn't understand was why it was such a bad thing to help my boyfriend work through his shame? Would it kill me to hold it for him while we sorted out our relationship? Weren't relationships all about making compromises so you didn't die alone next to a tin full of baby ashes?

The group's appetite for revelation surged. They tried to guess the secret: Embezzling? Bankruptcy? Secret wife? Gambling? Check-kiting? Pedophilic impulses? The very group of strangers Brandon entrusted me to protect his secret from now suspected him of possible money laundering and child molestation. I looked at Dr. Rosen and begged him to make them shut up, but he shook his head and insisted they were helping me carry the shame.

"They're showing you the price you're paying."

I looked at the faces in the circle. The levity from moments before had vanished. How I longed to tell them what Brandon had told me. I could tell his secret, and Max would laugh and say something about the myth of the sexually insatiable male. Lorne would say something snarky about the flipping. Patrice would rub my arm and coo soothingly, and Grandma Maggie would point at her wedding band. Brad would work in a question about Brandon's financial portfolio. I loved my group more than I loved Brandon, but I couldn't take them all home with me at night. They couldn't be my date for the next law school reunion. They couldn't hold my hand at night or start a family with me. They couldn't keep me from dying alone.

Dr. Rosen asked me what I was feeling. My voice broke as I said it.

"Lonely."

35

The Monday before Thanksgiving, I sat through group quietly while everyone discussed the complications of their Thanksgiving plans: Max was in trouble with his wife for not ordering the right kind of bread crumbs for the stuffing. Patrice's daughters were in town, but spending too much time with their father. Grandma Maggie's stepson from Arizona violated her house rules by smoking pot in the basement. Dr. Rosen listened and offered feedback to each of them. Several times he looked at me, but I kept my face impassive.

Max tapped my toe with his brougham. "You're quiet."

I nodded and shrugged.

"So? What're you allowed to tell us? Can you say what your Thanksgiving plans are?"

I swiveled in my chair to check the clock on the wall behind me. Five minutes left. Could I ignore his question for the next three hundred seconds? The truth was, I didn't have plans. And while there were plenty of people—Clare, Rory, Marnie, Patrice, Lorne and Renee—who would gladly take me in, I was ashamed to have to scrounge for a seat at someone's table. I'd told my family I was staying in town with the guy I was dating because I assumed Brandon and I would be together. But Brandon had announced on Friday night that he was leaving the next day for a week-long trip with his family. There'd been no time to process all of my feelings—the shame, loneliness, hurt, and anger. They sat bundled like a homemade explosive under my rib cage.

"Where's Brandon?" Max asked.

I looked at Dr. Rosen, hoping he knew I was about to blow from the shame of facing another holiday with nowhere to go even though I had a boyfriend. It was Italy with Jeremy all over again.

"Go ahead," Dr. Rosen said. He knew.

I shook my head, resisting.

"You want to keep it all to yourself?" Dr. Rosen said as he glanced at the clock. Two hundred seconds left.

"No!" I screamed. NO! NO! NO! NO!

"No, what?" Dr. Rosen kept his eyes on mine.

No to all of this—to gagging myself for a guy who didn't want to spend the holidays with me after months of dating. No to Brandon telling me about his trip forty-eight hours before his flight. No to this loneliness. No to flipping and having no voice and sitting through group, isolated, lonely, and stuffed with secrets. Dr. Rosen was looking at me the same way he looked at me after I got back from the trip to Germany. He was still worried about me, his little failure. He should hate me. I hated myself.

"What do you want?" he asked.

"Stop being nice to me!"

"I won't stop loving you and neither will this group."

I squeezed my eyes shut. I hated all of them for what they had: in-laws they loathed, forgetful spouses, drug-addicted stepkids. Stuffing recipes. Family. Places to be, people to be with. If I opened my eyes, I would see their faces as I admitted I had nowhere to go. I collapsed onto my legs, grabbed my hair with my fists, and pulled. Hard. The sharp, physical pain brought relief. My fists were full of hair I'd pulled out of my head.

I wanted therapy to be linear. I wanted to point to measurable improvements with every year I put in. By this point, after five years and two months, I should be immune from the fury that made me pull hair out of my head with my own fists.

Patrice put her hand on my back. "Please don't hurt yourself. Come to my house."

"I don't want pity! I want my own! I want my own family! I thought you would help me, Dr. Rosen!" The windows vibrated with my screams. I was the sobbing woman with fists full of hair in group therapy again. Would I ever be anything else?

"Can you stay with the hurt?" Dr. Rosen asked.

"No!" There were zero seconds left in the session. My head pounded.

"Stay with the hurt."

I stood up and grabbed a ceramic flowerpot from the windowsill. I hoisted it over my head with both hands and brought it down on my head—right where my forehead met my hairline. White-hot silence stunned me before the rush of pain to my head. I let the pot slip through my hands. The dirt, dotted with tiny white balls, rained on the carpet along with a hunk of eucalyptus. Dr. Rosen grabbed my wrists and guided me back to my chair. I didn't struggle. I fingered the welt already forming on my head. The room fell silent, except for my ragged breathing. "Say it, Dr. Rosen: 'We'll stop there for today.' It's over."

It was two minutes after nine. Nobody moved. Without looking up, I asked, "What do I do?" I was asking all of them. We weren't meeting again for a week. A sob lodged in my chest broke through. "I thought I was getting better."

"Don't hurt yourself anymore," Patrice said. "Please."

"Christie—" Max hesitated. "Keeping Brandon's secrets isn't working."

I nodded and opened my palms, hoping that the gesture might save me from myself. Dr. Rosen suggested, as usual, that I be around other people as much as possible over the holiday weekend. Go to meetings. Sleep on Lorne and Renee's couch. Like a preschooler, I should make playdates with people from group or recovery meetings.

At five after nine, Dr. Rosen took a deep breath and clasped his hands together. We all stood up for the regular closing. I held out my right hand, now streaked with my own blood, to Patrice. Dr. Rosen grasped the other. Tears trickled down my cheeks, and my head thrummed with my pulse. After we let go, everyone moved in slow motion. I bent to pick up my bag, keeping my back to the group. I was embarrassed about my tantrum, the bloody wound on my head, my nonlinear movement in therapy.

"Can you all stick around for a few minutes?" Dr. Rosen said. Max, Brad, Patrice, Maggie, and Lorne stood silently in front of their chairs. "I want to get Christie some medicine for that cut." Dr. Rosen pulled a small first-aid kit out of his file cabinet. He squeezed some ointment onto his finger and rubbed it on my forehead. He patted my head tenderly. "You're going to be okay." He repeated it twice. "It's fortunate you have a very hard head."

I slid open the curtains to let the bright December sun fill the room. The Pacific Ocean rolled toward the shore like a frothy tongue. The sand shimmered in the midmorning light, and the Ferris wheel on the dock sparkled against a perfectly cloudless sky.

It was Christmas Day, and Brandon and I were in Santa Monica.

After the flowerpot incident, I summoned the courage to be more direct. As soon as he returned from his Thanksgiving trip, I told Brandon straight up: I'd like us to be together for the next holiday. It wasn't a test or a demand—it was simply what I needed. He suggested we go to LA for a few days. "I know a great hotel on the beach," he said. He never asked about the bruise on my forehead.

Dr. Rosen appeared agnostic about my relationship with Brandon— he never hinted that I should let go of the secrets—but all of my group mates were skeptical. They would speculate among themselves during sessions. About the secret, whether he was still flipping me during sex, how long we would last. *Is she even enjoying this relationship?*

On vacation, Brandon and I were loose and loving. He joked more and hummed while he shaved. We had more sex and sang along to songs on the radio and ate dishes with fresh avocado. We saw *The Pursuit of Happyness*, the movie where Will Smith played a destitute salesman who ends up with an unpaid internship at a prestigious brokerage firm and eventually becomes a wealthy businessman. Brandon held my hand the whole time. The movie proved that seemingly impossible transformations could happen. Under the bright California sky, the ocean as my witness, I let happiness seep in.

cir

"I'm meeting my mom for brunch at the Peninsula on Sunday." Brandon paced around my living room one January night as I scrolled through work e-mails on my BlackBerry. "Do you want to join us?"

My head jerked up. I dropped my BlackBerry on the counter. Brunch. The Peninsula. His mother. "Yes. Yes, I do want to brunch with you and your mother at the Peninsula."

It was the first week of January, and everything in Chicago was still and frozen: ice-laden trees, slick roads clogged with old snow, the frigid metal rail leading to the El train. But underneath my wool sweater, my down coat, and my fleece hat, I was humming with life. I'd never met a Mother at a five-star hotel brunch before. My heart warmed my body. I hinted to my group that things were going well. "Maybe I'm having a fancy brunch on Sunday with a friend and his mother." Subtle.

The morning of breakfast, Materfamilias's driver picked us up in her long black Mercedes. Her fur coat was so thick that it was hard to see her head underneath all the mink. She shook my hand and offered a slight smile. After we ordered, we talked about Barbara Kingsolver novels and ordered the same entrée: egg-white frittata with farm vegetables and goat cheese. She kept the mink draped on her shoulders, but her smile widened, and she laughed at my jokes.

Later, Brandon reported that his mother enjoyed my "lively company." I assumed that the next step would be meeting his younger brother, who lived in London full-time, and then he could meet my parents when they visited in the spring. In every vision of my future, I Photoshopped Brandon into the frame. Just out of the frame, I could feel my group members and Dr. Rosen cheering me on, even though no one could see them but me.

36

Brandon stopped kissing me on the lips. When I asked him about it, he said that my breath turned him off, even after I brushed, flossed, and rinsed with mouthwash. Hurt, I brushed harder, swilled more mouthwash. Still no kisses.

Then he started working longer hours. He booked meetings out of town and declined my offer to drive him to O'Hare. We still had sex about once a week, and my face always met the pillow. One hundred percent flipping. And every single time, my voice failed—it sat quivering and useless on the pillow next to my head. At work, I'd imagine rearing up and saying something—anything—the next time he flipped me. Or bringing it up in the car, over dinner, in a text. I'd promise myself I wouldn't sleep with him if I couldn't discuss how we were having sex. But in his bedroom, on his fancy white sheets, I couldn't utter a single syllable.

In group, I stayed silent too. I wanted so badly to spill my guts and ask for feedback. It had been so long since I'd filled them in that I could no longer imagine what advice they'd give me. Would they tell me to ask for kisses on the mouth? To discuss how the flipping made me feel? To accept him exactly as he was? To let go altogether? It terrified me that my connection to my group members and their voices was dissolving into memory.

Sunday mornings with Brandon still felt normal. We still slept in, read the *New York Times*, and went to the gym. For those few hours, passing the paper or high-fiving after a run on the track, I trusted that the relationship was stronger than whatever was going on with Brandon's work. Real relationships had ups and downs. I'd heard that from everyone. Our hearts might not perfectly match, but surely there were enough grooves to attach.

On a Sunday in early February, we ran into Brandon's college friend Bill in front of the gym. The three of us stood in the parking lot, bouncing to keep warm as fat chunks of snow fell from a cashmere-gray sky. I listened as Brandon and Bill talked about mutual friends, orthopedics, and the Dow Jones.

"How's Marcie doing?" Bill asked Brandon. I'd met Marcie—one of their mutual college friends—in the fall when she was in Chicago to meet buyers of her exclusive line of high-end eyeglass frames. I'd been envious of her long curly hair, her killer leather jacket, and her funky-framed glasses. Next to her New York chic, I felt like a midwestern lump of dough.

"I'll see her in two weeks," Brandon said. News to me.

"In New York?" Bill asked.

"Actually, Cancún."

If my life was a movie, I would have spit out my food or spewed a mouthful of soda all over someone's face. My boyfriend of ten months had just casually announced his upcoming vacation with another woman in another country. I must have misheard. Brandon didn't notice my shock. A few minutes later, Bill touched my shoulder, said good-bye, and walked away. Brandon walked toward the gym. I didn't move. After a few steps, he turned to ask me what was wrong.

"Are you serious?" My voice sounded low and powerful. I spoke from my deepest place.

"About what?"

"You're joking, right?" I turned and walked toward my car. I was done.

By the time I opened the driver's-side door, he'd caught up to me. In the car, I looked straight ahead as I put the key in the ignition and turned on the heat full blast. I cupped my hands over my mouth and breathed warm air into them. A random CD was in the player, and I cranked the volume all the way up. He slid into the passenger's seat and turned down the volume.

"Christie."

I turned the volume back up. He punched the power off and held my hand away.

"Why are you so upset?"

"Please get out." He didn't move. For once I wasn't hysterical, even though I knew by sundown I would be single. "Don't play dumb. It's a bad look. Also, Cancún is where Texas high schoolers go to puke for spring break—"

"She has a meeting and asked me to come—"

"Tell me what's going on or get out of my car." He sighed heavily, which made me want to punch his face. It was all such a burden for poor Brandon.

Then he said things like "You should be with someone who wants to be with you," and "You deserve better."

"If you want to break up, do it like an adult."

"I'm telling you that you deserve someone who wants to be with you."

"You're saying that's not you."

He didn't answer.

~

"You don't look so hot," Max said.

I still had on the same clothes from the day before—a sweater, now wrinkled, and shirt, now untucked. "Brandon and I broke up last night."

Gasps. All eyes wide.

"Are you hiding any sharp objects?" Lorne asked.

I held my hands up in the surrender pose. No weapons. I had no urge to hurt myself or smash my stuff. This breakup, unlike the others, carried something novel: a strong whiff of relief. Now I could stop pretending that Brandon was my soul mate and get on with my life. When I told them about Marcie and Cancún, no one seemed shocked.

"Dr. Flipper has major issues," Lorne said.

"Money can't fix crazy," Max said, shooting a look at Brad, who remained steadfastly convinced it could.

Dr. Rosen stared at me long and hard.

"I know what you're going to say," I said to Dr. Rosen. My palms were open, all fight drained out of me. Dr. Rosen opened his palms. A mirror image of mine.

"I'm listening."

"You're going to say that this group loves me. My other group loves me. That you love me. That I'm going to be okay." Of course he would insist that this—sitting in this circle in my rumpled clothes turning my thoughts and feeling over to him and the group—was enough.

"Wait—" Lorne's face lit up like a jack-o'-lantern. "Can you tell us his secret now?"

I looked at Dr. Rosen, whose face was wholly inscrutable. I wanted to tell them everything—to go back to the way it was before I picked Brandon over them, but not like this. Not to satiate Lorne's curiosity, and not while I was still so raw. I shook my head—I'd tell them later. I started to shiver uncontrollably. My teeth chattered like pennies falling on marble. My knees jolted up and down. I hugged my arms into my body and tried to sit still. It was impossible.

"What's going on?" Dr. Rosen asked.

I shook my head. No amount of effort could stop the shaking that was growing more violent.

"Give her a blanket," Patrice said. I glanced in the corner at Dr. Rosen's sad collection of 1970s fringed pillows and a ratty old brown blanket that screamed *smallpox*.

"No thanks," I said through clattering teeth.

Dr. Rosen stood up and moved his chair back. He sat on the floor with his legs hips width apart and opened his arms wide.

"Oh boy," Max murmured under his breath.

"What're you doing?" I asked.

Dr. Rosen smiled broadly. "I have an idea." He opened his arms wider. "My sense is you need to be held. You're on the edge of a new identity and a new way of thinking about yourself." He stretched his arms wider.

"He's offering to hold you," Max said.

"How?"

Max tossed me a pillow. I walked over to where Dr. Rosen was sitting and handed him the pillow, which he positioned like fig leaf. I knelt and then eased myself onto my butt. I stuck my feet out so they were perpendicular to his body. He bent his left knee so it was supporting my back and his right knee formed a bridge over my outstretched legs. I was still shivering, hands and legs jerking.

"Breathe," he said.

I inhaled until it felt like my chest would explode. I slowly let the air out, molecule by molecule. The shivering continued but with less force. A wave of shame about being in this room with another failure on my docket washed over me. I let it. I didn't try to outrun it in my mind or spook myself with thoughts about dying alone. Dr. Rosen held me. I let him.

After a few minutes, I put my head on Dr. Rosen's shoulder. He put his arm on my back and held me closer. I buried my face into his shirt like a child and began to rock back and forth. He patted my back gently. On and on I rocked. I went to some other place—some preverbal time when I was rocked to sleep as a little girl before I had language and knew the words *failure* and *loser*.

The group continued as usual: Lorne told a story about his ex-wife, and Max said something about his daughter's college application. They were all right there, but I was far away—I was a child, a toddler, a baby. When Dr. Rosen spoke, his neck vibrated against my scalp. I kept my eyes closed, but when they flickered open now and then, I saw Dr. Rosen's watch, Max's shoes, the mottled carpet. Twenty minutes went by. Then twenty more.

At some point, Dr. Rosen said, "We'll stop there for today." We were still on the ground, and now group was over. I opened my eyes and sat up. My hip flexors ached, and I wasn't sure I could get to my feet by myself. Max grabbed one hand, Brad the other. I stood up and joined the circle.

37

To help me move past Brandon, Dr. Rosen gave me two prescrip-
tions: to feel my feelings anywhere, anytime, and to commit no acts that
required safety goggles. I agreed and decided I would be single differently this time. I would embrace and explore it. I would let go of the
story that being single was a death sentence or a fatal disease. At night,
I'd sit on my couch and stare at the Chicago skyline. When my fingers
itched to throw something that would shatter, I would call Rory, Lorne,
or Patrice. I'd crawl through the loneliness to their familiar voices that
promised comfort.

One night, the stillness felt like a curse, and no one was around. I
paced from my kitchen to my bedroom, where I stood in the doorway
staring at my bed and imagined the ghosts of Jeremy, the Intern, Alex,
and Brandon hovering just above my comforter. *Good-bye*, I whispered,
and then turned to my laptop, where I scrolled through furniture stores
looking for a new bed. I liked the symbolism of a new bed for this new
chapter of my life, whatever it held. Even if it only held me.

Click. Click. Click.

Now I was the new owner of a giant sleigh bed, a heavy, curved
monstrosity in light oak set to be delivered in two weeks. A warm gust
of triumph made me raise my fist. I'd dreamed this bed for my betrothed

young cousin the night I cut up Dr. Rosen's teddy bear, but now I'd claimed it for myself.

A week later, I gave myself a challenge to say yes to any social invitation. Period. No qualifications. In some cosmic way, word must have spread about my new resolution because invitations rolled in. Did I want to see a country band I'd never heard of with a friend from work? Did I want to accompany Nan to the store to replace her dildo? How about catching a Preston Sturges black-and-white movie at an old bank that had been turned into a movie theater ten miles west of Chicago? Yes, yes, yes. *I'm in. I'm alive. I exist.*

On Presidents' Day—a below-freezing morning in February—I woke up in a fog of shame and anger. My fists curled and my head throbbed.

This is it. Here's where I skid off the ledge. Brandon and I were supposed to be in New Hampshire for a wedding—had we stayed together we'd be there now. Brandon had probably taken Marcie and they were doing whatever you do in New Hampshire in mid-February: Tapping trees for maple syrup? Ice fishing? Fucking by a fire? Before me stretched an empty day: the office was closed, and I had no plans other than group. Looming holidays had always been my undoing. I could hardly breathe. To beat back the despair, I laced up my running shoes and headed outside.

The sky was still inky gray and the temperature hovered around ten degrees. A coat of ice slicked the sidewalks, so I ran in the street. The air was so cold and thin that breathing took extra effort. By the time I reached the lakefront path, the sun was rising over the half-frozen water. With every step, my breath huffed out in a puff of white air. This run teetered on self-abuse—the world was frozen all around me—but I decided: If I saw another runner in the next two minutes, I would keep going. If not, I would get in a cab and sit in a coffee shop around the corner from Dr. Rosen's office until group started.

A half mile ahead, I spotted a lone runner in a green jacket, and I followed her like the North Star.

Left foot, right foot, breath.

Left foot, right foot, breath.

Follow the green jacket. The green lights. Go, go, go.

When the sun made its full appearance on the horizon, I stopped to stare at the blazing, defiant fist rising out of Lake Michigan. I shook my fist back at it. As I rounded the turn where Wacker meets Lake Shore Drive, I stopped, hands on my knees, and tried to slow my breath. Something was happening. My whole body felt inexplicably warm—from the inside.

Then, staring at that fist of light, I heard a voice. "You are okay." I looked over my shoulder. There was no one. Whose voice was that? Never once in my life did I think such a seditious thought: that I was okay just as I was, even without a plus-one, a lover, a prospect, a beloved, a partner, a family of my own, a gleaming future filled with people who truly knew me.

Frost was forming on my nose, so I had to keep running. My pace doubled. The speed of a quiet surrender. *I'm okay, I'm okay, I'm okay*—with each thump of my pumping heart. It was a revelation. And they kept coming. Brandon didn't own my okay-ness; neither did anyone else. Even Dr. Rosen. He couldn't make me okay. All he could do was show up for the sessions and bear witness to all the shenanigans that composed my personal life, offering to hold me when the pain threatened to break me. I was okay, or okay enough, for the first time in my entire life. Because I said so.

I wasn't going to mention these thoughts in group because I thought they were fleeting. But then it happened in the middle of group. Lorne was reading the latest court order related to his custody fight and that feeling came over me again—the sensation of okay-ness right here, right now.

"Y'all, something's happening to me."

Patrice touched my cheek with the back of her hand. "You're freezing."

"I had a revelation, but it's hard to describe. It was like someone was talking to me, but it was me. I told myself I'm okay. Like right now, this very second, I'm okay." Dr. Rosen's face curved into a bemused smile. "Even if the Big Relationship never shows up, even if I have to adopt a child as a single woman, and even if I fail at every romance from this day forward—I'm okay. I get to live and go to work. And I get to come here."

Dr. Rosen leaned toward me. "We've all loved you like that—just as you are—for a long time."

They had always loved me. So did my Tuesday group. They stuck by me even when I raged, detonated self-pity bombs, keened, snotted, fought, and monopolized the sessions with my tribulations. I wouldn't die alone. These people would surround me. They would help my family plan a proper burial. They would say nice things about me and explain Baby Jeremiah to my confused, grieving mother.

I visualized my heart and saw slashes from each group session I showed up for, from each man I dated, from each squabble with Dr. Rosen or with a group mate. Each "fuck you" to Dr. Rosen was a nick. Each screechy voice mail, each temper tantrum during a session, each dramatic hair pull and broken dish. Nicks, gashes, hash marks, chips, gouges, striations. My heart, a messy, pulpy thing, was scored from each attempt, each near miss, each lunge toward other people, those who loved me back and those who didn't.

In addition to my policy of saying yes, I started expressing exactly what I wanted from other people as a way of making amends to myself for having been voiceless with Brandon. Never again would I abandon myself in a sexual situation. But to keep that vow, I had to start speaking up in nonsexual situations. *I want to hang out this weekend*, I e-mailed my friends, instead of the safer *we should hang out*. When a coworker, Anna, responded with a plan to see a Rusted Root concert at House of Blues, I filled in the blank calendar square. My voice, expanding into the void, began to shape my life.

Then I sent another e-mail. *There's a group of us going to a concert, and I want you to come.* I hit send, and then laughed. Did I really just send an e-mail to John out of the blue? John was the guy from Skadden, the one I'd used to test Brandon. The e-mail was a voice lesson. Right before I'd hit send, I'd smiled at the line: *I want you to come.* I'd never said that to any man before.

I had no hidden marriage agenda, no secret hope that John and I might hit it off. He just popped into my head. After hitting send, I got back to work without compulsively checking my e-mail for a response. Honestly, I didn't care if he joined us or not.

After I'd canceled dinner with John back in the fall, I thought I'd never hear from him again. But six weeks before Brandon and I broke up, John offered me an extra ticket to see Puccini's *Turandot* at the Lyric Opera. When I told Brandon about it, he of course was unperturbed. At that point, I wasn't testing him—we'd already brunched at the Peninsula. But then, three days before I was supposed to go out with John, Brandon called me at work to ask if I had plans for the evening. It was a Wednesday night in the snowy dead zone of early January—my plan was to swaddle myself in flannel and curse Chicago weather patterns. He asked if I wanted to see *Turandot* that night. His parents' season tickets. Fourth row center. In our typical dysfunctional way, neither of us mentioned that I was seeing the same opera on Saturday night with John. I smiled through the conversation because Brandon was showing me that he cared about me. About us. Maybe he felt a little bit threatened by John.

Three nights later, I watched the same opera from the second balcony with John and his two friends. After the opera, John's friend Michael drove us all home, the CD player blaring "Nessun dorma." From the backseat, I listened to Michael and John discuss the best dessert places in Chicago. All night I'd been thinking John was more attractive than I remembered, but then it crossed my mind that he might be gay.

Asking a potentially gay guy to join an outing to a concert: low stakes.

I'd love to see the concert. Let me know what time.

Six hours before the concert, I went to group in a foul mood. Embracing my new life, the way I was doing it, was exhausting and expensive. Concert tickets, a new sleigh bed, sushi dinners for one—none of it was cheap. I was so tired of all of it, I was so frustrated. I yelled at Dr. Rosen. Lots of *fuck you*'s and *this doesn't work* and *why can't you admit you can't help me?* Nothing Dr. Rosen or the group members said got through to me. A single thought pounded through my mind: *I hate how fucked up I am.*

After group, I stormed back to my office, dreading the concert where I'd have to paste on a smile and be social. Six o'clock came and went. I remained at my desk. Then it was almost seven. I was supposed to meet everyone, including John, in twenty minutes. I called Rory from my office and cried as the sun melted behind the Chicago River, leaving my office dark save for the glow of my computer. No one was around other than the cleaning crew. "I'm sick of saying yes."

"Can you go for an hour? Just one." Rory stayed on the phone until I agreed.

Before leaving work, I went into the bathroom to check the damage from an hour of crying. All of my makeup had washed off. I didn't have a brush, lipstick, or anything resembling a beauty product in my possession. I finger-combed my hair into a bun that I hoped looked sexy and devil-may-care, not like proof of my ongoing existential crisis. On the walk to the bar, I found an old Burt's Bees lip gloss in my coat pocket, which felt like the universe throwing me a sparkly mauve bone. There were lingering patches of snow on the ground, but you could smell spring preparing her entrance. The closer I got to the bar where we were meeting, the better I felt. I remembered that I was okay. And I could go home to my sleigh bed after one hour.

Anna and the others were huddled around the corner of the bar. Someone slid an oversize square plate of cheese and dried fruit toward me. I stuffed creamy Roquefort and smoked Gouda into my mouth. John walked in ten minutes later. A flicker of worry: Would I have to babysit him? As he made his way to the bar, I took in his confident stride, his calm smile. He greeted the coworkers he barely knew and side-hugged me. He smelled like fresh air and clean clothes. This guy could take care of himself; I could leave whenever I wanted.

"Sorry, I'm late." He leaned toward me so I could hear over the din at the crowded bar. "I just bought a new bed and had to wait for the delivery." I told him about my new sleigh bed. There was something suggestive about the bed talk and it stirred something in me. Maybe he wasn't gay.

More friends arrived, and our group reshuffled around the bar. I kept ending up next to John.

I watched him. He didn't say much, but his eyes sparked with life as he followed the conversation. When it was time to walk over to the House of Blues for the concert, again, John and I fell into step. His style was simple: blue sweater, jeans, lace-up black dress shoes with a rounded toe. His jacket was warm, but neither trendy nor businessman serious. I didn't sense any dark secret stash of shame in him—no well of loneliness or hint of a dark side that would be tempting and maddening to try to fix.

In my purse, my phone buzzed with a text from Rory checking to see if I'd made it home. From the bathroom, I texted her back: *Still out and almost having fun!*

The House of Blues was jammed with sweaty drunk people in sweaters and boots. John bought me a bottle of water. I found myself actively hoping he wasn't gay. He reminded me of someone, but I couldn't place who. A vague connection tickled at my consciousness. I didn't mean to grill him. It was just a question. A harmless question to a guy I was enjoying talking to.

"Do you have a religion?" I have no idea why I asked that question in those words.

He raised his brows in amusement. "I didn't see that question coming." He took a swig of his water before answering. "I was raised Jewish."

Everything went still and silent: The dance floor. The bar area. The people setting up the stage. In an instant that stretched into the next day, I froze too. This guy, whom I had blown off months before, then wrote off as gay, but now wanted to kiss, reminded me of Dr. Rosen. It was the Jewish thing that pushed me into revelation. Suddenly it was so obvious. They were both introverts with sharp senses of humor and a gentle but solid masculinity they didn't have to flaunt. Simple style that didn't flash their status or the current trends. Both had an air of confidence that, at times, bled into cocksureness. And their directness—they were not men who would ignore an elephant in the room. Good God—standing before me was a young, single, age-appropriate, gainfully employed man who reminded me of my therapist.

The rest of the concert was a blur of sweating, dancing, and losing myself in the music. John stood off to the side taking in the whole scene. At two o'clock in the morning, he walked me home. The city streets, dotted with snow flurries, were empty except for a nocturnal dog walker. I felt something I'd never felt with a man before: calm, quiet, happy, and excited. I wanted to be close to him. I wanted to fall asleep listening to his voice. I wanted to hear what he thought about all the people we knew in common and where he'd traveled. I liked him, and it felt like a secret power collecting under my skin. We laughed again that we'd both bought new beds in the past forty-eight hours. It meant something—the two of us with our new beds. A good omen.

The next day John left a voice mail: "I don't know if you're single, but if you are, then we should hang out."

The excitement I felt about John was a steady pillar of hope, one that could guide me, not distract me and obliterate everything else in my life. It was quieter than the gale-force winds of the Intern and Reed. It was brighter and rose higher than the flat line of my desire for Brandon. But it wasn't overwhelming. I still had an appetite. I slept normally. I wrote briefs at work and went to 12-step meetings.

"He's Jewish, single, handsome, gainfully employed, liberal, kind, and just bought a new bed." I ticked off all John's positive traits to the group. "We're going out tomorrow night."

"And he took you to the opera," Max said. "I'm calling it now: John's the one."

"Don't do that." Too much pressure. "It's just dinner."

I sat back in my chair and matched Dr. Rosen's smile, beam for beam. "He reminds me of you."

Dr. Rosen rubbed his chest.

La Scarola looked like a dive from Grand Street, but inside it was bright, smelled of garlic frying in butter, and bustled with waiters running trays of lasagna and fried calamari through its haphazard aisles. Dozens of people loitered by the front door, but John spoke to the host, who showed us right away to a quiet table in the corner. We split the angel hair pasta with shrimp and the pasta arrabiata. The conversation drifted from the stuff we did in college, how we felt about the partners we worked for, how often we went home to visit our families. My gaze never once drifted beyond the world of our table for the next three hours. I was genuinely surprised when the houselights came on and the music stopped. "I'm sorry," our attentive waiter said, "but we must

GROUP 253

sleep." I'd just spent almost three and a half hours with John and hadn't called any of my group members from the bathroom. My heart still held the steady joy I first felt when he walked me home the other night.

At the end of the date, John squeezed my hand, which sent a jolt straight through my whole body. Back at home, I didn't send a long e-mail debriefing to my groups or call Rory about my food. I climbed into my sleigh bed and drifted off to sleep with a smile on my face.

The next day at work I focused on the brief I was working on and ended the day with a 12-step meeting. I'd had the best date of my life and was still able to function. Before going to bed, I checked my e-mail and saw one from John.

I think I just went on my last first date.

I read the line again and again and then tiptoed over to my bed, as if a sudden move might make the expansive feeling in my chest disappear. I put my head on my pillow. I'd waited all these years for a chance to build a relationship with someone without drama, doubt, alcoholism, or protective eyewear. Now that opportunity was sitting in my in-box.

I put my hands over my heart—my beautiful, scored heart.

38

I waited for John to get drunk and urinate on me, but he didn't like alcohol. He didn't play video games, have a wife, or follow strict religious rules. When he told stories about growing up in LA, I listened for signs he was enmeshed with his mother or subconsciously enraged with his father, but he didn't appear to be anything other than emotionally steady and hardworking. There seemed to be no extreme elements in his personality. He worked out, but moderately; he had a corporate law job that required long hours, but he worked only as hard as the task required; he watched his finances, but wasn't cheap. I braced to be bored by his stability, for my body to curl into itself like a winter leaf. But being with John was like eating a perfectly seared piece of Arctic char, rosemary roasted potatoes, and grilled asparagus. Filling, tasty, nourishing. My tastes had changed, and John was delicious. He made me feel like I could stretch out like a starfish, bursting with life.

"There has to be a catch," I said to Dr. Rosen and my groups. "How did I go from Brandon to this in just a few weeks?" I thought you had to wait months after a breakup to find a healthy relationship. "Is he my rebound guy?"

"Ask him about his past relationships—whether he had them and how they ended," Dr. Rosen said. "You might see evidence that he's afraid of commitment."

Lorne groaned. "Don't do that. Guys don't want to discuss 'fear of commitment.'"

"Don't worry, I'll be super casual when I bring it up."

That night, John started a fire after dinner while I huddled under a white wool blanket. He settled next to me on the couch and closed his eyes—he'd worked past midnight the night before.

I threw off the blanket and faced him. "Have you had any long-term girlfriends?"

He opened one eye and looked at me. "We're going there right now?"

"I'm wondering if you've ever . . ."

"Been serious with anyone?"

"Right. Like committed, and if so, what happened?"

"Is this a test?"

I nodded. He laughed in his good-natured way and then described his two serious girlfriends. One from right after college, and one from a few years later. He described both women as good people whom he would probably still be friends with if they weren't ex-girlfriends. The first relationship fizzled because she cheated on him, and there was too much drama. In the second, they broke up because they were too much alike.

"It wasn't exciting to be with someone who thought and acted just like I did."

While I might bring him more drama than he had a taste for, we didn't have to worry that we were too much alike. I wasn't moderate about anything, and I spun through more emotions in an hour than he did in a month.

During the second week of dating, John and I were parked in front of my building, kissing—neither of us wanting to say good-bye for the night. I was seized by the impulse to confess.

"I go to twelve-step recovery meetings for an eating disorder. I also go to group therapy three times a week. If you don't like the sound of that, then we should part ways right now. And I don't keep secrets from

my group, so don't even ask. They're going to know the size of your
penis and whether you flip me during sex." I braced for a tense negoti-
ation.

"The flip thing sounds like a good story." No signs of angst on John's
part.

"I'm serious about the group thing."

He shrugged. "Talk about whatever you need to in therapy."

"And I don't suck dirty dick, like ever."

"Duly noted." He smiled like *what else you got?*

I put my hand on his cheek. Where did he come from?

We kissed again, but then John pulled away and looked down at his
hands. His expression was serious.

"What is it?" I asked.

"I already knew about your therapy and your twelve-step meetings."

"What? How?"

"I read some of your essays. The ones you saved on the Skadden
system."

Oh my God, I'd forgotten about those. Sometimes, while waiting—
occasionally for hours—for partners to get back to me with edits on a
brief, I'd write essays, scraps of stories. Stuff about growing up in Texas,
going to Catholic school, and anecdotes about group therapy. I saved
the writing under my name on the firm system with deceiving titles like
"Tate Billing Information" or "Tate Litigation File." I thought they were
well-hidden Easter eggs.

"You found those?"

He blushed. "I wanted to know more about you."

"By reading 'Tate Billing Info'?"

"It worked."

We went back to kissing. But then I stopped us again. My conscience
ached like a sore muscle.

"I saw *Turandot* with my ex three nights before I saw it with you."

Surprise spread across his face. "But you acted like you didn't know
anything about it." Before the opera, John invited me over to his house
to present a PowerPoint he'd prepared about Puccini's life and the plot
of *Turandot*. He'd added a cartoon video of Puccini's car accident right

before he completed *Madama Butterfly*. I'd been utterly enchanted by the work he'd put into educating me on the opera so I could enjoy it as much as he did. I wasn't about to raise my hand and tell him I'd just seen it from the fourth row.

"I didn't want to hurt your feelings."

"It takes a lot to rattle me."

"Have I?"

"Almost."

After three weeks of dating, I got up to leave John's place one night well past midnight. He told me I was welcome to stay, but I wasn't quite ready. It had only been six weeks since I had slept in Brandon's bed.

"We don't have to have sex," he said.

"I'm just not ready."

He walked me out to my car and held me underneath the navy sky.

"I'm not up for having sex with someone who isn't in love with me. I'm not interested in that." My beautiful clear voice.

"I do love you, you know," he whispered in my ear.

"What?"

He looked me in the eye and said it again.

"How do you know?"

"I can feel it."

"We've only been dating three weeks."

"So I've known for three-ish weeks."

We eventually progressed to spending the night at each other's house and stayed up talking and doing "everything but" until morning's first light bled through the curtains. Whenever we got to the part of the night where either we were or weren't going to have sex, I pulled away. "I'm still not ready," I would say, unable to explain why. He was infinitely more suitable for me than any of the men I'd ever slept with or groped in a suburban mall parking lot, but I couldn't move forward sexually.

"Why are you torturing him and yourself?" Max said. "I feel so sorry for him."

"What are you afraid of?" Everyone wanted to know, including me.

Dr. Rosen pointed out this was the healthy relationship I'd been waiting to find myself in. I was using my voice, setting boundaries, and staying in my body when I was with him. He thought I was scared of sex because it would bring me and John even closer. For once, I fully agreed with him, but I still wanted to know: "Why can't I just have sex with him already?"

"*Mamaleh*, you will when you're ready."

And then one spring night, I no longer needed to keep John at a distance. Our bodies fit together. The physical part of our relationship was an extension of all the things we were already doing—talking, eating, laughing, kissing, touching, and sleeping. For the first time, I understood that sex was a big deal for me not because it involved private parts or because the nuns told me it was one of God's major preoccupations or because my mother told me I'd wind up in hell if I did it before marriage. It was a big deal because with sex, I gave John my body in a singular way, and he gave me his. Together, we shared the pleasure of that exchange. And even though he was kind, committed, and loving, it was super hot.

39

When my thirty-fourth birthday rolled around, John and I had been dating for only four months. I hoped for a dinner that required a reservation and some heartfelt words on card stock, signed *Love, John*. Dr. Rosen hinted I might get an engagement ring, but I cut him off. The last thing I needed was the weight of expectations on my four-month-old relationship. The joke was on Dr. Rosen when John gave me a Sonicare electric toothbrush and a homemade wooden picture frame. Lovely, but not gemstones that announced "lifetime commitment."

Several months after my birthday John and I took a two-week trip to India with his high school friends. Nothing like a trip to a third-world country where you can't always control your bowels to solidify a relationship. John held my hand during Diwali fireworks, helped me find tampons in a Goa supermarket, and carried the souvenirs for all my group members in his carry-on, including a brass Hindu symbol that represented luck and fortune, which happened to look like a backward swastika. That was for Dr. Rosen.

In December, John and I spent our first Christmas-Hanukkah in Los Angeles with his family. During his family's epic thirty-person Hanukkah gift exchange, his mother gave me a Victoria's Secret gift certificate, and his grandmother gifted me a white marble box with intricate tile from her long-ago trip to India. John's cousins taught me how to make latkes, and his brother showed me old family pictures of their Russian forebears—stern men with long beards and black hats and women in black dresses with high collars. When John set the camera on the tripod for a group photo, I stood next to him, and he put his arm around me. I folded into the welcoming arms of his family.

We stole away from the official celebration one afternoon for a quiet walk on the beach in Orange County. The brilliant California sunshine on the hot white sand almost hurt my eyes—it was the same ocean that Brandon and I had walked along just a year before, the same water that stole David's life. It was comforting to see it still churning toward the shore. I rolled up my jeans and slipped off my boots so I could feel the sand, warm and gritty between my toes. We stopped at a rocky ledge to watch the ocean. There, underneath a surreal blue sky, I scanned the beach for celebrities and their dogs. John was quiet, until we headed back to the car.

"I want to move forward. With you." He said words I'd never heard a man say to me: *engaged* and *certain* and *together* and *future*. I held my hand over my galloping heart.

un

On a Monday morning in March, I walked into group a few minutes late and sat in the empty seat to the right of Dr. Rosen. I sat quietly, not overly gesticulating or calling attention to my left hand.

"I'm sorry, I'm almost blinded by the ring on Christie's finger," Dr. Rosen said when he'd waited long enough for me to speak up. Laughing, I jumped out of my chair and spun around the room sticking my hand in everyone's face.

"Not too big, not too small," Max said approvingly.

Patrice held my hand up to the window to see it in the sunlight.

Grandma Maggie beamed. "I knew it, kiddo."

I'd never cared about jewels, but this ring was so much more than its stones. John and I designed it together. There was a larger stone in the middle, flanked by three smaller ones on each side. The big stone represented me and John; the three smaller stones on either side were

Dr. Rosen and my groups. Those three smaller stones were the foundation of my life. They'd introduced me to myself, my appetites, my rage, my terror, my pleasure, my voice. They made me a real person. There was no "John and me" without them. Every single day of my marriage would be a tribute to the work I'd done in group, and I could not separate my romantic relationship from the hours and hours I'd spent in group, growing up and growing into my life.

"I *cannot* believe that John puts up with you," Lorne said, winking at me. "Good job finding a man who doesn't have to flip you every night."

Dr. Rosen had oohed and aahed over my ring and offered a genuine mazel tov that landed on my heart like a blessing. I could tolerate this mazel tov in a way I could not take in the mazel tov he offered for my class rank seven years earlier during my first appointment. Now I knew that Dr. Rosen loved me and that I deserved his praise and whatever "mazel" was. But I longed for more. An explicit blessing. Not permission, but consecration. I looked at him and said, "I want something more from you."

"What did you have in mind?"

"Not exactly sure."

"Talk about it in your groups and see if you can get clarity."

Dr. Rosen answered the door to his tidy white town home in jeans and brown sandals that exposed his toes. Were you supposed to see your therapist's bare feet? I thought not, so I directed my attention to his bright kitchen. But then I felt my head practically crack open with pain—a ferocious stress headache from having dinner with my fiancé at my therapist's house. I'd felt vaguely nauseated as John drove us out to Dr. Rosen's quiet suburban neighborhood, but now all I wanted was a cold compress and extra-strength Motrin. I squeezed John's hand and tried to steady my nerves. *It's perfectly natural to have dinner at your therapist's house.* I handed Dr. Rosen's wife a bouquet of light pink peonies that she smelled and said were her favorite.

"Can I use your bathroom?" I asked, not because I had to go, but because I wasn't ready to make small talk over apps with the man I planned to marry and the man who'd witnessed multiple temper tantrums and pinworm-inspired monologues. I sat on the toilet and massaged my temples, willing the pain around my skull to dissolve. I counted the number of toilet paper squares I used (six) and the pumps of liquid soap (three). The temptation to swing open the medicine cabinet made my fingers itch, but the prospect of confessing my snooping next week in group held me back.

As I cruised through the living room on the way back to the kitchen, I wanted to look at the books on the shelves, the pictures in frames, the tchotchkes on the coffee table, but I was too scared. You're not supposed to surveil your therapist's personal possessions. Plus, what if I saw embarrassing things, like Nicholas Sparks novels or pictures of Dr. Rosen and his wife posed with Goofy on a Disney cruise?

Mercifully, his wife invited us to sit down. She spoke with a thick Russian accent and smiled warmly. Between John's and my plates was a wrapped present. "Open it," Dr. Rosen said, smiling. John pulled off the paper and held up a white tile with colorful painted flowers and script that read *Shalom Y'all.* They'd found it on their recent trip to Israel and loved that it celebrated both of our heritages: Texan and Jewish. I couldn't even summon words—all I could do was stare at the script, absorbing the fact that when Dr. Rosen traveled across the globe, he still continued to hold me in his mind. Me and John.

Dr. Rosen lit two candles and said a prayer in Hebrew. Then, as we'd discussed in group, he put his hands on my head and recited the Hebrew blessing over a child. The press of his hand on my head stopped the pulse from my headache, but when he moved on to John, the pain roared back. As Dr. Rosen said the prayer over John's head, tears sprung to John's eyes, making me tear up as well.

Dr. Rosen's wife apologized that parsnips were not in season. I looked at Dr. Rosen, who smiled at me. A week before, Dr. Rosen had asked me in group what my favorite foods were and I answered by starting to cry. Foods were coming to mind, but the words were stuck as pictures in my head.

I remembered when I first got into recovery for bulimia and latched on to dozens of rules so I wouldn't fall back into bingeing and purging. I didn't eat sugar, flour, wheat, corn, bananas, honey, or potatoes. I didn't eat between meals or after nine at night. I never went back for seconds of anything and never ate standing up. Shortly after I got into recovery, my parents and I drove from Dallas to Baton Rouge for my brother's college graduation, and my dad stopped for lunch at Lea's Lunchroom in Lecompte, Louisiana—my parents' favorite pie shop. The only thing on the menu was honey-cured ham sandwiches and four kinds of pie. I asked the waitress if they could take the shredded iceberg lettuce from the ham sandwiches and make me a salad. Not possible, she said. Starving, I ordered two ham sandwiches, ate the lettuce with salt and pepper, leaving the ham and bread behind. My plate looked like a crime scene. I watched as my parents ate their ham sandwiches and split two pieces of pie, one chocolate and one lemon. I didn't know how to ask them to take me somewhere to get food I could eat. I didn't know how to tell them my belief that adhering to my food rules kept me alive. All I knew how to do was sit in my chair and smile stupidly as my empty stomach growled and begged me to take up a fork and load it with pie.

In group, Dr. Rosen employed eating metaphors with me from day one. But this dinner at his house wasn't a metaphor: it was Dr. Rosen and his wife feeding and blessing me and John. He wanted to feed me exactly what I wanted. My favorites. In group, Rory had told me to close my eyes and shout out my favorite foods. I squeezed my eyes shut and ground my fists into my eye sockets as I whispered, "Parsnips. Mango. Salmon. Potatoes."

Dr. Rosen's wife served a brilliant-orange carrot soup with a dollop of melting cream in the center. I swirled my spoon around, and the cream dissolved. It tasted rich and earthy. Dr. Rosen listed all the ingredients in each dish, even though I had let go of most of my food rules by then. The salmon was perfectly pink, and the potatoes had a touch of rosemary and salt. As they carried empty plates to the kitchen after we ate, Dr. Rosen and his wife spoke softly in another language that sounded half Russian and half Hebrew.

I don't remember uttering a single word the whole night, though I must have spoken. I was all sensation: My throbbing headache. The flavors on my tongue. John's hand on my leg. The feeling of wanting to cry for no reason other than that the night was so lovely, the food so delicious, the occasion so improbable. I remember that it seemed like Dr. Rosen's wife was in charge as she told him where to find the silver spoons for the tea and the knife for the cheese. What a thrill to watch someone boss Dr. Rosen around! I couldn't wait to tell Max.

For dessert, Dr. Rosen placed a wooden cutting board with several hard cheeses, grapes, and dried cherries in the middle of the table. I popped a grape into my mouth. Its slick sweetness beat my headache back by an inch. The last bars of daylight streamed through the window making shadows on the table. Dr. Rosen said sometimes they saw deer in their wooded backyard. My body ached with fullness. I'd taken in so much; I was ready to go home.

On the way back to Chicago from the suburbs, I reclined the seat and cranked up the a/c, aiming the vents at my face. I cried all twenty-one miles back to the city. John held my hand.

"Is this happening?" I cried. John held my hand tighter.

"Where did you come from?" I cried some more.

Mile after mile, I cried. Feeling pouring out of me. "I can't believe any of this is happening. How did I get here?"

John held my hand as the city skyline sparkled beyond the windshield.

"I feel afraid," I said as we pulled up to my place.

"Of what?" John asked.

"You." He raised his eyebrows and smiled. "We're stuck with each other now. I feel a strange loneliness. I'm not sure where I am." John squeezed my hand as if he understood.

I thought once you got engaged, you were filled with certainty and bliss about the person you were marrying and the life you were building. I thought that finding the man I would marry would cure my deep loneliness. But I didn't feel pure bliss. I felt whispers of fear and loneliness. I was still me.

"All these years, I've been the single-est person everywhere I went—group, law school, Texas friends, family. Christie—unattached, single, no-plus-one Christie. I hated that role, but now that it's no longer mine,

I feel like I'm free falling. Like I'm losing something. It feels like I'm not special anymore, now that I'm not crying in all corners of Chicago about my shitty love life and unpopulated weekends. Now I'm just like everybody else. Does that make any sense?" Where did the apples go? The worms? The purple towel that I'd ripped the threads out of? Who was I now and where did the old me go?

John brushed my cheek. "You still cry more than most people. That probably won't ever change."

40

Barack Obama was hours from winning the title of Forty-Fourth
President of the United States. All of Chicago went bonkers—jubilant
people were streaming from their offices downtown to Grant Park, waiting for Obama to take the podium as the president-elect. Raj popped
his head into my office around four and offered me an extra ticket to
the rally. I turned him down, even though John and I campaigned for
Obama in Wisconsin and were dizzy with joy at his victory. Physically, I
didn't feel like myself and hadn't for a few days. That afternoon, I'd had
to mute a conference call because I was about to go off on an opposing
attorney who insisted our client was liable for fraud. I'd punched my
desk so hard that my stapler clattered to the edge. An hour after the call
I was so walloped by fatigue that I put my head down on my desk and
slept for twenty minutes. I suspected flu and was convinced if I went
down to Grant Park in the cold November air, I'd end up hospitalized
with mono.

That night, John and I ordered takeout and waited for Obama's
speech. The TV cameras panned to the crowd assembled five miles from
our house, and I regretted not being there. John saw friends he knew
from law school standing five feet from Oprah. "That could be us!"
What was wrong with me? It was the most historic night of my lifetime,

and I'd opted to sit on the couch, braless, shoveling a Cobb salad in my mouth with my feet propped up on two Crate & Barrel boxes—early wedding presents from John's aunt.

McCain's face filled the screen to concede the election. He was flanked by a perfectly coifed Cindy McCain in a yellow suit and flawless red lipstick. McCain wasn't my candidate, but when he put his hand over his heart and bid his supporters farewell, sobs from way down deep pressed forward, racking my whole body. Into our new red chenille blanket, I cried for poor John McCain as if he were my most beloved friend. I could not stop crying, no matter how much I tried to convince myself that McCain would one day know happiness again.

The next thing I remember is John shaking my shoulder. "You're going to want to see this," he said, turning up the volume. I lifted my head—where the hell was I? "You were crying about McCain, and then you fell asleep." We stared in awe as Obama spoke. Again, tears streamed down my face. This time: pure joy.

The next night, I fell asleep right after dinner again, only to find myself staring at the bedroom ceiling at two in the morning. John stirred and opened his eyes. I told him I had to pee. "While I'm there, I'm taking a pregnancy test." He laughed and wished me luck as if I was joking.

I squatted down and rifled under the sink for the purple box with the generic drugstore pregnancy test. We'd had unprotected sex on the fourteenth day of my cycle, so it was possible. But so many women I knew were struggling to conceive while on Clomid that I didn't think there was any chance I was harboring a fetus. My ob-gyn warned it might take a while because I was over thirty-five. I peed on the stick and then crawled back in bed.

"So there's a bun in the oven?" John asked in a good-natured but mocking tone.

"Probably twins. We'll need a bigger place."

After three minutes, I elbowed him. "Go check." I wasn't getting out of the warm cocoon of sheets and comforter to confirm a negative pregnancy test. I flipped my pillow and laid my cheek on the cool side. I heard John pee, and then: silence. He stepped into the doorway, his head backlit by the bathroom light, his face obscured by the shadow.

"I think there may be two lines."

"Ha-ha." I wasn't even positive my period was late—I'd lost track because October had been busy with out-of-town settlement negotiations on a new case with Jack. I snuggled deeper under the covers and waited for John to join me, but he stood in the doorway, staring at the pee stick. He was serious. I threw off the covers and lunged at the stick.

Two lines, bright as peppermint stripes, showed through the little circle.

I screamed and danced with joy. A baby! A baby! A baby!

Lucky peppermint stripes. Lucky us.

41

You've been to a wedding. You've seen pearl-colored dresses, black ties, bridesmaids in jewel tones. You've heard string quartets and heart-felt vows. You know the drill: a procession with music, readings, vows, and a pronouncement on behalf of the state.

Here's what I want you to see from our wedding:

See me and my six bridesmaids, four of whom were Rosen-patients, running through Chicago's Millennium Park so the photographer could snap pictures of us in front of "The Bean" before the sun faded across the western sky. See us dashing across the lobby of an office building with cool hexagonal mirrors on the ceiling, laughing still, and filling in the bewildered photographer: "We are going to see my therapist!" See me, six weeks pregnant in white strappy heels and a dress tight across the bodice from all the first-trimester carb loading I'd been doing.

See Dr. Rosen in his smart gray suit and shiny black shoes opening the door to a chorus of seven screaming women treating him like a rock star we'd been escorted backstage to meet. See Dr. Rosen smile and usher us back to the room I knew better than any other space on the planet with its fritzy light in the back corner, the coffee stain by the window, the askew mini-blinds. See that he'd arranged the chairs in a circle—just like for a session—except it was a Saturday night, ninety minutes before my wedding. See him take a seat in his usual chair and ask us where we'd been. See him ask me if I was ready. *Yes, I'm ready.* See me close my eyes and take in a deep breath as first-trimester nausea roils through my body. Hear me exclaim with a twinge of panic: *I forgot my crackers!* See Dr. Rosen disappear through the door and return with a red plastic cup full of milk and cereal. Muesli. Hear me say, *Is this what you eat before morning sessions? You seem more like a toast guy.*

See me and John standing together in a side room before the ceremony. See us embrace and hold the moment between us. See how much love my scored heart holds within its swollen boundaries. See me and John walk together down the aisle—there is no giving away, only choosing, accepting, showing up. Hear us promise to build a home and life together with the support of the people who love us. Hear us speak our family into being.

See us vowing before our witnesses. See me resting my palm against my belly, where our baby's heartbeat clocked in at one hundred and seventy-five beats per minute.

You've also been to wedding receptions. You know all about centerpieces, chair covers, and calligraphied place cards. You've tasted appetizers with mushrooms and Brie, dry champagne, and buttercream frosting. You've heard toasts to the new couple and the opening bars of "Brown Eyed Girl."

Here's what I want you to see at our wedding reception:

See table five, where Dr. Rosen and his wife sit flanked by Max, Lorne, Patrice, and their spouses. See table six ringed with the women from my Tuesday-afternoon group. See table seven, where Rory, Marty, and Carlos pass pasta and fish to one another. See each of them embrace me throughout the night, wishing me well, and holding me tight—just as they always have.

From the miracle department, please see Reed and his wife, Miranda, weaving through the crowd toward me after the second course. *Congratulations,* they say. See me hug them both, dumbfounded at what the human heart can do, how it can surprise and delight, how it can rejoin, regenerate, forgive, and connect across oceans of hurt, canyons of loneliness. *Thank you for coming. It means so much to me.*

Most weddings are a blending of families like my Texas Catholic clan and John's Jewish family from the West Coast. Every dance floor at every wedding is a blur of bodies, some that belong to one side and some that belong to the other. As John's family members scooped me into a chair and lifted me above their heads for the hora, I saw our reception from above. My parents and siblings gamely clapping along on one side, absorbing a custom that didn't belong to them. Dr. Rosen and his wife amid a throng of his patients, linked arm in arm as they circled us, singing the words they knew by heart. John's brother, parents, and cousins waving their napkins in the air. As "Hava Nagila" played on, the chaotic, joyous scene below me became a collage of loving faces and arms holding me and John up.

In the weeks leading up to my wedding, I asked Dr. Rosen if we could share a dance during the wedding. I wanted to honor the work I'd done with him in group that made my life with John and our baby possible.

"I don't want to step on your father's toes."

"Don't worry, of course my father will get his own dance. Ours can be later. A traditional, mid-reception, therapist-patient waltz."

"Talk about it in your groups."

The more I discussed it, the more I wanted to dance with Dr. Rosen. I wanted to commemorate that I'd showed up for hundreds of therapy sessions and was no longer the isolated young woman with nothing but billable hours in her future. After all the crying, gnashing, rending, and screaming, it was now time to dance.

I wanted to dance.

Right after John and I got engaged, Clare asked me if I would have eventually ended up with John even if I hadn't gone to group all these years. I said, *I doubt it,* but what I really mean to say was *No fucking way.*

Hear the opening bars of the iconic song from *Fiddler on the Roof*— the one the father sings about the swift passage of time and the blossoming of seedlings to sunflowers. See me leading Dr. Rosen to the dance floor from his seat next to his wife. See him twirl me left and then right, and then no more twirling because of the surging, first-trimester nausea.

See the dance floor ringed with my group mates, past and present, who knew exactly what this meant to me and perhaps to Dr. Rosen. When the music ends, hear him give me one more mazel tov. Hear me say, *Thank you for everything. I'll see you Monday.*

Because this story doesn't end with a wedding.

The next day, John and I hugged our families good-bye and sent them to the airport. Snow flurries swirled all afternoon, and the late-November sun didn't even pretend to shine. At home, John and I sank into bed, surrounded by presents and leftover cake. John's heavy eyes succumbed to sleep, but I couldn't settle. I picked buttercream roses off the cake and popped them into my mouth. I called Rory and then Patrice.

"Now what?" I asked them. "I feel weird, and yes, I know weird's not a feeling." I loved John and was happy to be married, but I also felt lonely and exhausted and anxious. Weird. Kind of like I wanted to bawl into my leftover wedding cake.

They both told me what I knew they would. "Bring it to group."

Everyone was in their usual seats. My body still trembled with excess adrenaline from the weekend filled with family, friends, joy, and cake. I was still in shock that I was pregnant and dizzy in love with our little fetus.

Max opened the session by asking why the DJ made such a production out of my dance with Dr. Rosen. Patrice asked if my sister enjoyed the jaunt to Dr. Rosen's office before the ceremony. Brad and Lorne teased Dr. Rosen about the cut of his suit, and Grandma Maggie praised Dr. Rosen's wife's merlot-colored gown.

And then, just like that, we moved on. Lorne reported on the latest with his ex-wife and the kids, and we debated whether Max should follow up on a lead for a new job. Dr. Rosen transferred his gaze from member to member around the circle while the rest of us did our best to offer our whole selves to one another. I felt my heart beating—its scored surface protecting the chambers, the ventricles, the atria, the valves, the aorta. I held my hands close to my chest and listened to the music of my group.

POSTSCRIPT

Ten Years Later

Before I sneak downstairs, I kiss my daughter's head. She stirs and whispers, "Bye, Mama," without opening her eyes. "See you to-night." Her little brother in the room next door continues to sleep deeply even as I tussle his hair and kiss his cheek. They don't expect to see me on Monday mornings. They know I have an early appointment with Dr. Rosen. They're old enough to be curious. "Why do you go there?" "What do you do?" "Do you ever wish you could have Dr. Rosen all to yourself?" I don't know what they picture when I tell them I sit in a circle with Dr. Rosen and my group mates—people they've known all their lives—and we talk and listen, and sometimes cry and yell. And no, I would never trade individual sessions for my group. Sometimes, on Monday nights at dinner, my kids will ask about Patrice or Max. I laugh to think of my children holding the images of my group mates in their heads just like I do.

In the kitchen, I throw my lunch in a bag and then race out the door to catch the six fifty-five train. As the train lumbers downtown, I think about what issues I'll discuss in group. I should probably tell them about the spat John and I have had the past two times he'd returned home from a business trip. As he wheels his suitcase into the foyer, the kids besiege him with hugs and requests to show him their art projects, their spelling tests, their new dance moves. He slips out of his coat and gives them his full attention. Oohing and aahing. Beaming the full bright light of his love on them. From the kitchen, where I'm washing dinner dishes or prepping lunches for the next day, I love hearing them reconnect. I know those hearts; they belong to me and to each other. The fight comes later, after John has read to them and checked their math homework, and they are fast asleep. It happens when we collapse into bed, and I launch into a story about a grievance at work or a perceived slight from a friend. John strains to keep his eyes open, but he's been up since five, attended various meetings, traveled across the country, and then parented through the bedtime gauntlet. His drawn face tells the story of the miles he's traveled. Intellectually, I understand how weary his bones must feel, how sleep drags him by the ankles into sweet respite. But I also want him to listen to me. I want him to save some of his bright-light energy for me. Dr. Rosen will ask me how this makes me feel, and I'll say, "Lonely for John and ashamed that I'm jealous of my kids." Max will smirk and say, "This is the life you wanted, remember?" Then the group will offer suggestions on how John and I can reconnect when he comes home without ignoring his physical limitations or the kids' needs. Someone will probably suggest that John and I schedule a sex date for the day after he returns.

I can also let the group know about the conversation I had with my supervisor at work on Friday. I surprised myself by saying, "I work really hard and do a good job. I don't need more money or a corner office, but I would like a thank-you." I'd filed a record number of briefs in the past thirty days and wanted acknowledgment. Brad will give me a thumbs-up, and then push me to ask for that corner office. And the raise. Patrice will high-five me for asking for what I want. At work, I struggle to set boundaries and say no when asked to take on thankless tasks with no discernible upside, but at least I spoke up to ask for acknowledgment.

The group will also get a kick out of the meltdown that happened at my house over the weekend. My kids had a piano recital, an activity they ranked behind teeth cleaning and flu shots. When it was time to head to the recital hall, the kids protested by putting on raggedy shorts and pajama tops. John and I explained that the event called for slightly more formal clothing, emphasizing that we should respect the other students, the teacher, and all the work they'd done to prepare. "Think of dozens of times you practiced 'When the Saints Go Marching In.'" They reacted by stomping and slamming doors. They refused to walk down the street next to us. I was sure I'd get a handwritten letter, like the one I got when I wouldn't let them buy Skittles in bulk: *Dear Mom, Thank you for ruining our lives*, but there was no time to take pen to paper. I'll report to group that I managed to celebrate my kids' intense emotions, instead of insisting they stuff them back into their little bodies. I'd actually channeled Dr. Rosen for a good twenty minutes before I lost my composure and hissed at them to get it together through gritted teeth. We arrived at the recital late, each of us fuming.

It still scares me, other people's anger, but I know it's part of intimacy. I know it's okay to let it be. I breathe through it the best I can.

All my basest impulses still live inside me, lying in wait. Impulses to keep my ever-wacky relationship to food a secret. Impulses to demonize John for making the reasonable decision to put his energy into parenting after a few days away. Impulses to dive into unremitting despair instead of taking a breath and feeling whatever emotion is trying to surface. Impulses to suck up frustration and invisibility at work instead of having a measured conversation about what I'm thinking and feeling, what I want and need. Impulses to do anything to keep other people from feeling angry at me. I still need help overriding those impulses. I need help figuring out what two-syllable word best describes my feelings. Telling the truth of my desire, even when I'm ashamed of it. Tolerating other people's intense feelings. Tolerating my own.

Sometimes I run into former Rosen-patients. "You're *still* with Dr. R?" they ask. "Yep, I'm one of the lifers," I say with an impulse to explain that it's not that I'm hopelessly fucked up or stuck in crisis mode. I have the attachments I craved when I first crawled into Dr. Rosen's office; now I need help deepening them. And I've dreamed new dreams. A more creative life. An intimate relationship with my two children as they pass through middle school, high school, and beyond. A graceful path through the impending corporeal chaos of menopause and the stress of caring for aging parents who live three states away. Dr. R and the group guided me through my early adulthood issues. Why not the middle-aged stuff? Don't I still deserve support, witnesses, and a place to bring my confusion and inner turmoil, even if I no longer pull out my own hair or drive around hoping for a bullet to the brain? And what about my love and attachment to Dr. R and my group mates? Why would I cut that off just because our pull-yourself-up-by-your-bootstraps culture says therapy should get you up and out in thirty sessions or less? Dr. R offers us tenure if we want it. I do.

When the train pulls into the station, I walk two blocks west to Dr. Rosen's office. Up ahead, I see the new guy who joined our group a year ago. He's in his midthirties, a brilliant physician who speaks six languages, and is sick and tired of being alone. He has no close friends in Chicago to hang out with on the weekends, and his specialty is falling for women who ghost him after the second date. In group, he despairs that nothing will change his lifelong patterns. He fears he will never have a family of his own, that it's too late for him. I borrow the moves of my group mates, who consoled me for so many years. I pat his arm when he shares the pain about yet another woman who won't return his texts. I say soothing things when he reports doing something he didn't want to do to win the affection of a woman who isn't available. *I've been there. I did that too. Have you heard about the dirty dick I sucked?* I answer his calls on Sunday afternoons or Tuesday nights when he buckles under the weight of his loneliness. I tell him I have no doubt he is in the process of transforming his life. In group, when Dr. Rosen assures him that coming to group and sharing himself is enough, he looks at me, and I nod my head.

"I promise. It's enough."

ACKNOWLEDGMENTS

When I was writing this book (and the four others that live in my computer), I thought of "the publishing industry" as a group of terribly fancy New Yorkers with Anna Wintour bangs and clothes from Barneys or boutiques I'd never heard of and could not pronounce. I never pictured the faces or bodies or hearts of the people I hoped would one day open the gates for me. Now I will never picture publishing without thinking of the hearts and minds that have touched this book and changed my life forever. Their minds are sharp, their hearts generous. And they poured them both into this book during a harrowing, uncertain time for the entire planet. They also have names. Thank you to Lauren Wein for the thoughtful editing and all the ways you saved me from some very poor choices, particularly in the sex scenes. Thank you to Amy Guay, Meredith Vilarello, Jordan Rodman, Felice Javit, Morgan Hoit, and Marty Karlow for bringing your hard work and expertise to the book.

Thank you to Amy Williams, who always makes me laugh while also wearing so many hats: agent, big sister, mother, friend, fellow traveler. I'm so blessed to have you on my team.

This book would not exist without the oceans of love and support from Lidia Yuknavitch and her Corporeal Writing program. The writers whose understanding of story and body changed the course of this book and my life include these midwives: Mary Mandeville, Tanya Friedman, Lois Melina Ruskai, Anne Gudger, Jane Gregorie, Anne Falkowski, Emily Falkowski, Kristin Costello, Helena Rho, and Amanda Niehaus. Special heart shout-out to Zinn Adeline, who gently contributed her careful reads and incisive comments, especially the one about how my jokes were distracting from the real story.

Thank you to Tin House for pairing me with the generous and talented Jeannie Vanasco in Winter 2019. And special thanks to my workshop mates: Wayne Scott, Sasha Watson, Melissa Duclos, and Kristine Langley Mahler.

To my favorite soul sister who inspires me every single day as a writer, mother, daughter, wife, podcast creator, lawyer, and all-around baller: Carinn Jade.

Way back in the day, I started writing online with a group of madcapped writers who taught me about voice, hooks, arcs, and aspects of the craft that I felt in my bones but had been too scared to practice. Thanks to the Yeah Write crew: Erica Hoskins Mullinex, William Dameron, Mary Laura Philpot, and Flood. Thanks to my early writing groups who had to slog through some pretty tortured drafts: Sara Lind, Samantha Hoffman, and Mary Nelligan.

Gratitude is not a debt, but I can't help but feel like I owe so much to the writers and friends who read drafts of this book, some of them more than once: Krista Booth, Amy Liszt, Andrew Neltner. You're saints, you really are. Joyce Polance read multiple drafts and was always game for a conversation about the pain and ecstasy of trying to get a story right. This book wouldn't exist without her generosity, support, and wisdom. Frank Polance is pretty swell too.

I'm grateful to all the babysitters we had through the years whose labor made it possible for me to write this book. Thank you to Sabrina, Tiffani, Christian, Brittney, Molly, Hailey, Mattie, Kathi, Dayane, and Gesa.

Thank you to Irvin Yalom, whose life work make it possible for a woman like me to get help in group therapy and then tell the world about it.

Special thanks to Marcia Nickow, Psy.D., who read an early draft

and urged me to keep going. Sara Connell's commitment to and belief in the power of writing brought immense pleasure and joy to the
final stages of this project. Eternal gratitude to Dr. Dana Edelson for
taking time off from saving people's lives to help me proofread this
book.

I'm pretty sure my therapist knows I'm grateful, but I'll say it again:
I gave you enough money over the years to buy a deluxe yacht, but you
gave me an entire life, so I guess we're even.

My group mates have put up with so much shit from me all these
years. I love them with my whole heart. Special shout outs to my favorites: R.S., T.L., C.C., D.E., J.T., S.M., K.S., M.N., J.S., K.B.B., J.P., C.G.,
A.R., B.A., S.M., S.N., and S.K. And to M.C., who is no longer with us
but whose loving wisdom continues to guide and comfort me.

I'm grateful to every person who shares their recovery stories both
inside and outside meetings. They mean everything to me. I'm forever
grateful to Dax Shepard for his commitment to honesty and truth-telling
about addiction and alcoholism several times a week on his podcast
Armchair Expert.

When my parents heard about this book, they said the words that
every writer hopes their parents will say: "It's your story. You have the
right to tell it however you want." I'm grateful for their years of support
and all the gifts they've given to me.

To Doug and Alex Tate for their support and enthusiasm, which I
hope never to take for granted. I'm glad you are my family.

Thank you to Leslie Darling, Michael Lach, Keme and Jamail Carter,
Thea Goodman, Marc Dubin, Caroline Chambers, Betty Seid, Maria
Tamari, Davey Baby, Carol Ellis, Karen Yates, Steve and Celia Ellis, and
The Writing by Writers Program.

My kids are going to be mortified if they ever read this book. No
one wants to read about their mother's sex life. The good news is
that I've given them ample material for their own therapy sessions. I
thank them for making me a mother. To be present and to love and
be loved by them are the reasons why I stay in recovery and continue
in therapy.

Lastly, to my main man who has more patience and know-how than anyone I know. Thank you for loving me and for championing my story-telling and my voice. I feel so lucky every single day. Everyone who goes into therapy in hopes of finding a relationship is dreaming of someone as bighearted and steady as you are. Thank you for being part of the ending of this book and the center of my happiest days.

ABOUT THE AUTHOR

Christie Tate is a Chicago-based writer and essayist. She has been published in the *New York Times* (Modern Love), the *Rumpus*, the *Washington Post*, the *Chicago Tribune*, *McSweeney's Internet Tendency*, *Eastern Iowa Review*, and elsewhere. Kiese Laymon selected her essay "Promised Lands" as the winner of the *New Ohio Review*'s nonfiction contest, which was published in fall 2019.

GROUP

in

Christie Tate

This reading group guide for Group includes an introduction, discussion questions, ideas for enhancing your book club, and a Q&A with author Christie Tate. The suggested questions are intended to help your reading group find new and interesting angles and topics for your discussion. We hope that these ideas will enrich your conversation and increase your enjoyment of the book.

INTRODUCTION

Christie Tate is a high-achieving workaholic with an apartment in an up-and-coming Chicago neighborhood and the highest-ranking student in her law school class. She also spends the majority of her waking hours daydreaming about her death. Bemoaning her inability to be intimate and encouraged by her eccentric therapist, Dr. Rosen, Christie embarks on the mortifying and revitalizing journey that is group therapy. Throughout the course of this addictive, painfully funny memoir, Christie grapples with the challenge of radical honesty as well as Dr. Rosen's seemingly ludicrous mandates. Baring her soul about everything from her eating disorder to her sexual misadventures, Christie endeavors to believe Dr. Rosen's promise: in order to embrace the messy realities of human connection, she requires not a cure, but a witness.

TOPICS & QUESTIONS
FOR DISCUSSION

1. Christie begins *Group* by detailing the first time she "wished for death." She spends the rest of chapter 1 describing the contrasts of her life—an unwitting outsider might assume she has it all, yet internally she struggles with profound loneliness. Were you surprised to find that Christie could struggle so much with her self-worth given her success? Have you ever felt others' perception of you did not match your own perception of yourself?

2. One of Christie's biggest reservations about participating in Dr. Rosen's group is the fact that secrets are discouraged. How does this central tenet of Dr. Rosen's group sessions affect the ways she interacts with her fellow members and how she forms relationships with the other patients? Think back to a time in your own life when

you committed to something that was emotionally uncomfortable for you. Was it worth the risk?

3. In chapter 6, Christie describes how once during a meeting, no one says a single word for the entire ninety-minute session. What do you think was Dr. Rosen's intent with this exercise? Is this kind of silence productive or a waste of time?

4. When Christie leaves an indignant voice mail on Dr. Rosen's answering machine, he uses the moment to "celebrate" her anger (p. 93). What are the benefits of uplifting feelings that are, in Christie's words, "ugly, irrational, petty, reckless, spiteful, and spewing" (p. 94)? How does expressing this anger freely affect her relationship with Dr. Rosen and the group?

5. Recall some examples of where the body as a site of externalized trauma figures prominently in *Group*. Can you think of reasons why Christie's reaction to pain is sometimes so physical?

6. Christie recounts the dysfunctional and frustrating details of several romantic and sexual relationships throughout *Group*. What lessons does she learn from each affair, and how are they demonstrated in not only her love life but also her life in general? Could you relate to any of her relationship struggles in particular?

7. Dr. Rosen's methods are unorthodox, and Christie expresses doubt about their effectiveness throughout the memoir. This is especially true when Christie dates Dr. Rosen's other patients, Jeremy and Reed. Do you think Dr. Rosen ever oversteps boundaries or becomes too invasive? Do you agree with how Dr. Rosen distinguishes between keeping a secret, which is toxic, and maintaining privacy or having boundaries, which is not necessarily unhealthy?

8. In chapter 28, Christie and Max engage in an intense fight in front of Dr. Rosen and the other group members during a session. At the end of the chapter, they reconcile with a wordless hug. How do these moments of catharsis influence Christie's feelings about and openness toward relationships?

9. When he offers to hold Christie after she and Brandon break up, Dr. Rosen observes, "You're on the edge of a new identity and a

new way of thinking about yourself" (p. 243). Can you think of inflection points in your life when you reevaluated the way you exist in the world?

10. Soon after Christie vows to say "yes" more and reclaim her voice in her daily life, she reaches out to John, resulting at long last in a healthy, loving relationship. In what ways is Christie's therapy about understanding and respecting herself? How do those two concepts—attaching to others and connecting to yourself—interact?

11. The three parts of *Group* correspond to the three groups Christie joins along her therapy journey. Reflect back on how Christie and her approach to the struggles she faces evolve over the course of the book. In your opinion, what are some key moments that demonstrate to you that group therapy was working for Christie?

12. Christie's relationship with her three groups—the members within them and the dynamic as a whole—defines her transformation from a loner with an "unscored heart" (p. 7) to someone who accepts help when she struggles to "tell the truth of [her] desire" (p. 275). Think about your own "group," whatever that means to you: it could be friends, family, community members, coworkers, and beyond. How have those individuals contributed to your growth? If you could thank them for the role they have played in your life, what would you say? In what ways has your own group served as a witness for you as you struggle, both through quotidian challenges and major life upheavals?

13. For readers who have never experienced group therapy: After reading *Group*, why do you think Christie felt moved to share her experience? Did the book change any preconceived notions you had about group therapy? Do you think you would be a good candidate for this type of therapy? Why or why not?

14. For readers who have experienced group therapy: What did you appreciate about Christie's depiction of group therapy in *Group*? Is/was your experience similar or different? How so?

ENHANCE YOUR BOOK CLUB

1. Split your book club members into four groups and assign one of Christie's former boyfriends—Jeremy, Alex, Reed, and Brandon— to each group. Discuss the trajectory of each relationship, the lessons Christie learned, and your reaction to each man's behavior. If you were Christie, would you have acted similarly, or would you have made different decisions in the course of the relationship? If Christie were your friend, what advice would you give her? Come back as a big group to share what you discussed.

2. As a group, brainstorm a list of memoirs about therapy and/or mental health. In terms of tone, narration, and structure, how are these selections different from or similar to *Group*? You can also expand the list to include fiction, film, and other art forms that depict characters battling mental illness.

3. There are a wealth of colorful characters in this book, including Christie, Dr. Rosen, the group members, and her flings. As a book club, cast a film adaption of *Group*. Who would best inhabit each role and why?

A CONVERSATION WITH CHRISTIE TATE

Q: This is not only your debut—it's also an extremely vulnerable memoir about how you learned to be vulnerable with others. What inspired you to write *Group*? Did you have qualms about disclosing your life to an even wider circle of strangers?

A: I started *Group* in November 2015 after writing a novel that was a mess I didn't know how to fix. The worst part about the novel is that it ended with a terrible sex scene between the protagonist and her therapist, and Dr. Rosen had me bring the manuscript into group and read the sex scene. I can still hear my group mates' groans. With my disastrous novel on my hands, I took a month off from writing and read everything I could get my hands on about how to write a novel. Then, one day I could see the whole arc of *Group*: from driving around dreaming of death to dancing at my wedding with my new husband, family, friends, Dr. Rosen, and my group members. Because I could see it so clearly, I had the courage to begin writing.

Oh yes I did have qualms. Honestly, I still do at times. I wonder if I'm making a jackass of myself by telling the world how I acted like a fool all those years. Most days I'm grateful for the qualms because they remind me that I've told the truth. Hemingway emphasized the importance of "writing hard and clear about what hurts." The qualms tell me I've done that. As I was writing, fears would rise up, and I would turn to my literary and artistic heroes who write candidly about themselves and their bodies. Lidia Yuknavitch, Kiese Laymon, Roxane Gay, Samantha Irby, and Sarah Hepola. And beyond books, I felt inspired by women writers and comics like Ali Wong, Phoebe Waller-Bridge, and Leslie Jones. Their stories about their bodies, desires, sex lives, sorrows, struggles, and ambition have entertained and comforted me. They've also made me uncomfortable. They've changed how I understand myself and my body. True stories are a gift to the world, and I committed to offering mine because I've loved others who did it before me. It's scary, of course, but it should be. I respect readers enough to tell them stories that scare me.

Q: In chapter 4, we meet the first group members who will accompany your journey to a scored heart. By the book's end, you've participated in volatile confrontations, called members to confess when you binged or masturbated, and dished the unsavory details of many romantic duds. How do friendships created in group differ from friendships you make outside of therapy? How have group members featured in the book reacted?

A: When I think about my relationships with my group members, I want to invent a whole new language. When you've screamed into someone's gaping mouth or called them while still naked after disappointing sex with a man you don't particularly like, the word "friend" feels too flimsy—it's too "Snoopy and Woodstock on a Friendship Day" greeting card. The word "family" isn't right either, because there's no one in my family I'd call under those delicate circumstances. The people in my group have seen me literally yank the hair out of my head and cry until my snot ran into the ugly brown carpet in Rosen's office. None of my friends outside of group have seen that. Sure, I can describe it after a session, but it's not the same as being a real-time witness. Once you've been in group with someone, you have hundreds of inside jokes and a shorthand that is hard to develop in friendships where you don't sit together for one hundred eighty minutes each week learning to get real. It's very hard to re-create that deep-in-my-bones intimacy outside of group. I've done it with my husband and my children, but hardly any other people.

I sent my group mates an early draft. They all seemed vaguely amused I wanted to tell this story. Only two of them read it. None of us thought it would go anywhere. Once I revised the manuscript three more times and got an agent, I sent them an updated draft. In group, we discussed what it would mean if my book about our group was published. Several members were worried that I'd outed them or disclosed their personal issues. I revised the manuscript again, excising anything personal about my group mates. I wasn't willing to put a book out that harmed my relationship with any of them. Four of my group mates read the updated manuscript and reported feeling relieved about how I protected their privacy. One guy reported feeling hurt he wasn't featured more prominently, and another member didn't read it because he doesn't want it to get in the way of our relationship. At times, it was excruciating to hear their projections or fears that I would exploit them or hear them wish I wasn't writing about group at all. But as you would expect, we worked through the issues over many sessions, and they, along with Dr. Rosen, helped me navigate the issues of privacy, disclosure, and truth telling.

Q: Dr. Rosen is many things: Harvard educated, infuriatingly confident in his unconventional methods, and a stickler for his "no secrets" directive. What was it like to reckon your evolving relationship with

Dr. Rosen on the page? Would you encourage skeptical readers to embrace some facets of his unique approach?

A: In some ways, writing about Dr. Rosen was the easiest because he's so extreme and unconventional. Those early memories and conflicts are seared into my brain because they were so strange. I remember the white shirt he was wearing when he leaned in and told me to pray that he dies. A writer dreams for someone as startling and peculiar as Dr. Rosen to enter her life. And because his entire life's work is to help addicts and stuck people let go of their secrets, I always knew I had full permission to write anything I wanted to about him. That kind of radical freedom allowed me to pour my memories onto the page. Plus, I still see him twice a week and get a front row seat to his mannerisms and personality: the shrugs, the *mazel tovs*, that laugh. He's so uniquely and consistently himself—so odd, so unashamed of his unorthodox methods, so arrogant, and so committed to his beliefs—that he never grew hazy in my memory. He's entertaining to write because who could believe this guy? Get a henna tattoo on your belly that says "I hate my breasts"? Bookend your masturbation? The stories almost write themselves.

I know from the reactions I got from friends outside of group or writers who read early drafts of the book that people will have very strong reactions to Dr. Rosen. The word I hear most often in relation to him from outsiders is *abusive*. Someone once wrote me to explain how abusive it was for Dr. Rosen and his wife to attend my wedding, even though John and I invited them. I hear all the time that it was abusive for him to "allow" me to date Reed. Other therapists who hear these stories and practice differently give me major side-eye when I share how Dr. Rosen operates. And I totally get it. I know the Rosen-world is not familiar or comfortable for everyone. I've had friends schedule a session with Dr. Rosen, see him once, and then decide he's not for them. Too weird. Too out there. Too intense. Some people, because of their history, do not feel safe in a therapeutic setting that does not offer strict confidentiality. And I totally respect that. I'm certainly not advocating this therapeutic setting for everyone.

I would encourage skeptical readers to consider whether an additional amount of disclosure—whether a group of their own choosing, a friend, a spouse, an individual therapist—might bring them a measure of freedom and release from shame. I truly believe that the closer we hold a secret, the sicker we become. The secret takes over our lives and separates us from other people. The deepest, most crippling secret I carried had nothing to do with breaking laws or hurting animals or sexual deviance. My secret was my nightly binges on eight to ten apples. I believe I could have leaped forward in my life if I could have told someone from my 12-step program about my Red Delicious addiction. But I had too much ego, fear, and shame to tell the truth before group. There's no reason people can't practice self-disclosure outside of a formal therapy group. And anyone can turn over their food—or spending, fantasizing, masturbating, gambling—to another person. You just need a cell phone or e-mail address and a consenting witness.

Q: Much of *Group* is devoted to the embarrassing, painful pitfalls inherent to navigating sex and relationships, and you don't hold back. How does it feel to share intensely intimate moments—sex dreams, bad dates, messy breakups—with a large audience? Did finding John affect your perspective as you looked back on bad exes?

A: When I was nineteen, I fainted in the shower while bingeing and purging leftover pizza rolls alone in my dorm room. I thought I would be dead within the year. The fear drove me to a 12-step program for disordered eating, and the first thing I learned there was that telling the truth in meetings or to my sponsor could literally save my life. And it did. The only reason I was able to let go of purging every day is because I became willing to disclose my most deadly food secrets to other people in meetings and listen to theirs.

In group, I landed in another community where telling the truth was a transformative, life-saving act. While I resisted at first, I learned that the more I shared about myself and my history, the more my group understood and knew me. That's how they came to truly love me. My relationship with them, myself, and my body began to change for the better. It was a messy and uncomfortable process, but my life was undeniably better.

Not surprisingly, I ended up in a writing community that also values telling true stories, particularly stories about the body and how it moves through and experiences the world. Because so many writers I know through Lidia Yuknavitch's Corporeal Writing program write stories about their bodies, it no longer feels radical or scary to write about my Luther Vandross dream or the bad sex I've had. The more I have healed from sexual shame and body hate, the more I can celebrate all of my experiences. It is an act of self-love to transform those experiences into stories.

From my first day in treatment, Dr. Rosen assured me that I would find the partner who fit me one day, and I would be grateful for each so-called failure I had along the way. I wanted to believe it, but I didn't fully. How could I? I was still chasing married men in group or dating a guy who couldn't have sex while looking at my face. But when I started dating John and no longer silenced my voice or hid parts of myself, I understood how much I'd changed. I understood what gifts each of the relationships had given me. Only then could I join Dr. Rosen in being grateful for them. My relationship with John is in a different stratosphere than what I was doing with any of the other men. But I couldn't get to John without the gifts from the other relationships.

Everyone asks how John feels about *Group*. From the beginning, he's been fully supportive of all my writing. When he read the latest draft of the book, he offered three pieces of feedback. First, he said that he loved the book and was extremely proud of me. Then, he urged me to be sure I felt comfortable with all the privacy issues so that I could enjoy the publication journey without fear of hurting someone in the process. Finally, he said that our children would not be allowed to read *Group* for many years. Those responses perfectly capture John. He's generous with his love and praise, while also considering practical issues and long-term goals. And of course he's a devoted father.

Q: From battling bulimia to coping with the Hawaii memory, you outline the origins of significant trauma throughout *Group*. What was it like to return to that headspace during the writing process? Was it at all cathartic?

A: Writing about Hawaii makes me tremble and weep every single time. I think of the three of us kids on the beach—Jenni, Sebastian, and me—and I want to huddle them up and hug their terrified, broken hearts. I want to be the adult on the beach who could have held them while the tragedy was unfolding. When I wrote the scenes about Hawaii, I felt such deep respect for the grief that lives in me forever from that experience. I'm so grateful that Dr. Rosen and my group mates have never once minimized the experience or suggested I get over it or stop dwelling on it. It was absolutely cathartic to write about it and tell the full story. Writing about the experience helped me forgive myself for the ways in which it's still hard to attach to people because I'm so afraid of one day losing them.

As for my eating disorder, I found it much easier to write about my active bulimia because it's been so long since I purged. It was harder to write with specificity about the other parts of my eating disorder—weird food rigidity and bizarre habits with fruit—because I still do those things. These days, I do a weird thing with orange peels that I'm super ashamed of, but I can't seem to stop. Interestingly, when I asked readers for feedback on early drafts, I expected them to comment on my sexual shenanigans or about what a weirdo Dr. Rosen is. But every single woman who read *Group* mentioned the apples. And the more people ask me about it, the more human I feel about all those apple binges. My writing about those nights has opened the door to intimate conversations with other women about the things they do with food. So writing about disordered eating was one kind of catharsis, but the real change inside me happened when I discussed it with other women.

Q: As readers, we watch you secure professional success, persevere through mature—if flawed—romantic attachments, and settle into the rhythms of Dr. Rosen's world over the course of nearly a decade. In your opinion, how much of *Group* is about growing up and knowing yourself?
A: I absolutely think of this book as a bildungsroman. When I showed up in Dr. Rosen's office, I was a child in so many ways. I didn't know how to eat or speak up, and I had no idea how I felt about anything. I was missing very basic skills and self-knowledge that "normal" people learn by the time they reach their midtwenties. There's a saying in

12-step recovery meetings that the moment you begin your active addiction, you stop growing emotionally. I began actively bingeing in fifth or sixth grade, and I didn't get into recovery for bulimia until age nineteen. I missed a huge chunk of emotional growth during the years I was stuffing Girl Scout cookies and crescent rolls into my mouth. Plus, even after recovery, I still held on to secrets and buried trauma, which didn't leave much room for building skills in healthy relationships. Emotionally, I was still a teenager when I started group.

So much of knowing oneself happens through being in touch with your feelings. I was twenty-seven years old before I realized the word *shame* applied me, even though shame had driven most of my choices all my life. Before group I'd never expressed anger directly to anyone. I'd never told anyone I was hurt, and I had no idea I was lonely. How could I possibly know myself when I was so emotionally shut down? The process of learning what I felt with my group as my witness introduced me to my true self. And if group therapy had given me just that—a true, intimate relationship with myself—it would have been enough.

Q: While memoirs about the therapy process are less common, there is a huge canon of nonfiction books by women who took risks to pursue pleasure and more meaningful connection. How do you think *Group* enriches this genre? Do you have any favorites?

A: Oh, all praise the women writers who came before me. This subject also makes me weep with gratitude. Samantha Irby's writing about her body, particularly her experiences with IBS and digestive distress, have changed the world. When women tell the truth about their bodies—that they cramp, shit, explode, orgasm, tremble, shudder, release—it allows the rest of us to release the shame we've been taught to carry about those functions. Her three essay collections are favorites. Of course, my favorite all-time book is *Chronology of Water* by Lidia Yuknavitch. Until I read her memoir in March 2016, I had never read female desire written with such specificity and corporeality. And oh boy, no one writes a sex scene like Lidia Yuknavitch. Her fight to reclaim her life from the drowning waters of her past and her abusive father inspired me so much that I read her book once a year. I also love the work of Melissa

Febos, who also writes about female desire and sexuality in *Whip Smart* and *Abandon Me,* both of which are sacred texts to me. Roxane Gay's *Hunger* also stunned me and made me consider questions about how we make our bodies safe after trauma and what the cost of that safety is.

And I love a good recovery memoir. Erin Khar and Erin Lee Carr both wrote excellent books about addiction and recovery. As I was writing, Sarah Hepola's *Blackout* was a north star, because she too was unflinching in her depiction of her alcoholism and the dark places it took her. Esmé Weijun Wang's *The Collected Schizophrenias* is another favorite for its combination of both the scholarly and personal investigation of a much-misunderstood diagnosis. I love Wang forever for letting us into her experience of living with schizophrenia.

Group opens the door to a room that many people don't know exists. I like to say that group is just really crowded therapy. People are familiar with traditional one-on-one therapy. *Sopranos* fans went to therapy with Tony Soprano. Lorelei Gilmore went to therapy with her mother. *In Treatment* showed how intense the therapeutic relationship can be. But there aren't many cultural depictions of out-patient group therapy. Before I joined a Rosen-group, I thought group therapy was only for hospitalized people. I pictured Angelina Jolie and other adolescent girls, smoking and screaming in a sterile hospital rec room like *Girl, Interrupted*. I had no idea that group therapy was a transformative tool that a lonely, high-functioning law student could use to address her misery and untreated trauma. I hope *Group* offers a realistic depiction of true change, which for some of us takes many years of learning new skills and unlearning bad habits and modes of thinking.

Q: Instead of ending *Group* with your wedding and first group session as a married woman, you include a postscript. In it, you describe how being a Dr. Rosen "lifer" helps you deepen attachments and provides you with a community to bear witness to your evolving life. Why did you decide to include this "Ten Years Later" update?

A: I ended with the epilogue for two main reasons. First, I didn't like concluding with a wedding because it suggests that the route out of my difficulty was solved by finding a man. We as a culture are actively working to undo the damage that "just snag a man" stories have wrought. Second, I wanted readers to know that I still attend group. Twice a week. As I've evolved in group, I dreamed new dreams and now I want and need support for those new dreams. And I still go because I love those people. In addition to my husband and my children, Dr. Rosen and my group mates are the loves of my life. I'm attached to them, and I want to continue to show up as their witness and to allow them to witness my ongoing evolution. The last thing I want a reader to think when they close the book is that I'm cured and now just live my best life, going to work and sailing through life. No, I still go to group. Sometimes, I still gnash my teeth and pull out my hair. These days my distress isn't about loneliness or lack of attachment. But I'm still me—I still get overwhelmed, I still have an eating disorder, I'm still impatient about dreams that remain out of my reach. I still need Dr. Rosen and the group. I still have a lot to learn about attachment, commitment, and vulnerability.

Most of the non-Rosen-world people I know who go to therapy eventually graduate and move on. With Dr. Rosen, the goal of therapy isn't graduation but deepening attachments. I started group therapy desperate for help with relationships. Now my life is full of relationships, but I have new challenges. Like how to deepen the relationships I have. How to balance my professional and personal life. How to show up for aging parents. How to manage family conflicts. How to parent my children without passing along my shame and fear. Just because those challenges haven't driven me to suicidal ideation does not mean I don't need or deserve help with them.

Q: If you could give the Christie we meet in chapter 1 a single piece of advice, what would it be and why? If you told her that she would publish a memoir about her experience in group therapy, how do you think she would react?

A: Oh, sweet Christie from chapter 1. I drove her so hard all those years of chasing achievement and approval. I recently found a note I wrote to myself—most likely a Dr. Rosen prescription to write to my former self—making amends for how mean I was. One of the lines was: "I'm sorry for putting time tables on your head, for trying to strangle you, pressuring you to hurry up and be okay already." If I could give her advice, the first thing I would do is tuck her into bed, nice and snug, and then rub her forehead softly, assuring her it's okay to relax. I'd promise her it's really, truly going to be okay. In those days, I never, ever talked to myself like that. I was more like a psychotic college basketball coach, frothing at the mouth, shouting at myself to "fucking get myself together."

As for bona fide advice, I'd also tell her that she has exactly what she needs to move forward: her voice. "Use it, and keep using it to let people know what's going on with you. Tell the whole truth, like about the apples. Holding back isn't working, so you might as well speak from your darkest corners."

Chapter 1 Christie would never believe she would one day publish a memoir. If you told her that, she'd blather on about how she was a nobody who went to Texas A&M University, insistent that publishing belonged to "real artists" who live in the East Village and graduated from Sarah Lawrence or the Iowa Writers' Workshop. If you insisted it were true, chapter 1 Christie would assume you were joking. I was a ninja back then—I could make compliments and well wishes and affirmations disappear before they landed anywhere near my heart.

Q: What are some lessons or ideas about identity, community, love, and therapy you hope readers take away from reading _Group_?
A: Foremost, I want readers to know that group therapy is a potential tool for life transformation. I've seen it in my own life and in the lives of my group mates. These days, there are so many options for healing and finding meaning: energy work, individual therapy, drum circles, acupuncture, meditation, sound therapy, biofield tuning, EMDR, ayahuasca jungle retreats, rock climbing, tai chi, and other options I've never heard of. Group therapy is the process that stuck for me, and I hope that readers who feel similarly stuck might feel hope in knowing about an option that might work for them. When I joined group in 2001, I had very little money and bare-bones insurance—I couldn't afford individual therapy. The lower cost of group therapy made it possible for me to participate after telling myself for years that therapy was out of the question for me financially.

Of course, not all readers are going to race to group therapy when they finish the book. But the principles I learned in group can be applied to anyone's life. Someone struggling with food could ask a friend if they could call them every night and tell them what they ate. Asking for a witness to whom you can tell the dark, scary truths haunting you is something anyone can do. Dr. Rosen taught me that sharing my feelings, including anger and hurt, was a way to draw closer to people. At the time, that statement blew my mind. I thought the only way to have a healthy relationship was to hide all the "unpleasant" feelings. For readers who are watching me learn that lesson in *Group*, they might be able to experiment with telling someone in their life that they feel angry or hurt instead of swallowing their feelings in service of keeping the peace.

I learned how to love others and to let myself be loved in group, and it happened because I showed up day after day and asked for help and let out my feelings, as messy and loud and painful as they were. Dr. Rosen and my group mates witnessed it all. But there are other places that people can find witnesses who will hold them with love and attention when they are hurting. I can imagine finding witnesses in school or church groups, writing groups, book clubs, sporting groups. Conceivably, there are infinite ways to find another soul you trust enough to expose yourself. Even if it's just one other person, I believe transformation is possible.

When I came into group, I had a rigid sense of my identity. I knew I was a go-getter who strived to be the valedictorian in every situation. I saw myself as a baller on the outside, but hopelessly broken around relationships. I believed I could have recovery from bulimia and a good career but that was it. That was all I was getting. Dr. Rosen and my group mates challenged that story from the moment I started group. They never signed on to my vision of dying alone surrounded by law firm pay stubs and feral cats. I hope readers believe it's possible to find people in their lives who will help them let go of the old, false stories holding them back.